Religion in Ancient Etruria

This work, published as part of a program of aid for publication, received support from the French Ministry of Foreign Affairs and the Cultural Services of the French Embassy in the United States. Cet ouvrage, publié dans le cadre d'un programme d'aide à la publication, bénéficie du soutien du Ministère des Affaires Étrangères et du Service Culturel de l'Ambassade de France aux Etats-Unis.

THIS BOOK WAS ALSO SUPPORTED BY FUNDS MADE POSSIBLE THROUGH THE GENEROUS SUPPORT AND ENDURING VISION OF WARREN G. MOON.

# Religion in Ancient Etruria

Jean-René Jannot

Translated by Jane Whitehead

THE UNIVERSITY OF WISCONSIN PRESS

The University of Wisconsin Press
1930 Monroe Street
Madison, Wisconsin 53711

www.wisc.edu/wisconsinpress/

3 Henrietta Street
London WC2E 8LU, England

Copyright © 2005
The Board of Regents of the University of Wisconsin System
All rights reserved

5   4   3   2   1

Library of Congress Cataloging-in-Publication Data

Jannot, Jean-René.
    [Devins, dieux et démons. English]
    Religion in ancient Etruria / Jean-René Jannot ; translated by Jane K. Whitehead.
       p. cm.—(Wisconsin studies in classics.)
    Includes bibliographical references.
    ISBN 0-299-20840-0 (hardcover : alk. paper)—ISBN 0-299-20844-3 (pbk. : alk. paper)
    1. Etruscans—Religion. I. Title. II. Series.
BL740.J3613   2005
299′.9294—dc22      2004024545

# Contents

Illustrations   vii
Translator's Note   xiii
Preface   xv

1   The *Etrusca Disciplina*   3
2   Rites of Divination   18
3   Sacrificial and Funerary Rites   34
4   The Afterworld   54
5   Sanctuaries   72
6   The Buildings   96
7   Worshippers   125
8   Gods   143
9   The Divine   171
    Conclusion   182

Notes   187
Thematic Bibliography   203
Glossary   215
Illustration Credits   219
Index   221

# Illustrations

1.1. Mirror from Tuscania: Pava Tarchies teaches haruspicy, beginning of the third century (Florence, Museo Archeologico Nazionale)  5

1.2. Mirror from Bolsena with a scene of divination: Cacu prophesying before the Vibenna brothers, 325–300 B.C. (London, British Museum)  6

1.3. Sarcophagus of Laris Pulenas, end of the third century (Tarquinia, Museo Archeologico Nazionale)  7

1.4. Text of the inscription of Laris Pulenas  7

1.5. Fragment from the *liber linteus* of the Zagreb mummy, second century (Zagreb, National Museum)  9

1.6. Sarcophagus from the Tomb of the Sarcophagi at Cerveteri showing a folded *liber linteus*, fourth century (Vatican, Museo Gregoriano Etrusco)  10

1.7. Gold plaques from Pyrgi: foundation text of Thefarie Velianas, sixth to fifth century (Rome, Museo Naz. di Villa Giulia)  11

1.8. Fragment from the text of the Capua tablet, fifth century (Berlin, Staatliche Museen)  11

1.9. Division of celestial and terrestrial space according to the *etrusca disciplina*  12

1.10. Marzabotto, site of the city, sixth century  14

2.1. Bronze liver found near Piacenza, end of the second century (Piacenza, Museo Civico Archeologico)  19

2.2. Drawing of the inscriptions on the Piacenza Liver indicating the domains of the gods  19

2.3. Cinerary urn of Aule Lecu: the deceased holds a liver, second century (Volterra, Museo Guarnacci)  19

2.4. Roman haruspex depicted on a fragment of molded ceramic (*terra sigillata*) from Arezzo. 25–15 B.C. (Tübingen, Institut für Klassische Archäologie)  20

2.5. Chalchas Mirror, from Vulci: soothsayer consulting a victim's liver, around 400 B.C. (Vatican, Museo Gregoriano Etrusco)  22

2.6. Tinia brandishing one of his lightning bolts against a giant, end of the sixth century (Perugia, Museo Archeologico Nazionale)  26

2.7. Rock incised with the representation of Tinia's lightning bolt: a marker for a place struck by lightning, sixth century? (Orvieto, Museo Claudio Faina)  26

2.8. Vel Saties, probably observing the flight of a woodpecker to draw an omen before a military encounter, around 330 (Rome, Villa Albani)  28

2.9. Inscribed rock, from Arezzo, Santa Croce: *Aplu puteś tur Fartnś*  31

2.10. Mirror from Chiusi: Aliunea (Albunea) fixing in writing the word coming from a head rising out of the ground, around 300 B.C. (Siena, Museo Archeologico)  32

Illustrations

3.1. A folded *liber linteus* supporting a priest's hat, end of the fifth century (Berlin, Staatliche Museen)   35

3.2. The Capua tablet, a liturgical calendar, lines 8–17, beginning of the fifth century (Berlin, Staatliche Museen)   36

3.3. Reconstruction drawing of the Magliano lead tablet: chthonic deities are evoked, fifth century (Florence, Museo Archeologico Nazionale)   37

3.4. Relief from Perugia: priests and a scene of sacrifice, beginning of the fifth century (Perugia, Museo Archeologico Nazionale)   38

3.5. "Campana" plaque from Caere: an altar and an incense burner are visible, sixth century (Paris, Musée du Louvre)   38

3.6. Fragment of a sarcophagus or cinerary urn from Chiusi with sacrifice scene: altar with blazing fire and an incense burner, beginning of the fifth century (Paris, Musée du Louvre)   39

3.7. Mirror from Palestrina with sacrifice scene: musician and sacrificial aide calming the future victim, fifth century (Florence, Museo Archeologico Nazionale)   40

3.8. Tarquinia, Tomb of the Baron: offering (libation?) to a god or a deceased woman, end of the sixth century   41

3.9. Amphora of the Micali Painter depicting a religious procession with dancers and Sileni, end of the sixth century (London, British Museum)   42

3.10. The Arezzo plowman: a scene of agriculture or of the foundation of a city? around 400 B.C. (Rome, Museo Naz. di Villa Giulia)   45

3.11. The dead person lying in state (*prothesis*) under a tent, beginning of the fifth century (Copenhagen, Ny Carlsberg Glyptothek)   46

3.12. Dance of lamentation on a funerary relief from Chiusi, beginning of the fifth century (Copenhagen, Ny Carlsberg Glyptothek)   46

3.13. Tarquinia, Tomb of the Funeral Bed: banquet *kline* occupied by two cones bearing garlands and crowns, mid-fifth century (Copenhagen, Ny Carlsberg Glyptothek)   47

3.14. Tarquinia, Tomb of the Triclinium. Dance of reanimation during or after the funeral banquet, mid-fifth century (Rome, Deutsches Archäologisches Institut)   49

3.15. Guglielmi Altar, from Vulci: a stele in the form of a tomb, third century (Rome, Museo Naz. di Villa Giulia)   51

3.16. Melone del Sodo II, Cortona, the stairway of the tumulus, about 560   53

4.1. François Tomb, Vulci. Trojan prisoners slaughtered by Achilles before the shade of Patroclus, in the presence of Agamemnon, Charu(n), and Vanth, around 330 (Rome, Villa Albani)   55

4.2. Ossuary from the former Paolozzi collection from Chiusi: the deceased magically surrounded by a dance of lamentation, seventh century (Chiusi, Museo Archeologico Nazionale)   57

# Illustrations

4.3. One of two "couple" sarcophagi from Caere, end of the sixth century (Paris, Musée du Louvre)   58

4.4. Sarcophagus of Seianti Hanunia Tlesnasa: idealized portrait. From Chiusi, third century (London, British Museum)   59

4.5. Tarquinia, Tomb of the Augurs: *tanasar* in front of the door of the tomb or the Afterworld, around 520   60

4.6. Tarquinia, Tomb of the Bulls: a young man riding a hippocamp toward an island, end of the sixth century   61

4.7. Tarquinia, Tomb of the Blue Demons: the last stages before embarkation on the ship to the Afterworld, fourth century   62

4.8. Tarquinia, Tomb of the Aninas: Charu(n), holding his mallet, mid-third century   63

4.9. Tarquinia, Tomb of the Aninas: Vanth, holding her torch, guards the door of the tomb, mid-third century   63

4.10. Tarquinia, Tomb 5636: Charu(n) and Vanth, the door of the Afterworld, and the deceased bidding farewell to the living or greeting the shades of his parents, second century   64

4.11. Tarquinia, Bruschi sarcophagus. The final stage of the journey to the city of the dead under the direction of Charu(n) and Vanth, third century (Tarquinia, Museo Nazionale)   65

4.12. Tarquinia, Tomb of Orcus: Aita and Phersipnai enthroned in Hades, end of the third century   67

4.13. Cinerary urn from Chiusi: gate guarded by a female genie of the Afterworld, third century (Palermo, Museo Archeologico Regionale "A. Salinas")   69

5.1. The Portonaccio Sanctuary at Veii: view of the altar   73

5.2. Tarquinia: ruins of the urban temple called Ara della Regina, southeast corner, sixth to third century   76

5.3. Tarquinia: relief plan of the Ara della Regina   77

5.4. Tarquinia, Ara della Regina: pediment decoration—horses of the chariot of the dawn (Tarquinia, Museo Archeologico Nazionale)   78

5.5. Orvieto (Volsinii): plan of the Belvedere Temple, fifth century   78

5.6. Marzabotto, urban sanctuary: podium of the great altar, sixth to fifth century   79

5.7. Fucoli: acroterion from the right corner of the pediment, mid-second century (Chianciano Terme, Museo Civico delle Acque)   84

5.8. The "Pyrgi tablets," gold leaves with Etruscan and Punic inscriptions, beginning of the fifth century or end of the sixth (Rome, Museo Naz. di Villa Giulia)   90

5.9. Plan of the Murlo complex, second building, beginning of the sixth century   93

5.10. One of the seated acroterial figures from the second building at Murlo (Murlo, Antiquarium)   94

## Illustrations

6.1. Urn of Ceicna Fetiu, from Volterra: Pelops sacrifices the charioteer Myrtilos (Florence, Museo Archeologico Nazionale) 97

6.2. Altar of the Hellenistic temple at Fiesole, with characteristic molding, third century 97

6.3. Altar of Punta della Vipera in the form of a U: axonometric drawing 97

6.4. (a) Terracotta model of a distyle temple, from Satricum (Rome, Museo Naz. di Villa Giulia); (b) plan of the Etruscan temple, according to Vitruvius 99

6.5. Hut urn in sheet bronze: residence of a "chief," the probable model for the first temples, eighth century (Rome, Museo Naz. di Villa Giulia) 100

6.6. Model of the Tuscan temple, following Vitruvius (Rome, Istituto Archeologico) 102

6.7. Rock-cut tombs in the necropolis of Norchia, possibly a formal model for Etruscan stone buildings 103

6.8. Decoration of the temple of Velletri, Tempio delle Stimatte: reconstruction of the terracotta revetment plaques, end of the sixth century 104

6.9. (a) Model of a temple with an open pediment: *antepagmentum* and *mutuli*, from Nemi; (b) Small temple of Alatri, reconstructed in Rome in the gardens of the Villa Giulia (Rome, Museo Naz. Di Villa Giulia) 105

6.10. The Capitolium of Cosa: building of the Roman colony adopting and perpetuating Etruscan norms, reconstruction by F. Brown 106

6.11. Plan of the temples of Le Ferriere at Satricum: superpositions and enlargements 107

6.12. North Sanctuary of Pyrgi: plan 108

6.13. Pyrgi, peripteral Temple B: axonometric reconstruction, around 510 B.C. 109

6.14. Dancer with a bird's head: antefix from Temple B at Pyrgi, around 510 B.C. (Rome, Museo Naz. di Villa Giulia) 110

6.15. Pyrgi, Tuscan Temple A: model, 480–460 B.C. (Rome, Museo Naz. di Villa Giulia) 111

6.16. *Antepagmentum* of Temple A at Pyrgi: the Seven against Thebes, 480–460 B.C. (Rome, Museo Naz. di Villa Giulia) 111

6.17. Plan and façade of the Tuscan temple at Sant'Omobono dedicated to the Mater Matuta, sixth century 112

6.18. Terracotta plaque from the temple at Sant'Omobono: procession of chariots, gods, heroes, and personages of power, end of the sixth century (Rome, Antiquarium Comunale) 113

6.19. Sant'Omobono roof acroterion or votive group: Hercules and an armed goddess, probably Minerva, sixth century (Rome, Antiquarium Comunale) 114

6.20. Probable plan of the Temple of Jupiter Optimus Maximus, end of the sixth century (Rome, Capitolium) 115

6.21. Hypothetical reconstruction of the acroteria on the peak of the Portonaccio Temple at Veii, last decades of the sixth century 116

6.22. Turms/Hermes: large acroterial statue from the *columen* of the Portonaccio Temple at Veii, end of the sixth century (Rome, Museo Naz. di Villa Giulia) 117

# Illustrations

6.23. Aplu/Apollo: large acroterial statue from the *columen* of the Portonaccio Temple at Veii, end of the sixth century (Rome, Museo Naz. di Villa Giulia)   118

6.24. Leto/Latona carrying the infant Apollo: acroterial statue from the *columen* of the Portonaccio Temple at Veii, end of the sixth century (Rome, Museo Naz. di Villa Giulia)   118

6.25. Heracles contending with Apollo over the Keryneian hind: acroterial statue from the Portonaccio Temple at Veii, end of the sixth century (Rome, Museo Naz. di Villa Giulia)   118

6.26. Orvieto, Belvedere Temple: podium and plan, second half of the fifth century   119

6.27. Orvieto, Belvedere Temple: old man (soothsayer or Nestor?) from the second decorative phase of the pedimental decoration, beginning of the fourth century (Orvieto, Museo Claudio Faina)   120

6.28. Orvieto, Belvedere Temple: seated goddess from the second decorative phase, beginning of the fourth century (Orvieto, Museo Claudio Faina)   120

6.29. Model of a distyle temple with a full pediment depicting Dionysus and Ariadne, from Vulci, third century (Rome, Museo Naz. di Villa Giulia)   121

6.30. Talamonaccio, pediment of the temple at Talamone: the Seven against Thebes—assault and defeat of the Argive chiefs, middle of second century (Florence, Museo Archeologico Nazionale)   122–123

7.1. The haruspex Vel Sveitus: votive bronze with dedication, fourth century (Vatican, Museo Gregoriano Etrusco)   126

7.2. Coin of Volsinii (Orvieto): priest wearing a pointed hat (*apex*); reverse: sacrificial instruments, third century (Paris, Bib. Nat., Cabinet des Médailles)   126

7.3. Priest wearing the characteristic hat, preceded by an *aulos*-player: monument in the shape of a house, beginning of the fifth century (Chiusi, Museo Archeologico Nazionale)   127

7.4. Chianciano, limestone (*pietra fetida*) base: procession of men carrying the insignia of rank or office, beginning of the fifth century (Rome, Museo Barracco)   130

7.5. Stele from the region of Fiesole depicting a priest, end of the sixth century (Berlin, Staatliche Museen)   131

7.6. Small terracotta votive from Caere: musician playing *aulos* in a sacrifice, second century (Boston, Museum of Fine Arts)   132

7.7. Repoussé bronze from Bomarzo: sacrifice performed by Sileni in the presence of a god, end of the sixth century (Rome, Museo Naz. di Villa Giulia)   132

7.8. The Chimaera of Arezzo, end of fifth to beginning of fourth century (Florence, Museo Archeologico Nazionale)   135

7.9. So-called Laran/Mars of Todi, votive statue of an offerent, fourth century (Vatican, Museo Gregoriano Etrusco)   137

7.10. Votive statue from Monte Acuto Ragazza holding a phiale for libations, beginning of the fifth century (Bologna, Museo Civico Archeologico)   139

# Illustrations

7.11. Bronze child. Ex-voto from the shore of Lake Trasimene, in Sanguineto, around 150 B.C. (Vatican, Museo Gregoriano Etrusco)   141

7.12. Anatomical ex-voto: a right foot, beginning of the second century (Tarquinia, Museo Nazionale)   141

8.1. Aplu, the "Ferrara Bronze," from the Po plain, first quarter of the fourth century (Paris, Bib. Nat., Cabinet des Médailles)   144

8.2. Aplu: head of the "Lorenzini Kouros," end of the sixth century (Volterra, Museo Guarnacci)   146

8.3. Menrva/Athena Promachos, middle of the fifth century (Paris, Musée du Louvre)   148

8.4. Funerary Turan from the chthonian sanctuary of La Cannicella, Orvieto, sixth century (Orvieto, Museo Claudio Faina)   149

8.5. Mirror with Turan, Atunis, and secondary deities of Turan's circle, end of the fourth century (Saint Petersburg, Hermitage Museum)   150

8.6. Bronze handle from Spina: doubled Turms serving Tinia and Aita (Ferrara, Museo Archeologico)   152

8.7. Aita and Phersipnei attending the sacrifice of Trojan prisoners for Patroclus, mid-fourth century (Orvieto, Museo Claudio Faina)   154

8.8. Tinia/Zeus, from a model by Pheidias, fourth century (Orvieto, Museo Claudio Faina)   156

8.9. Mirror from Tuscania: Nethuns, Usil, and Thesan, fourth century (Rome, Museo Naz. di Villa Giulia)   159

8.10. Votive statuette depicting Selvans, god of the wild border, third century (Cortona, Museo dell'Accademia Etrusca)   161

8.11. Statuette of Culsans, god of doorways, found at Cortona, first half of third century (Cortona, Museo dell'Accademia Etrusca)   163

8.12. Mirror from Volterra: Uni nursing Hercle and becoming his mother, around 300 (Florence, Museo Archeologico Nazionale)   166

9.1. Lasa with Amphiarios and Aivas, mid-fourth century (London, British Museum)   174

9.2. Fury or Vanth, a winged female genie holding serpents, around 420 (London, British Museum)   175

## Translator's Note

English is a rather brittle language. It is strongest when it is most direct. Because French preserves more inflections from its Latin origins, it seems to have greater tensile strength and can support multiple relative clauses or participial expressions that flow, one into another, in long streams. Professor Jannot's fluid prose in *Devins, Dieux et Démons* was exuberantly Gallic, and my attempts to render it literally in English only sounded stilted. When I began to break up the long sentences and refashion the impersonal expressions and periphrases, the language became more English, and, with the poetry removed, more academic in tone. It also became more concrete, denotative; and from this another problem arose: the need sometimes to state explicitly a logical or causal connection where there had been only a participial modifier.

Thus what started as a grammatical challenge turned into a quasi-scholarly exercise. I worked to clarify the connections so that the translation would clearly distinguish the author's conjecture from fact and that, in both the text and the footnotes, it would document the sources upon which both conjecture and fact were based. (The excellent copyeditor Jane Barry played a significant role in this.) The period of time between the publication of the French volume and the completion of the translation also allowed Professor Jannot to incorporate new scholarship (including his own), to correct inconsistencies and errors, and to respond to insightful criticism from reviews. The resulting English version, then, is not simply a translation, but a thoroughly updated revision of the original. While the poetic qualities of the French version are here somewhat dampened, the poetry of the Etruscan religion itself shimmers.

Throughout the French text, Professor Jannot uses the word *l'Au-delá*, the Beyond, to denote the Etruscans' concept of the place of the dead. The traditional term Underworld, which is generally used for the Roman and Greek place of the afterlife, seemed inappropriate in that the Etruscans appear to conceive of death as "away"—across a body of water—not "below." The term Afterlife, also traditional, conveys a state of existence but not a sense of location. "The Beyond" evokes the U.S. Air Force, somehow. Thus I have settled on the term Afterworld, which makes room for the rather concrete, though fantastic, geographies of Etruscan belief.

It has been an honor to work with Professor Jannot, who is not only an erudite and creative scholar, but also a very generous one. Every communication with him was a delight, even when our computers translated each other's Greek fonts into gibberish.

We have resolved this last problem by transliterating all the Etruscan names into Roman letters; this simplification will also make the volume more accessible to nonspecialists. For citations from the ancient texts we have tried to use the latest Loeb

## Translator's Note

translations, because they are most readily obtainable and they have the added advantage that they allow the reader who wishes to check the ancient source the convenience of reading both the original and a translation at the same time. Now Professor Jannot's deeply insightful work on the fascinating and little-known subject of Etruscan religion may have the wide English-speaking readership that it deserves.

# Preface

This brief study deals with a complex, and hence fascinating, subject: the religion of ancient Etruria. Etruscan civilization was steeped in the sacred; rites governed every action, whether religious, public, or private, from the most important to the most ordinary. Religious power was tightly intertwined with political power; daily life was ruled by complex rituals; and the power of the divine was omnipresent. This study thus touches on virtually the entire history of the Tyrrhenian world.

The present volume is directed primarily to an educated public and to students beginning their university study; it does not refer to the highly specialized methods of Etruscan epigraphy and philology, nor does it involve the reader in complex iconographic analyses. We wanted it to be easily accessible—to present in a straightforward style information from the most recent studies on the most complex questions. You will find, not a series of working hypotheses, but as coherent as possible a collection of generally accepted scholarly conclusions.

Syntheses on this question are rare. The most recent, excellent though it is, dates to 1975 and has so far not been superseded.[1]

During the last twenty years, however, research on specific issues has multiplied at all levels: archaeological documentation; the interpretation of texts; the publication of engraved bronze mirrors, which are a veritable mine of information and an inexhaustible source of unresolved questions; and the analysis of figural iconography, which opens new areas of study, including, in particular, ideological analysis. The *Lexicon Iconographicum Mythologiae Classicae (LIMC)* has made available virtual small monographs by very authoritative scholars on Etruscan divinities. Finally, there have been new views into old problems,[2] and new attempts at analyzing divination, aspects of Hellenization, and the relationship between religion and politics.

But access to new data remains difficult: the bibliography, published in various languages, is relatively scattered and its use in effect reserved to specialists. Only a few recent general works contain chapters on the subject of Etruscan religion.[3] It is clear

# Preface

that there is a demand for precise new information and a need for an explanatory overview.

We have attempted to approach most of the large questions, and to give iconographic and textual documentation on each point, as well as a comprehensive and current bibliography. Thanks to the research of the last twenty years, it now seems possible to sketch out some orientations and interpretations that may offer a more coherent image of Etruscan religion.

Rather than review all of the previous scholarship on the subject, our efforts are directed toward showing the uniqueness of this civilization, which the whole of ancient tradition characterizes as fundamentally religious. Livy (5.1.6) calls it "the nation which was devoted beyond all others to religious rites and all the more because it excelled in the art of observing them." And Arnobius makes this severe judgment: "Etruria, the begetter and mother of superstitions" (*Adv. Nat.*, 7.26).

We shall attempt to present the truly original character of the beliefs, cults, and religious practices of Etruria. Beginning with the revealed texts that codified relations with the divine world, we shall show how the conceptions of the universe and of humanity are inseparable from that of the divine and how the consultation of signs and divination translated its structure. We shall explain the role of ritual in daily activities and in the form of the city. Finally, in describing the gods, we shall go back in time to the process of individuation that marked their birth and their emergence from an originally impersonal existence.

The general picture will appear remarkably different from that presented by Georges Dumézil almost forty years ago,[4] and if the gaps in our knowledge seem greater than our certainties, current research, in allowing us to pose different questions, will ultimately lead to a fuller understanding. We hope that the complex and moving nature of this area of research will instill in young scholars the desire to pursue it.

Is it a translation, another edition, or something like a new book ? The three at the same time.

I first have to thank Jane Whitehead for braving the extremely difficult translation of an old fashioned French style. My French text is full of conditional forms, concessive sentences, half-negations, and shades of meaning that seemed to me necessary when speaking of this highly hypothetical subject. It has been a challenge for Jane to translate, find equivalences, and sweep away the French-looking forms. She needed Job's patience to work with me! It is a splendid work.

In fact, this is a second revised edition of my French book: a lot of small errors, approximations, or even mistakes have been corrected thanks to the excellent remarks of the University of Wisconsin Press reviewer. One ought to be read by an exigeant specialist before publishing.

A new bibliography, new footnotes, new illustrations, a new formatting of the text

## Preface

and photographs, and, of course, up-to date information about recent discoveries make not really a new book but a new style of book. If I have to produce a second French edition, I wonder if it would not be convenient to translate the American edition.

Finally, I wish to thank the team at the University of Wisconsin Press, and especially Justin Johnston, Lindsay O'Malley, Raphael Kadushin, Sheila Moremond, Adam Mehring, and Jane Barry. So many people are responsible for this book that they should be listed on the cover, with my name in a very small font.

Many thanks.

# Religion in Ancient Etruria

CHAPTER 1

# The *Etrusca Disciplina*

The religious knowledge of the Etruscans was contained in a group of texts collected into books and called generically the *etrusca disciplina*.[1] These texts, known today only from small and out-of-context fragments, are of the utmost importance. They were regarded *a posteriori*, by the Etruscans themselves, as both the theoretical foundation and the justification for Etruscan civilization as a whole.

### KNOWLEDGE REVEALED

The Etruscan religion has often been called a "revealed" religion because it has "prophets" such as Tages and Vegoia. This term is both accurate and ambiguous. What is "revealed" is not the existence of god; it is not even a theology, a mythology, or an explanation of the order of the world. It is exclusively a series of rites and sacred techniques that permit one to enter into contact with the world of the divine, and to receive its signs and its complex cosmology, which defines the space in which the gods act. It is a revelation of cultic and divinatory practices, of religious customs and acts. These were eventually written down and formed a veritable literature.[2]

*Tages*
Several stories involve supernatural contacts with the world of the gods, the most famous being that of Tages. Cicero and Ovid preserve the story:[3] while he was working his field, a peasant of Tarquinia discovered, to his astonishment, a child with the features of a sage old man, a *puer senex*, emerging from the earth in the middle of the furrow that the farmer had just plowed. A consecrated place in front of the famous Ara della Regina Temple at Tarquinia may mark this founding event (see chapter 5). This story clearly shows that the Etruscans wanted to present themselves as autochthonous. The child expert in things divine is a very widespread theme, even extending into Christianity.

The farmer could not help but cry out, and at his call came all the inhabitants of Etruria, or, more exactly, "all the peoples"—that is, the Twelve Peoples comprising

## The *Etrusca Disciplina*

the *nomen etruscum*, who thus would appear to be religious dependents of Tarquinia. They then received from the lips of this earthborn child-sage named Tages the immense knowledge of sacred things that would become the religious patrimony of the whole Etruscan people. The words of Tages were collected, transcribed, and disseminated, and they came to form the basis for the religious science of the *principes* of Etruria: those local kings whose political power was founded in part—probably in great part—on the knowledge of ritual. One might say that from this time on all the kings of Etruria had the same beliefs and the same customs.

In all likelihood it was thus that the Etruscan people was formed and defined: that *nomen etruscum* whose uniqueness had so impressed the ancients. This, too, is how the most prestigious of the sacred books appeared—the *libri tagetici*, whose redaction was believed to have been undertaken by Tarchon,[4] the mythical founder of Tarquinia. If one credits the various traditions, only the *libri haruspicini* can be traced to this source with any certainty, but the *libri acherontici* are frequently included with them, since they were also part of Tarquinian tradition.

This topographic precision is important. Revealed at Tarquinia and carefully compiled by one of its kings, the precepts of haruspicy seem strongly attached to that city where, at the beginning of the Imperial period and under the stimulus of Roman power,[5] the college of sixty haruspices was later reestablished. A relatively late (end of the fourth or beginning of the third century B.C.) engraved mirror (fig. 1.1),[6] found in a tomb at Tuscania, depicts Tages, called *Pava Tarchies*, wearing the hat of the haruspex. His left foot is resting on a rock to ensure contact with the earth, the Etruscan goddess Cel, the mother of all revelation. He is holding a liver in his left hand and is bending over it, examining and interpreting signs on its lobes. He is surrounded by gods, among them the famous Veltune, who is identified with the Etruscans' chief or primary deity *(deus Etruriae princeps)*, Voltumna (Varro, *Ling.* 5.46). Also present is a young man labeled *Rathlth*, who seems to have some of the attributes of Aplu/Apollo. Tarchunus, holding the long cane that is the sign of his rank, is centrally placed. He is attentively watching the "lesson" in haruspicy given by the mythical author of the *libri tagetici*.

### Vegoia

These sources chiefly rely on Tarquinian traditions. But other cities had their prophets and their revelation, too. At Chiusi, a prophetess named *Vegoia* (or *Vegoe*), whom some describe as a Muse, revealed the laws and practices relative to hydraulic works, surveying, and delimiting property,[7] and transmitted these rules to Arruns Veltymnus. Also attributed to her were the most important texts on the interpretation of lightning.

It is tempting to believe that this tradition of a revelation at Chiusi was part of the religious patrimony of a local royal family and contributed to its prestige. The fragments that have come down to us evoke a sort of cosmology and mention the calcu-

# The *Etrusca Disciplina*

1.1. Mirror from Tuscania; beginning of the third century. Pava Tarchies teaches haruspicy, surrounded by gods, including Velthuna. Florence, Museo Archeologico Nazionale, Soprintendenza Archeologica per la Toscana Firenze.

lation of the Etruscan *saecula*. Ten of these time measurements were supposed to enfold the whole of Etruscan history. These texts became important; Augustus in fact had a copy transferred to the Temple of Palatine Apollo, where they lay next to the Sibylline Books and the Books of the Marsi. The prophetess Vegoia calls to mind the nymph Egeria, who similarly counseled King Numa at Rome.

### SACRED TEXTS AND GREAT FAMILIES

Thus it seems that the great families who ruled the city-states at their foundation enjoyed privileged relations with the world of the divine, and the prestige of this relationship reinforced their power. Several representations, difficult to interpret, depict the two Vibenna brothers, Aulus and Caelius, fierce opponents of the Roman regime of Tarquin. They are shown capturing or holding prisoner a certain Cacu,[8] who was a bard, soothsayer, or prophet, and who probably served the Etruscan tyrant of Rome.

The *Etrusca Disciplina*

1.2. Mirror from Bolsena with a scene of divination: Cacu prophesying before the Vibenna brothers. 325–300 B.C. The British Museum.

One such scene occurs on an engraved mirror from the end of the fourth century B.C., found at Bolsena and now in the British Museum (fig. 1.2). Here one can easily discern the preoccupied soothsayer, prisoner of the Vibenna brothers. His prophetic discourse is being transcribed onto tablets by an assistant named *Artile.* To control a soothsayer or a prophet, to possess the sacred books, to have access to the *etrusca disciplina:* this is to exercise the greatest and the only real power.

When the Etruscan cities lost their independence, when they became simple federated cities (*civitates foederatae*), or worse, *municipia*, the great families who continued to live there dutifully guarded these sacred texts, which were the sign of their nobility and the gauge of their former power. Augustus, wishing to restore the religions of a pacified Italy, sought to gather up these texts and collect them in Rome under his authority. By so doing, he would appropriate to himself the same sacerdotal and scriptural authority that was the property, and no doubt one of the bases of power, of the Etruscan aristocracy.

# The *Etrusca Disciplina*

1.3. Sarcophagus of Laris Pulenas, who presents his career inscribed on a *volumen*. End of the third century. Tarquinia, Museo Archeologico Nazionale.

1.4. Text of the inscription of Laris Pulenas. "Lars Pulenas, son of Larce, grandson of Larth, grandson of Velthur, great-grandson of Pule Laris Creice (the Greek) . . . he wrote this book of haruspicy (or this book on parchment)." The text next mentions his magisterial offices at Tarquinia, then indicates another type of priesthood: "He was in charge of the rites of Catha and Hermes (or interpreted them?)" A little later, Catha is associated with Pacha (i.e., with Bacchus). Finally, the text alludes to Culsl, a god of the door similar to Janus, for whom Lars Pulenas was probably charged with offering the contents of a vessel (for libation?). Although the text is still somewhat obscure, its allusions to multiple sacerdotal activities are certain.

But the traditional texts of Tages, Vegoia, or Cacu were not the only properties that the unifying Roman power wanted to possess. All the priests, magistrates, or important people pursued studies that we would term "theological." They wrote treatises on rites and liturgy and greatly increased the volume of exegeses and speculations. On a beautiful late third-century sarcophagus from Tarquinia (fig. 1.3), *L(a)ris Pulenas*, wreathed in a garland, reclines on the cushions of his luxurious couch and unrolls a *volumen* inscribed with nine lines.[9] The deceased seems prouder of his writings on sacred subjects than of his magisterial or priestly duties, and he makes it known: *an cn nethsrac*, "He compiled this book [of haruspicy]" (fig. 1.4).

In fact, the initial texts were continually modified and enriched with multiple additions. Cicero (*De div.* 2.50) mentions these, and Latin writers at the end of the Republic[10] may reveal traces of them. The most significant borrowings seem to have had two origins. One certainly comes from southern Italy, where late Pythagorean influences produced a new image of the Afterworld and a kind of philosophical-mystical speculation; the other, which may evoke ancient Anatolian and Mesopotamian connections, deals with divination and seems to derive from an oriental current of thought most commonly associated with Apollonios of Mende. These late additions are superposed, which makes it particularly difficult to interpret the fragments of text that have come down to us.

There was a moment, between the first century B.C. and the end of the first century A.C., when the *etrusca disciplina* was widely fashionable. Tarquitius Priscus was the author of *De rebus divinis*, in which he describes omens, *ostentaria*. Aulus Caecina

## The *Etrusca Disciplina*

from Volterra, a friend of Cicero and the son of the defendant in the *Pro Caecina*, was especially interested in the interpretation of lightning, a skill he learned from his father.[11] Nigidius Figulus and Julius Aquila translated from the Etruscan several books that were still accessible to them. Their translations, unfortunately almost completely lost, were known to the antiquarian Varro, "the most learned of Romans" (as Quintilian called him). They were also known to Cicero, who often alluded to them in the *De divinatione*, and to encyclopedists such as Pliny the Elder.

During the early Empire, the philetruscan emperor Claudius, thanks in part to his knowledge of the language, was still able to write lengthy *Tuscae historiae* in which the information drawn from religious writings was probably considerable. That is no longer possible for us. We do not even really know what subjects the sacred books addressed. This dilemma can be illustrated by the works of Attalus, a Greek author who was very probably from Pergamon. Seneca preserves some of his ideas and expresses a certain admiration for him. By utilizing fragments from the Etruscan scriptural tradition and mingling them with Hellenistic additions, Attalus, and other essayists who followed his example, built a theological and cosmological system that had only tenuous connections to the original Etruscan sources.

This sacred knowledge, however, survived for a long time after the other components of Etruscan culture had disappeared. In the middle of the fourth century A.C., if one believes Ammianus Marcellinus, Etruscan haruspices, claiming the authority of Tarquitius Priscus, interpreted the passage of a comet as having a military-political meaning; and in 633 the Council of Toledo forbade the clergy to employ the services of haruspices![12] Some of these texts had not yet been lost. Evidence of this is the work of John Lydos, who wrote at Byzantium toward the middle of the sixth century A.C. and still remains one of our best sources for Etruscan religion. It is difficult, as one may imagine, to reconstruct Etruscan religious literature on the basis of fragments that have only survived through later reworkings.

### A SACRED LITERATURE

What has come down to us directly is very limited and always fragmentary. It seems that Etruscan literary texts in general and the sacred texts in particular were written on perishable surfaces: papyrus scrolls and fabric books (*libri lintei*). Of the former nothing remains, only sculptural representations such as the one that *L(a)ris Pulenas* unrolls on his sarcophagus, mentioned above. Another image of a papyrus scroll, decorated with a scene of a hunt, is perused by a book-loving banqueter in a lost painting from Tarquinia.[13] On mirrors, vase paintings, and stone sarcophagi, the underworld goddess Vanth, and sometimes even *Lasa*, are frequently shown holding the papyrus scroll of fate. Of the fabric books, which seem to have been intended mostly for religious use, only fragments of the Zagreb mummy book remain (fig. 1.5). This is a long band of woven linen inscribed with an Etruscan ritual calendar, whose contents we shall discuss later. It had been used in Egypt for wrapping the corpse of a young woman, perhaps of Etruscan origin.

# The *Etrusca Disciplina*

1.5. A fragment from the *liber linteus* of the Zagreb mummy, a liturgical calendar inscribed on linen. Second century. Zagreb, National Museum.

Sculptural representations in stone, however, such as those on an ash urn in Berlin, on a sarcophagus in the Vatican, and in the Caeretan Tomb of the Reliefs,[14] illustrate the importance of these texts written on fabric. There must have been veritable libraries composed of books of this type. The prominent place they hold on some funerary monuments is evidence that they both held great value and conferred value on their owner. On the Berlin ash urn, the *liber linteus* is folded beside the deceased and topped by a priest's hat, while on the Vatican sarcophagus,[15] the linen book lies almost in contact with the deceased's head (fig. 1.6). The books were probably considered to be useful in facing the afterlife.

Fortunately, several fragments of religious writings were inscribed on nonperishable surfaces: for example, the gold dedicatory and commemorative plaques excavated at Pyrgi (fig. 1.7), and the "liturgical" calendar written on the Capua tablet (fig. 1.8), the *tabula capuana* (formerly called the "Capua Tile").[16] The latter was probably associated with a whole series of revelations by the Etruscan prophets collected in the *libri rituales*.

Etruscan "revelation" is highly unusual because it deals not with the nature of the divine but with the relationship between mortals and that which is not mortal. It

## The *Etrusca Disciplina*

1.6. Sarcophagus from the Tomb of the Sarcophagi at Cerveteri, showing a folded *liber linteus*. Fourth century. Vatican, Museo Gregoriano Etrusco 14949.

concerns space (how the world is perceived, measured, and organized); time (how it flows and is divided); and the establishment of communication with the world of the divine. The relations between mortals and gods are in large part determined by the questions the worshippers pose and the answers they expect, whether ethical, theological, practical, or ritual. Similarly, the authority of the oracle at Delphi, at least in the Archaic and Classical periods, was almost exclusively religious: one consulted Apollo on rites and sacrifices, on cults and sanctuaries. Apollo was perceived as an organizer of cult practices, the legislator of divine matters. The importance of the god of Delphi also illustrates the profoundly ritualistic character of Greek religious life in the Archaic period.

In Etruria, the revealed truths concern the order and functioning of the universe, its history and its future—that which determines the destiny of individuals as well as that of cities. The revelations of the prophets, like the responses of the haruspices, presuppose a cosmic structure in which the universe is dominated by an all-powerful, invisible divine world. The visible world is merely its language. The entire scope of Etruscan religion can be illustrated by a comment of Seneca the Elder, who stated that, for the Etruscans, events (such as the occurrence of lightning) "do not have a meaning because they happen, but rather they happen in order to express a meaning" (*QNat.* 2.32.2).

## The *Etrusca Disciplina*

1.7. Gold plaques from Pyrgi: foundation text of Thefarie Velianas. Late sixth or early fifth century. Rome, Museo Naz. di Villa Giulia.

1.8. Fragment from the text of the Capua tablet, fifth-century liturgical calendar on a terracotta plaque from Etruscan Campania. Berlin, Staatliche Museen.

As a result, every occurrence is the reflection of a hidden truth in the divine order. The science consists in reading and interpreting that apparently incomprehensible message. The Etruscans subjected every natural event to rigorous observation and careful description, from exceptional occurrences, called *ostenta* in Latin, which were regarded as specific signs from the gods, to the more ordinary, everyday phenomena, such as lightning or movements of birds, which were regarded merely as signs of current happenings in the divine world. They compared all the signs to the events that followed them and thus generated a veritable research field of interpretations, to which the late authors attest. These observations took place within a model of the world whose initial form, though refined over the centuries, originated in the legendary times of Tages or Vegoia. Likewise, the more simplified quadripartition of the sky used by the Roman augurs must date back to King Numa.

## The *Etrusca Disciplina*

### SPACE

Celestial space and its projection onto the earth are cut up into sixteen regions (fig. 1.9). We know this division of the world well, since it had already struck the ancients as remarkable and Pliny the Elder (2.143)[17] has given us a precise description of it. But is his description the result of speculation that dates from later than the third century B.C., and merely an elaboration of the simple four-part division of the sky that was common in Italian cultures and particularly at Rome, or is it a genuine ancient belief? The only indication we have that this division of space, this world model, was used in antiquity is the orientation of temples of the Archaic and Classical periods. If we look at the orientation of a temple that did not have to conform to an orthogonal urban plan and relate it to the characteristics and functions of the divinity to whom the temple was dedicated, we notice that its axis corresponds to that divinity's heavenly sector.[18] The allotment of divine sectors in celestial space is one of the

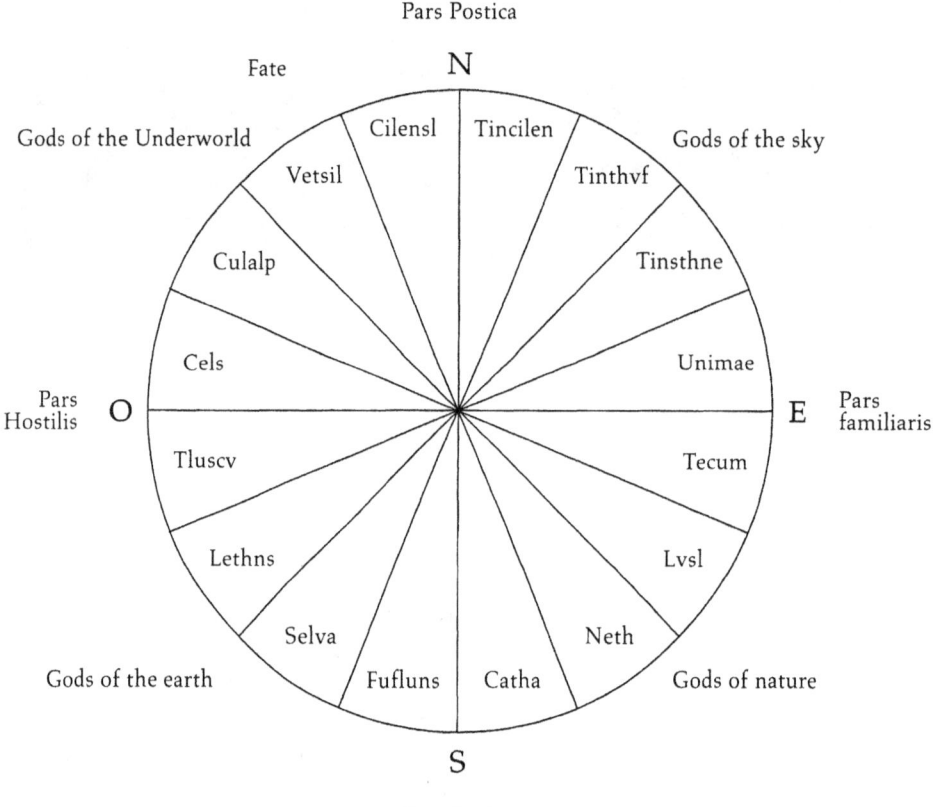

1.9. Division of celestial and terrestrial space according to the *etrusca disciplina* (as recorded by Martianus Capella, Nigidius Figulus, Pliny the Elder).

## The *Etrusca Disciplina*

singularities that, for lack of a better term, we shall call an Etruscan "cosmic theology." It is a characteristic unique to Etruscan divine topography (at least in the West) that this assignment of sectors of the horizon to various deities is paralleled in the microcosm that is the liver of a sacrificed animal. The sacred divisions seem also to have a correspondence in the measurement and division of land, which since the very dawn of Etruscan history obeyed religious rules. The rather late texts of the Roman surveyors *(gromatici)* recall this origin.

The division of the earth, of a city's territory, is an activity that arises from the sacred. Its practice is said to derive from a "prophecy" of the nymph Vegoia to Arruns Veltymnus, who thus believed it came "from Jupiter and Justice."[19] The prophecy spoke of the irremovable character of boundary stones and proclaimed that any alteration of them was a sacrilege. The control that the sacred held over the distribution of land and over the operation of *delimitatio* was so important that Tarquitius Priscus translated the books of Vegoia into Latin, and a fragment of them has come down to us:[20]

> Know that the sea has been separated from the sky. Now when Jupiter had claimed the land of Etruria, he established and ordained that the plains be surveyed and the fields bounded. Knowing human avarice and the passions that land excites, he willed that everything be marked with boundary stones. When someday someone, moved by the avarice of the ending eighth *saeculum*, will scorn the property that was allotted to him and will covet that of others, men by guilty maneuvers will violate, touch, or displace these boundaries. But whoever will have touched them [ . . . ] will be condemned by the gods.

The text clearly relates to specific circumstances and was probably written at the time of the agrarian troubles around 88 B.C., when there was talk of the redistribution of land. Nonetheless, it certainly repeats long-known formulae, and the cosmogonic allusion at the beginning is evidence of the tone of Vegoia's "books."

It is significant that the limits and boundaries that had been formulated in prophetic literature were placed under the protection of specific divinities. Selvans is the most important of them; to him are assigned two sections on the Piacenza liver (see chapter 8 and fig. 2.1), and numerous votive bronzes were offered to him. A late text attributes to him the invention of boundary cippi.[21] These marking stones, which often carry the word *tular* ("boundary"), are under his protection. It is equally probable that the same god protected oaths, at least when he is named *Selvans sanchuneta*.[22] The same text of Vegoia makes this connection: "This is why you must be neither of bad faith nor of deceitful language. Place our teachings in your heart."

Thus it becomes clear: the order of the world is held in place by the permanence of spatial allotment, which must be done according to Vegoia's rules and with the guarantee of good faith behind it. We seem to have come far afield from a theological cosmology, but we must turn our reasoning back: the earth, down to the smallest parcel, must be administered by humans according to the divine order.

## The *Etrusca Disciplina*

1.10. Marzabotto, site of the city: geometricized plan showing the religious and political organization of space. Sixth century.

Our documents are desperately poor, but the surveyed universe that we glimpse indirectly from a few texts is the clearest manifestation of divine omnipresence (fig. 1.10).

### TIME

The gods rule over space, and they also control the duration of the world. Here again, all the measurements, all the divisions, all the limits are religious. The life of cities, states, and peoples is no freer than that of individuals. The destiny that manifests itself through an omen on the day of a city's founding allows one to forecast the length of the city's life. Thus the Etruscans were persuaded that the existence of their people was limited in time, fixed forever, and destined to last ten *saecula*.

Divinities whose names had been borrowed from Greek myths assured the inexorable unfolding of time. Each year was rigorously counted, and Roman rites maintained that tradition: on the Ides of September, the anniversary of the dedication of the Capitoline Temple of Jupiter Optimus Maximus, the Praetor Maximus hammered a nail into the cella of Minerva. On a famous engraved mirror in Berlin, Athrpa/Atropos similarly pounds in, just above Meliacr/Meleager, the nail that marks the year (or the day) of his tragic death.[23] It is possible that the so-called stars

## The *Etrusca Disciplina*

*(HKKBM)* mentioned in the Punic text of the Pyrgi dedication plaques referred to the golden dating nails actually found by archaeologists.

The same reckoning Fate measured the time granted to humans, cities, and states. Each had been granted a determined lifespan, which it was useless to try to prolong. This "millenarian" fatalism must have weighed heavily on the politics of the city-states themselves, and the certainty of their fates ultimately became a veritable political weapon: every upset, every revolution, every annexation or conquest could be justified as inexorably predestined. One recalls that Augustus, and especially Virgil, whose Etruscan origins and Tuscan friendships are well known, toyed with the ideas of a golden age and the *saeculum*.

Just as the topographic organization of the world belonged to a divine order, its chronological organization also was sacred and fixed by divine authority. Time was calibrated by units that were sometimes fixed and equal, sometimes variable, according to circumstances and customs.

A human life, Censorinus tells us on the authority of the *libri fatales,* was allotted at most twelve periods of seven years each (hebdomads), a maximum of eighty-four years (*De die natali* 4.13). Simple observation sometimes contradicted that rule, and thus it became necessary to justify the anomalies. It was suggested that, under certain conditions, one might obtain a delay, a personal extension of one's lifespan. It was an impiety, however, to demand more of the gods than was reasonable. In order to attain the maximum age, a person might employ prayers and sacrifices. But while the maximum age was fixed and difficult to exceed, beyond that limit no one could know the predestined length of his life. Old people who managed to survive to a legendary age left the domain of the known and the predictable: "They depart from their spirit," Censorinus tells us, "and for them no more omens are given." In other words, their life is no longer ruled by the universal order that governs other humans.

These exceptions are worth lingering over. The possibility that one might be able to put off the decisions of fate suggests that one can establish a personal relationship with the gods. Nonetheless, contact becomes impossible when one passes the age limit of eighty-four. This limit indicates that fate is imposed on the gods themselves, or at least on those with whom humans can communicate through prayer or sacrifice, who are distinguished individually, and who are likely to be named or honored by mortals. It seems, then, that even Tinia/Zeus/Jupiter is not completely free. In order to throw his second lightning bolt *(manubia),* he must have the approval of the *di consentes* ("consenting gods"), and he may throw the third lightning bolt only with the authorization of the *di superiores et involuti* ("the higher and hidden gods"). Who are these unnamed gods, whose number is unknown and who have no image? Are they a primitive expression of divinity, older than and superior to Tinia himself (see chapter 9), or might they be identified as the very fate that dominates individualized gods? Remarkably, decisions concerning the life of humans (or of states) may thus be out of the hands of the most powerful deities.

## The *Etrusca Disciplina*

The largest of the time units is the "century," or, rather, what Roman tradition calls the *saeculum*. Etruscan history had ten *saecula*, of variable length: 119 years, 123 years, 44 years. That is because the length of a *saeculum* was defined as the lifespan of a specific man who is born and dies with it, but whom no one can know until a final omen distinguishes the day of his death as the end of the *saeculum*. Extremely complicated calculations were used to reckon the length, but in reality only extraordinary phenomena could indicate, *a posteriori*, that a *saeculum* had just ended. Patent signs marked the end of a *saeculum* and permitted the closing of an era; omens, astonishing or abnormal appearances, or better, a bundle of these phenomena collected together, constituted a kind of proof. The Latin authors called them *ostenta saecularia*. Thus in 88 B.C. the sound of a trumpet marked the end of the eighth *saeculum* (Plutarch, *Sulla,* 7). Similarly it was believed that the passage of the comet of 44 B.C. marked the end of the ninth *saeculum* (Servius, 9.45).

The *saecula* follow each other in a little-understood rhythm. In their mechanical succession they repeated, for the Etruscans, identical patterns in slightly different ways. What happened had happened before and would happen again: that was the conviction of the Etruscan people. And the importance of history, of knowledge of the past, even as transfigured in epic or myth, consisted in this.

It is possible that the Etruscans read certain Greek mythical stories, not symbolically as we once thought, still less allegorically (as did the learned in Europe during the Neo-Classical period), but analogically or even prophetically. The myth of Bellerophon killing the Chimaera[24]—depicted on gemstones, on sarcophagi, in the famous bronze group from Arezzo (see fig. 7.8), and perhaps on the pediment of the Portonaccio Temple—should not be read as an ordinary aristocratic symbol, but as an example and, above all, a precedent. The mythical horseman killed the monster that was menacing all of Lycia: this probably signified that an aristocratic hero would liberate his city from the disorder that threatened it. This teratomachia may also allude to the Etruscans' struggle against the Gauls. Likewise, the sacrifice of Trojan prisoners by the Greeks, which was the theme of departure for the paintings in the François Tomb at Vulci (see fig. 4.1), not only served as a substitute image for the actual act of slaughter that was believed to bring the deceased back to life; it also served as a paradigm, evoked from the most distant past, that had repeated itself in the historical massacre of the Romans by the people of Vulci two hundred years before the date of the tomb. The latter scene is represented on the facing wall. This paradigm may also have been repeated later in the slaughter of 307 Roman prisoners in the forum of Tarquinia in 358 (Livy, 7.15.11). Each of these historical massacres announced, like a precedent called to repeat itself century after century, the hoped-for victory of Vulci over contemporary Rome.[25]

This repetitive concept of history,[26] fostered by *saecula* of varying length and unknown rhythm, produced the collections of observations, the catalogues of omens—statistics, in effect[27]—that form an astonishing literary production. Signs were ob-

# The *Etrusca Disciplina*

served and described with extreme precision because one could only know after the event what they had been announcing. They could reappear, and the events that followed them could happen again. This serendipitous observation of phenomena is rigorously scientific, though in a completely irrational context. In effect, without identifying the causes, the Etruscans managed to conclude that the same signs announced the same events. If the signs repeat themselves, the events must also; thus it was important to identify them accurately. Time took on a repetitive, almost cyclic, dimension. Its character only amplified the Etruscan sense of predestination.

## FREEDOM AND KNOWLEDGE

What hope of freedom can there be in a space that is allotted forever and in a temporal fate that is predetermined? Refuge consists not in the hope—always limited and risky—of influencing fate, but in the attempt to know it. In other words, divine will defines the scope of human initiatives, but by learning where the boundaries lie, one can determine the field of one's freedom.

What questions did one ask the world of the gods? We must clearly distinguish two approaches, which can only be understood by analyzing the divinatory techniques that offered a privileged contact with the divine. One approach is active and results from a human search, a question, a request; the other is passive and only requires paying attention. In the latter, the gods have the initiative and send signs, while in the former it is the mortal who attempts to interrogate the gods according a code they have provided. The "divinatory" tool is not perceived as a series of magical protocols for action, but as a means to knowledge, authored by the gods who revealed it. It is in this spirit that we must read the words of Seneca quoted above. The knowledge conveyed by Tages, Vegoia, or Cacu thus appears to have been intended to define man's field within the strict limits of an order to which the gods themselves were subordinate.

CHAPTER 2

# Rites of Divination

THE PIACENZA LIVER

In 1877, at Decima di Gossolengo near Piacenza, a peasant working in his field found the famous bronze liver that is today one of the essential sources for our knowledge of Etruscan religion and divination (figs. 2.1, 2.2).[1] What was it doing there, on the outskirts of Piacenza, a Latin colony founded at the end of the third century at a point of contact with the Gauls of the Po valley? An examination of the object out of context gives us only a few clues. The letter forms are southern and relatively late; they suggest a date in the second or early first century B.C. To explain this late date, it is been hypothesized that the object was lost by a haruspex during the civil wars at the time of Sulla, and this theory, in spite of its fragility, seems adequate to many scholars.

The object is about 12 centimeters long. Its form is very stylized, but it clearly represents a sheep's liver. The rounded lower face is sharply separated into two lobes by a straight ridge. The perfectly flat upper face has three geometricized excrescences on its right side: a sort of pyramid with a triangular base (called by Latin authors the *processus pyramidalis*), a small hemispherical protrusion (*processus papillaris*), and finally the gall bladder, a round-bottomed semiconical form. This schematicization is standard. The liver is essentially similar to one in the hands of a late second-, early first-century B.C. haruspex, Aule Lecu, whom a Volterran sculptor depicted reclining on his cinerary urn (fig. 2.3).[2]

On the lower face of the bronze liver, two names are inscribed on either side of the line separating the two lobes. One is *Usils* (Usil is the solar disc, and the *-s* signifies the genitive), associated with a round sign that may indicate the sun. This lobe, then, would designate the sun or the day. The other lobe is inscribed *Tivs,* also in the genitive, and probably signifies the moon or night. Such a two-part division was used also in Mesopotamian hepatoscopy, or liver divination, but there it seems to have been a very generalized division.

The upper face, however, is divided into forty small sections, each carrying the

## Rites of Divination

2.1. Bronze liver found near Piacenza. End of the second century. A memory aid for a haruspex, or a model used for teaching? Piacenza, Museo Civico Archeologico.

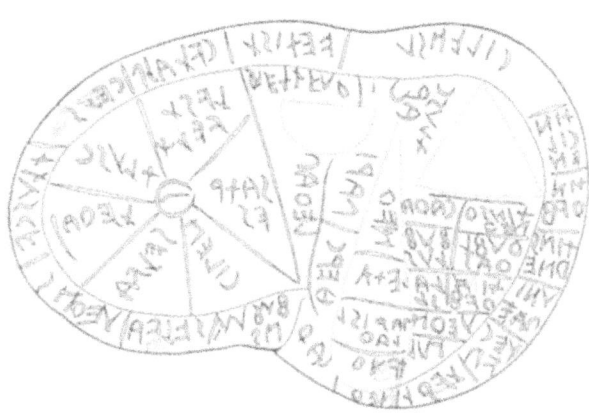

2.2. Drawing of the inscriptions on the Piacenza Liver indicating the domains of the gods.

name of a divinity. A ribbon of sixteen small sections runs around the external border. *Tinia*/Zeus/Jupiter is the lord of the first three regions of the sky; then comes *Uni*/Hera/Juno; and so on. It seems practically certain that these sections correspond roughly to the sixteen domains into which the late-period author Martianus Capella, writing at the beginning of the fifth century A.C., divides the heavens.[3] His description, though partly contaminated by elements from Platonism and oriental astrology, was nonetheless based on still-extant Etruscan beliefs. Cicero, Pliny, and

2.3. Cinerary urn of Aule Lecu. Second century. The deceased holds a liver, whose signs he interprets. Volterra, Museo Guarnacci.

## Rites of Divination

2.4. Roman haruspex depicted on a fragment of molded ceramic *(terra sigillata)* from Arezzo. 25–15 B.C. Tübingen, Institut für Klassische Archäologie.

Pseudo-Acron in his commentary on Horace confirm the value of Martianus Capella's information.

It is also probable that the placement of the sixteen sections on the surrounding border evokes a four-part division of space, which our late sources, distant and complicated though they are, attribute to Etruscan ideas of the universe (e.g., Nigidius Figulus in Arnobius, *Adv. nat.* 3.40). One can easily see here a *pars postica*, which corresponds to the north, a *pars antica* corresponding to the south, a *pars hostilis* to the west, and a *pars familiaris* to the east. The opposition of the two parts of the liver, one called "friendly" and the other "hostile," determined that auspicious signs on the *pars hostilis* be read as unfavorable to the questioner; conversely, inauspicious signs on that side were read as favorable to the questioner. The same game of opposition occurred with the *pars familiaris*.

It is customary, because of the positions of the inscriptions, to orient pictures of the Piacenza Liver so that the gall bladder and the two "lobes" are on the right. For the sake of convenience we shall keep that orientation, but as the urn of Aule Lecu, the Vatican mirror, and, to a lesser extent, a pottery fragment in Tübingen (fig. 2.4)[4] clearly illustrate, the haruspices held the liver in their left hand, with the gall bladder on their left. They turned toward the south so that the orientation of the liver corresponded to that of celestial space, which we have described above and which we shall discuss again in connection with lightning.

Rites of Divination

On the upper part of the right lobe (the one with the gall bladder), Tinia is mentioned three times with different *epikleses*, or surnames. Next comes Uni, followed lower down by divinities such as Tecvm, believed to be Menrva, and Cautha, who is surely a favorable solar divinity. She is probably, to cite Martianus Capella's gloss (*De nuptiis Mercurii et Philologiae*, 1.43–61), "the lively daughter of the sun." The lower left quarter is occupied by divinities related to the earth, food production, and perhaps chance: Fufluns/Dionysus, Selva, Tluscv. Finally, the upper left quarter seems to be the domain of the gods of fate, the Afterworld, and night. One finds Cel/Ge (the earth), then *Cvl* (the door or passage), whom we should probably identify with Culsu, the equivalent of the Latin Janus, and lastly Vetis/Veiovis and Cilens, the god of the night.

Inside this border the space is divided into twenty-four sections of various geometric shapes, each one inscribed with the name of a deity. The left lobe, certainly connected with the chthonian or at least the nocturnal world, is divided into six sections radiating out from the symbol of the moon. The right lobe is divided in a much more complex manner: a few sections occur on the gall bladder; others are arranged in a sort of checkerboard below the pyramidal lobe, and the divinities whose names are inscribed in this sector seem more or less directly connected with the gods on the right side of the surrounding border. It also seems that some gods might be the "guests" of higher gods. Thus we find under the pyramidal lobe the inscription *tinsthneth*, which a recent interpretation translates as: "Nethuns in the house of Tinia." This reminds us that temples in which multiple divinities (*synnaoi*) cohabit are not uncommon. In any case, there are numerous correspondences between the names in the border sections and those in the interior.[5] Let us cite only one example, that of Letham, who appears five times: on the surrounding border in the lower left, in one of the sections of the "wheel" in the left sector, in the lower part of a triangular section at the base of the *processus papillaris*, on the gall bladder, and in the lower part of the "checkerboard" on the right.

HARUSPICY

The placement of anatomical elements such as the gall bladder or the pyramidal lobe, as well as the clear representation of the veins, allowed one to locate with sufficient precision on an actual organ the different sectors identified by inscribed names. These careful details helped the haruspex position the signs that he was observing while he was holding the liver in his left hand, as did Aule Lecu on the Volterran urn (see fig. 2.3), Chalchas on the Vatican mirror (fig. 2.5), and a much later haruspex on a sherd of molded pottery (see fig. 2.4) in Tübingen. The Piacenza Liver served as a kind of model for understanding the liver of a real victim. This organ, essential to life, was in the eyes of the haruspices the reflection, or the projection, of the whole universe. Specifically, it reflected a *templum caeleste*, a sacred space where the gods manifested themselves. The liver is a kind of microcosm of the entire cosmos. Just as time repeats

Rites of Divination

2.5. Chalchas Mirror, from Vulci. The soothsayer is consulting a victim's liver. Around 400 B.C. Vatican, Museo Gregoriano Etrusco.

the units of its duration and the pattern of the *saecula* recurs, space offers identical patterns that are repeated at different levels. One of these patterns allows us to read the others.

By observing spots, morphological accidents, malformations, or the absence of one element or another, the haruspex could know the will of the gods. He began with a general examination of all the interior organs. The amount of blood, whether the heart was visible or not, whether it was surrounded by fat, the position of the spleen: these determined at first glance whether the general climate was auspicious. The color of the liver seems to have been an essential sign: a very dark organ was an unfavorable omen. The absence or malformation of the "head" (the pyramidal lobe) announced defeat or death. In contrast, light or "golden" colorations, which one might observe on the pyramidal lobe or the gall bladder, were very favorable signs. But occasionally the examination of the organs gave no response, no sign could be observed,

# Rites of Divination

and the gods were silent. The term for this was *muta exta* ("mute entrails"), and one either had to do without the gods' advice or ask again.

Rarely did anyone refuse to take the haruspices' advice into account. Always cited in this regard is Caesar, who, on the day of his death, was deaf to the haruspex Spurinna's warning of the absence of the *caput (kephale)* on the liver of the sheep that was sacrificed when the dictator entered the Curia (Appian, *BCiv.* 2.116). While Roman magistrates were content merely to take the auspices, Etruscan haruspices did not limit themselves to summary and generic opinions. They gave a careful reading that seemed a veritable communication with the world of the gods.

## EXSTISPICY

Divination by entrails, as Roman and Greek magistrates or military leaders practiced it, is merely the elementary observation of the *exta*. A general overview of the viscera told one whether the gods accepted or refused the sacrificial offering and, hence, whether they would protect the action that was about to take place. These sacrificial consultations, which Cicero reminds us preceded every important action in Rome, gave answers to precise questions posed by the augurs. The latter took the initiative to pose a question to the gods and expected a positive or negative response.

It was a different matter for the Etruscan haruspices, who, as practitioners of a revealed science of observation and interpretation, did not interrogate the gods but merely proclaimed the state of things and the equilibrium of divine forces. Whereas the Roman augurs provoked a divine response, Etruscan haruspices delivered a revelation or prophecy that was actually only a reading. In other words, while the function of the augurs presupposed a personal relationship with the gods, haruspicy necessitated a knowledge, a science, which was taught and handed down, refined and clarified, generation after generation, through classification, observation, and verification. Thus the reading of signs on the victim's heart, as Pliny says, did not become standard until the beginning of the third century, at the time of Pyrrhus' expedition. Thus, too, L(a)ris Pulenas (see fig. 1.3), who died around 200 B.C., seems to have written new treatises and refined the traditional haruspicy. This "science" can be acquired but not conferred. It is the property of a few, those born from the great aristocratic families. Caecina, Cicero's friend, possessed this organized and precise knowledge, unrelated to Roman augural practices. The famous orator wrote to Caecina that he admired greatly "the truly marvelous teachings that you have received from your father" (Cicero, *Fam.*, 6.6.3).

In Greece and even more in Rome, the summary observation of victims was done by whoever had need of divine advice: a civil or military magistrate, someone elected or appointed to political tasks. The Etruscan haruspices, on the other hand, were specialists in the world of the gods and drew their importance only from the quality of their science. Their role in the city was purely religious. In this respect they were closer to Chaldean *magi* and Mesopotamian specialists than to Roman augurs. This

## Rites of Divination

very resemblance poses a nagging problem, however, as do their methods of reading, mentioned above. Was there a direct contact and thus a close relationship between "Chaldean" hepatoscopy and Etruscan haruspicy? If such contact, completely unverifiable but very plausible, occurred, should we place it at the very origins of Etruscan civilization with Tages' "revelation," or should we instead posit a later stimulus for the essential borrowings, the diffusion of "oriental" beliefs in the Hellenistic period? If the latter, Etruscan hepatoscopic science, in its complex and refined form, would thus be a relatively late phenomenon, and we would have to look elsewhere to find Etruria's creative contribution to mantic practice.

### LIGHTNING

Among the heavenly manifestations that were believed to bear meaning, lightning occupied an essential place. Cicero considered the *libri fulgurales* one of the three main components of the *etrusca disciplina,* and all the ancient authors mention the importance of lightning. On the other hand, they are not in agreement on the origin of this discipline. General opinion attributed it to the nymph Vegoia, but Ammianus Marcellinus (17.10.2) judged that half of it came from Tages, the sage child of Tarquinia, while Arnobius (*Adv. nat.* 2.33) credited it exclusively to Tages.

As with the examination of victims' livers, the reading of lightning rests on a precise and extraordinarily detailed classification. Here again we are a long way from the vague presages drawn, in Greece and late Republican Rome, from claps of thunder, which were enough to cancel a meeting or suspend a debate. Cicero, reading the works of his friend Caecina, informs us of the techniques for observing divine space; Seneca—we do not know whether he really believed it or not—gives us exhaustive information on the points to which the Etruscans were particularly attentive.[6]

In a famous passage, Seneca (*QNat.* 2.32.2) contrasts Stoic and Etruscan attitudes:

> Between the Etruscans, the most learned of men in interpreting lightning, and us (Stoics), there is the following difference: we believe that lightning is produced because the clouds collide, but they believe that the clouds collide in order to produce lightning. In effect, because they attribute everything to the gods, they do not believe that lightning has a meaning because it happens, but that it happens in order to express a meaning.

This extremely important passage measures the fundamental difference between the "fortune-telling" cultures—Greek, Roman, or even contemporary (think of our horoscopes!)—and the Etruscans, who supposed that there was a mutual will to communicate between gods and humans. If we follow Seneca's opinion, natural phenomena are not, in Etruria, simple interpretable clues, but messages from the divine world.

The examination of these celestial signs demanded rigorous attention to minute detail. The basis of every observation was the division of the horizon into sixteen sectors (whereas the Romans divided the sky into four). Each of these sectors was the

## Rites of Divination

domain of a god or at least of a divine function, which ultimately is the same thing. These sectors probably extended up into the celestial vault.

This cartography of the sky, which, as a sort of property division, was attributed to Vegoia, was the prerequisite for every observation. One had to identify the point from which the lightning emerged and that to which it went, and then the direction of its return path. Whether the point where the lightning disappeared was close to or far from the point at which it started determined whether the message was more or less favorable. Furthermore, the shape, the course, and the color of the lightning were also important. The Etruscans could distinguish *manubiae albae* (white lightning), *nigrae* (black), or *rubrae* (red). They recognized those that came from Tinia (three kinds were attributed to him), from Uni, Menrva, Sethlans/Vulcan, or Laran/Mars. Finally Saturn, especially in winter, could generate chthonian thunder from the depths of the earth.

In fact, not all lightning seems to have been considered meaningful. Seneca distinguishes, in his philosophical way, lightning that has a meaning from that which does not, that which is humanly comprehensible from that which is not, and, finally, that which concerns humans from that which does not. Only that which concerns humans can be read, and it transmits messages that can be favorable, unfavorable, indifferent, or uncertain. This prudence, often regarded as coming from Etruscan doctrine, seems too Greek. It must be a late philosophical adaptation of the *etrusca disciplina*. Seneca's reservations are understandable: how can one make the sixteen sectors of the horizon coincide with the nine gods who threw the lightning? How can one coherently construe a system in which eleven types of lightning can all be included in other categories (e.g., according to topography or divinity)? The facts Seneca knew were the result of a complex fusion of very ancient elements with more recent additions, perhaps from Hellenistic or oriental astrology.

This extraordinary variety of signs became even more complicated when one took into account the lightning's effect. The Etruscans seem to have distinguished lightning whose message was permanent, perpetual, and remained valid throughout life from that which applied only for a precise and limited duration, and, finally, from that whose menace could be postponed for a period of six to thirty years, fixed in advance. Tinia had at his disposal three levels of communication corresponding to three types of lightning (fig. 2.6), three *manubiae:* sometimes he merely sent a message, which was generally favorable; sometimes he could only display himself by agreement of the *di consentes*, the college of anonymous and aniconic deities who controlled his actions; sometimes he threw his last and most terrible bolt, which announced catastrophic events and required the consent of the hidden gods (*di involuti*).

Lightning bolts could pierce or knock down, burn or blacken, and the places that they hit were the final clue to their meaning. If the bolt hit a very important public place, it acquired a meaning (usually involving death) for the whole city, but if it hit a private place, the interpretation of the message was generally limited to the private

# Rites of Divination

 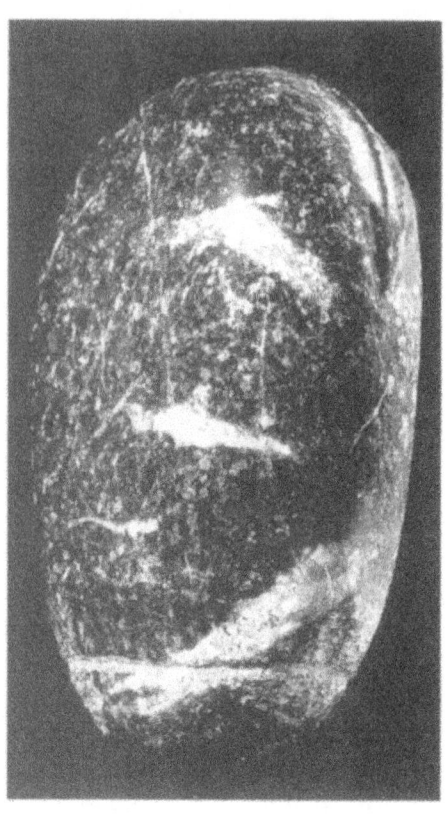

2.6. Tinia brandishing one of his lightning bolts against a giant. Side panel of a bronze chariot of Castel San Mariano, near Perugia. End of the sixth century. Perugia, Museo Archeologico Nazionale.

2.7. Rock incised with the representation of Tinia's lightning bolt: a marker for a place struck by lightning. Sixth century? Orvieto, Museo Claudio Faina.

sphere. Lightning-struck places or things had to undergo appropriate rites, comparable to burial, to protect ritually the trace of the gods' intrusion as well as to contain its effect. Lucan records (1.608) that all the marks made by the lightning were piously gathered and buried in the middle of an enclosure, where a stone box was dedicated to the god responsible (fig. 2.7). A sheep was sacrificed, and the place thus consecrated, the *locus religiosus,* was called *bidental,* a possible allusion to the victim roasted during the ceremony.[7]

The whole "science" of interpreting lightning and thunder was, like haruspicy, continually refined through experience. A rigorous observation of these phenomena and the events that followed them made it possible to verify the meaning of the messages that they communicated. Nigidius Figulus, who lived toward the end of the Roman Republic, wrote up a "brontoscopic" calendar—a series of observations of thun-

# Rites of Divination

der and the events it announced. The predictions drawn from these detailed observations and from this "scientific" system are often of a political nature, and are based on *a posteriori* observations.[8]

But the Etruscans' privileged relationship with lightning did not end there. Familiarity with these phenomena was perhaps the origin of the power that certain people boasted they exercised over lightning itself. Pliny the Elder (*HN* 2.140), who drew his information from Etruscan historiographic sources, tells of King Porsenna, who unleashed lightning against a monster named Volta, which was ravaging the territory of Volsinii. The naturalist's lack of critical judgment toward his sources is well known, so his mention of such an occurrence is hardly surprising; nonetheless this "power" was still claimed at the beginning of the fifth century A.C. by haruspices who tried to stop the advance of Alaric's Visigoths with a barrage of lightning (Zosimus, 5.41). It thus seems that there was a kind of tradition regarding the Etruscan haruspices' power to call down lightning.

This important phenomenon, of which we shall speak again later, relates directly to mortals' ability to act upon divine decisions or fate.

## AUSPICES

Observation of the flight of birds for divination, that is, the reading of the auspices, is generally considered a Roman rather than an Etruscan practice. In fact, its role in the foundation of Rome, when Romulus and Remus observed the flight of birds to determine the most auspicious site for the city, does much to support this opinion. Very ancient but much less well known examples of divine prodigies involving birds, however, are numerous in Etruria. One announced the destiny of Tarquinius Priscus. The message, akin to an omen, was given by an eagle and interpreted by an Etruscan woman:

> As Lucumo (the future Tarquin) and Tanaquil (his wife) were approaching the Janiculum, an eagle, slowly descending, took off Lucumo's hat, then [ . . . ], as if it had been assigned to do this by the gods, returned to put the *pileus* back on his head [ . . . ] Tanaquil, skilled as were all the Etruscans in the interpretation of heavenly prodigies, read the sign with joy. (Livy, 1.34)

This was an act of auspication—the interpretation of the flight of birds. Dionysius of Halicarnassus praised the "Etruscan science of observing birds" (*Tyrrhenike ornithoskopia*), which was well known in his time.

A remarkable depiction of this practice is the painting in the François Tomb in Vulci (fig. 2.8).[9] On the right wall, Vel Saties observes a bird in flight while, at his knees, a dwarf servant named Arnza[10] holds a female woodpecker attached by a string. Here we have one of the most eloquent representations of Etruscan auspication. A bird of a certain species, in this case probably a male woodpecker, is set free in the *templum*, the observation space. The female captive bird attracts the male back after the sign that he has transmitted has been interpreted.

## Rites of Divination

2.8. Vel Saties is probably observing the flight of a woodpecker—the bird of Laran/Mars—in order to draw an omen before a military encounter. The dwarf beside him holds a female bird to attract the male back. François Tomb at Vulci. Around 330. Rome, Villa Albani.

If Vel Saties is observing a woodpecker, it is because he is interrogating Laran, to whom that bird is sacred. It is thus clear that the subject of the consultation is war. The gods wanted to speak of war, and particularly the defeat at Cannae, when they sent a woodpecker to perch on the head of the praetor Aelius Tubero as he was rendering justice. The haruspices did not delay in interpreting this sign and decoding the menace that it contained, not only for Rome but also for the magistrate's family. Similarly, doves transmitted the messages of Turan/Aphrodite, and the eagle, naturally, those of Tinia. Certain birds, however, although they spoke in the name of a god, only gave signs to certain persons. Servius states that doves could only give auspices to kings.

The sector of the sky where the bird flew was a determining factor and, as it did for lightning, provided a major clue. The very precise methods of this system of observation demanded that the observer look toward the south from an unobstructed space, the *auguraculum,* very similar to the terrace on a podium, which antedated the *pars antica* of Etrusco-Italic temples. It seems certain that all these divisions are con-

# Rites of Divination

nected: those of the sky, of the Piacenza Liver, and of the horizon as described by Martianus Capella. The *etrusca disciplina* codified the general practice of interpreting celestial phenomena. The observation of the flight of birds, although it ultimately became a Roman specialty, was probably Etruscan in origin.

As the supernatural designation of Tarquinius Priscus shows, however, divine birds could act in extraordinary ways. Now let us discuss omens.

## OMENS

When the usual order of the world seems disturbed, when an abnormal event occurs, it cannot be an ordinary chance happening for this people who "attribute all things to the gods." It must be a sign. The key to the whole Etruscan concept of the world and of life lay in the certainty of a permanent communication with the gods. The observation of omens, which the Latins called *ostenta*, their interpretation, their "expiation," and the eventual elimination of the worldly disorder, were the domain in which the haruspices operated.

They distinguished omens, completely exceptional phenomena, from merely unusual signs that could recur. In the sign given to the young Tarquin (Lucumo), the eagle flying overhead is simple auspication and merely signifies the protection of Tinia. The fact that the eagle took off Tarquin's hat and then put it back on again, however, is an omen. It was interpreted as a promise of royalty.

According to Pliny the Elder and Macrobius, the Romans learned of these phenomena and their interpretation through the Latin translation of Tarquitius Priscus *(De rebus divinis)*. These authors believed that this knowledge and its rules had been written down by the Etruscans in the *libri rituales*.

Among the most ordinary, but also the most inauspicious omens were the births of deformed animals, such as calves with several heads, or monstrous or seriously abnormal children. A hermaphrodite was considered a deathly prodigy. These were closed up in chests and thrown into the sea. Deformed animals were destroyed whole and their remains burned on a fire specially lit from the wood of *arbores infelices* (deathly or sinister trees). Among the plants that had to be removed from gardens were the wild rose bush, the cornel tree, trees whose berries were black, and the wild pear, which was sacred to the infernal world. The ferns were also considered inauspicious. The laurel, on the other hand, in spite of the color of its fruit, was considered an auspicious tree that promised success.

Comets were also *ostenta*. Their periodicity, over a long space of time, did not make them ordinary celestial events, and they naturally augured ill.

"It rained milk, which might seem ordinary, but also blood, iron and wool," as Pliny says (*HN* 2.147), ". . . and even chalk" (J. Obsequens, *De prodigiis*, 47). These surprising meteoric occurrences were always interpreted by the haruspices as inauspicious signs.[11]

Rites of Divination

When nature emitted groans or unusual sounds, from the depths of the earth or from the sky, the haruspices found ways to interpret the prodigious voice. Trumpet blasts or the clashing of arms, rumblings from deep below ground, announced conflicts or changes of the *saecula*.

Unfortunately, all the examples we have mentioned are relatively late. They come from Roman sources, and they record interpretations of haruspices well after the Etruscan period proper. Can one legitimately project the data of the Republican, even the Imperial, period back into the distant past? The haruspices who accompanied the emperor Julian or those who offered their services to the bishop of Rome on the eve of the Alaric's sack: could they serve as models for our understanding of those who operated in the sixth century B.C.? Studies of the *etrusca disciplina* have always, probably by necessity, ignored the logical objections posed by this anachronism. We are condemned to use only late sources, since they are the only ones we have. Nonetheless, much of the information we utilize has been handed down to us in very archaic form. This encourages us to think that it comes directly from original texts of the *libri rituales* and was preserved by a religious conservatism over long centuries, well beyond Etruscan history properly defined.

LOTS

Judging from the techniques codified by the *etrusca disciplina*, one might too easily assume that there was a coherence in divinatory practice. There was much less than it seems. On the one hand, the reading of celestial signs, omens, and messages hidden in the entrails of victims was a science of interpreting revealed clues. On the other hand, the questioning of the future, destiny, or the will of the gods was often accomplished in a totally different manner. While the *etrusca disciplina*, unanimously admired by the ancients as a kind of science, formed the official framework of divination, the daily practice was often very different, and it reveals the importance of external influences.

Lots were consulted everywhere. These were little plaques of wood, bone, or bronze, or tokens, little metal balls with engraved inscriptions. They kept these small inscribed objects in a box, and the person who wanted to consult them drew them out at random. Each token or plaque bore the name of an oracular god. Most often the name was Śuri/Aplu (that is, Apollo, the mantic god *par excellence*), but we have a box of lots that was offered to Menrva, and we know that this practice was particularly common in the sanctuary of Fortuna at Praeneste. The response was usually written on the same lot. A token from Arezzo[12] ordered the consultant to make an offering to a rather enigmatic god named Farthan (fig. 2.9): *aplu. puteś. / Tur. Fartnś.*, "From Pythian Apollo: make an offering to Farthan." Other lots responded affirmatively or negatively to questions posed.

Here we see that the consultation of lots involved a different approach from the

# Rites of Divination

2.9. Inscribed rock from Arezzo, Santa Croce: *Aplu. puteś. Tur. Fartnś,* which can be translated, "Pythian Apollo: make a gift to *Farthan,*" or "Apollo (says): give to *Farthan* the (offering)."

one used in reading livers or lightning, for example. While the "signs" interpreted by the haruspices were given by the gods at their own initiative, so to speak, consulting lots demanded information from a god on a specific point. Now the initiative is human and the subject of the consultation chosen by the consultant. The mortal is no longer passively waiting, but actively seeking a response from a god.

### ORACLES

A very similar approach was involved in consulting oracles. A famous mirror in Siena (fig. 2.10) shows *Atunis* and *Euturpa* (Adonis and Euterpe) consulting an oracle coming from the mouth of *Urphe* (Orpheus). The hero's head, which seems to have been caught in a net by a fisherman named *Umaele,* emerges from the water at the consultants' feet. The words of this oracle are written on the tablets that a woman named *Aliunea* is displaying.[13] The protagonists of this scene, like many of the characters represented on mirrors of this period, are Greek, but here their Greekness is consistent with the nature of the oracular consultation. This same type of oracular prophecy is probably also illustrated on several other mirrors (see fig. 1.2)[14] and alluded to in several funerary reliefs[15] in which a certain Cacu is represented in the act of prophesying, probably in verse and with musical accompaniment, while an assistant writes down his vaticinations. On other representations, the same character appears to be the object of a battle between opposing political camps that are trying to gain mastery over his revelations (see chapter 1). This type of divination seems to be somewhat different from that codified in the *etrusca disciplina,* but it became increasingly frequent in later periods.

In fact, the great oracular consultations had occasionally been practiced in Etruria well before the superficial Hellenization of the third and second centuries touched Etrusco-Roman Italy. The most famous, which astonishes everyone who has worked on Etruscan divination, is the consultation of Pythian Apollo, which Herodotus

Rites of Divination

2.10. Mirror from Chiusi: Aliunea (Albunea) notes a prophecy, fixing in writing the word coming from the head, perhaps that of Orpheus, rising out of the water. Around 300 B.C. Siena, Museo Archeologico.

reports (1.167). Phocean prisoners from the sea battle of Sardinia were divided between the Carthaginians and the Tyrrhenians. The latter

> led them out of their city and stoned them. Since that time, any of the inhabitants of Caere who passed by the place where the Phoceans had been stoned, whether livestock, beasts of burden or men, became deformed, crippled, or impotent. Wanting to make amends for their mistake, the Caeretans sent to (consulted) Delphi. The Pythia ordered them to do what they still do to this day: they offer rich sacrifices to the shades of the Phoceans and instituted in their honor gymnastic and equestrian games.

The place of this "expiation" and the games and sacrifices seems to be Montetosto, identified several years ago and considered today a fine example of a politico-religious complex.[16]

This Delphic consultation, besides the fact that it resulted from an event in which

## Rites of Divination

the Greeks were involved, is of a very different nature from Etruscan divination. It seeks counsel from the god of Delphi on Greek religious practices that were foreign to the science of the haruspices but within Apollo's jurisdiction. There is nothing surprising here: Etruscan divination does not consult Greek gods; it interprets signs and omens. This event probably happened at an early time and required consultation of the Delphic oracle, the only one that Herodotus, writing from the Greek point of view, can logically mention. In this event, as in the scene illustrated by the Orpheus mirror or generally in the drawing of lots, the consultants posed precise questions to the gods and solicited responses. This procedure is Greek. It ultimately became Roman and even Etruscan after the third century, when Hellenic religious practices were widespread. But this attitude probably had no place in the *etrusca disciplina*, whose essence was quite different.

The Greek oracles clearly filled a need that the *etrusca disciplina* could not satisfy. Etruscan consultations at Delphi in fact must have been rather numerous to justify their constructing, in the *temenos*, the *thesauros* of the Agylleans—that is, a chapel to hold the offerings to the god from the people of Caere. One did not ask Apollo about the decisions of the gods, but one did ask him advice on what to do.

### DETERMINISM AND FREEDOM

The messages of fate and the gods' opinions, which the haruspices read in the sky, in omens, and in entrails, were not essentially changeable. They did not incite action. It was vain to try to bend or thwart the superior will, and the Etruscans were content merely to determine it.

At the very most one might try to slow down the decisions of fate. Our Latin sources speak of signs whose predicted events could be postponed. In the clearest case, that of the *fulgura prorogativa* ("delayable thunderbolts"), a person could hope for a delay of ten years maximum, and a city, a delay of thirty years. Here again, the role of divination was not so much to offer an opportunity for action as to offer knowledge.

Etruscan fatalism is often mentioned as responsible for the passive decline of Etruscan civilization. Clearly, the mechanisms of divination suggest that fate is unchangeable, though decipherable, and that one does not have the freedom to try to sway divine decisions.

CHAPTER 3

# Sacrificial and Funerary Rites

THE GREAT RITUAL TEXTS

Little remains of the *libri rituales*[1] that governed all of public life, and perhaps even many acts of private life. We suspect that it is in this section of the "Etruscan library" that the titles were the most numerous. In the Latin authors, we encounter scattered allusions to the *libri fatales,* which deal with the fate of individuals as well as groups, and to the *libri acheruntici,* which describe the Afterworld, the beings that inhabit it, its geography, its routes, and probably its workings. These books also contained rules for the management of society and the foundation of cities, and even treatises governing military affairs: the *libri exercituales* (Cassiodorus, *Var.* 11.1.6). The fragments attributed to the nymph Vegoia that dealt with boundaries very probably also belonged to the *libri rituales*.

*The Zagreb Book*

The ritual texts were usually written on linen fabric, as were the Roman magistrate lists, which Livy (4.20) says were kept in a temple of Juno: "our old annals as well as the books of the magistrates were written on fabric and placed in the Temple of Juno Moneta."

The luck of archaeology has preserved an example. A relatively late linen book (*liber linteus*), dating to the end of the second or beginning of the first century, came by chance to Egypt, probably during the first century B.C., and was cut up and resewn by an Egyptian embalmer, who used it to wrap the mummy of a young woman. This mummy, bought by a Croatian collector, became the property of the Academy of Zagreb. Only in 1892 was the true nature of this text discovered. It is a document of primary importance for us.[2]

It is a liturgical calendar, clearly identifiable by the formulae indicating dates: for example, *eslem.zathrumiś.acale,* June 18. It also contains numerous names of gods: in particular, Nethuns (Neptune),[3] and, less frequently, Veive (Veiovis) and Catha (the sun god). The text offers many examples of words formed on the root *sac* fol-

## Sacrificial and Funerary Rites

3.1. A folded *liber linteus* supporting a priest's hat. Hollow funerary group from Chiusi-Chianciano. End of the fifth century. Berlin, Staatliche Museen.

lowed by various inflections. This root clearly designates the sacred or consecrated character of an object or a place, as in *sacni* ("sanctuary"), which appears often. The book specifies the sort of religious acts that must be accomplished, but it is sometimes difficult to determine their exact nature. For example, one of the rites is designated by the root *vacl*, which appears more than ten times on the Capua Tablet in its more ancient and southern form, *vacil*. There it has the rather general meaning of "festival,"[4] but its translation is unfortunately imprecise.

Calendars of this type, which listed everything that had to be done ritually day by day, were the chief documents for the religious activity of a specific sanctuary or city. The acts were usually listed there in the imperative mood: the very relationship with the divine and the resulting cosmic balance depended on the exact performance of these prescribed actions.

The possession of these great fabric books was a mark of knowledge and religious power. Thus they figure quite visibly on the funerary monuments of several deceased personages of high rank. Behind the head of a reclining figure in the Tomb of the Sarcophagi in Cerveteri, a similar "book"[5] is carefully folded (see fig. 1.6), and on the bed of a high-ranking person from Chiusi, another book is noticeably positioned as a support for the hat worn by the important priests of this city (fig. 3.1).[6] One is tempted to read a symbolism into this latter composition: the idea that religious power rests on sacred knowledge.

These books, folded like a road map so that one could open them either to a double page or to a single one, were, as in the Tomb of the Reliefs at Caere,[7] the property of important persons, and represent both the mark of their social position and the tool

## Sacrificial and Funerary Rites

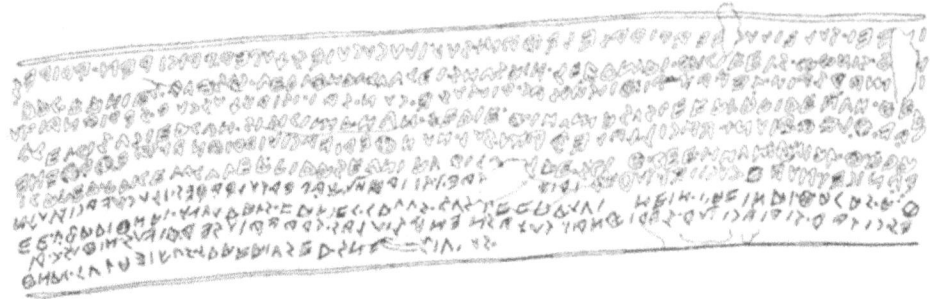

3.2. The Capua tablet, a liturgical calendar, lines 8–17: rites of Letham in the sanctuary of Hamae, festivals of Uni and Calu. Beginning of the fifth century. Berlin, Staatliche Museen.

of their power. The delicacy of the material on which the texts were written required that these books be private property or at least of very limited access.

*The Capua Tablet*
The object usually called the Capua "Tile," dating from about 470 (see fig. 1.8 and fig. 3.2),[8] is a calendar incised onto a terracotta plaque, a *tabula*. It was meant to be hung, so it must have had a public function. The text, which reverses direction at the end of each line in the pattern called *boustrophedon*, is not easy to decipher. One wonders if it actually could be read when it was displayed in the temple.

This calendar of the ceremonies of a Campanian sanctuary lists an average of four religious acts per month. The cult of Letham, a very important god of whom we are completely ignorant, holds the most significant place. In the first months of the year there are five rites dedicated to him. In March rites are dedicated to unknown deities who seem to share the month's festivals with him (or her: we do not even know the sex of this god), since rites offered to Letham are listed just before and just after them. One also finds rituals dedicated to gods of apparently little importance, such as Calu, or practically unknown gods, such as Afe, Qanur, Savcne, Fulinusne, and Savalsie (see chapter 9). Is this a sign of provincialism, or rather is the deep religious reality of Etruria suddenly revealed, thanks to this text, at Capua?

In fact, the content of this calendar reveals the extreme complexity of the rites. They are called by different names, which we shall discuss later in connection with the different types of sacrifices. This liturgical text also defines the relative importance of the rites. We know by the mood of the verbs that prescribe them which ones must absolutely take place as opposed to those that should be celebrated. From the multiplicity of divine names and the variety of acts of piety listed we sense the complexity of this religion as well as the extent of our ignorance.

*The Magliano Lead Tablet*
The text engraved on a bronze disk known inappropriately as "the Magliano Lead Tablet" (fig. 3.3) contains only dedications to infernal and celestial deities. Nonethe-

## Sacrificial and Funerary Rites

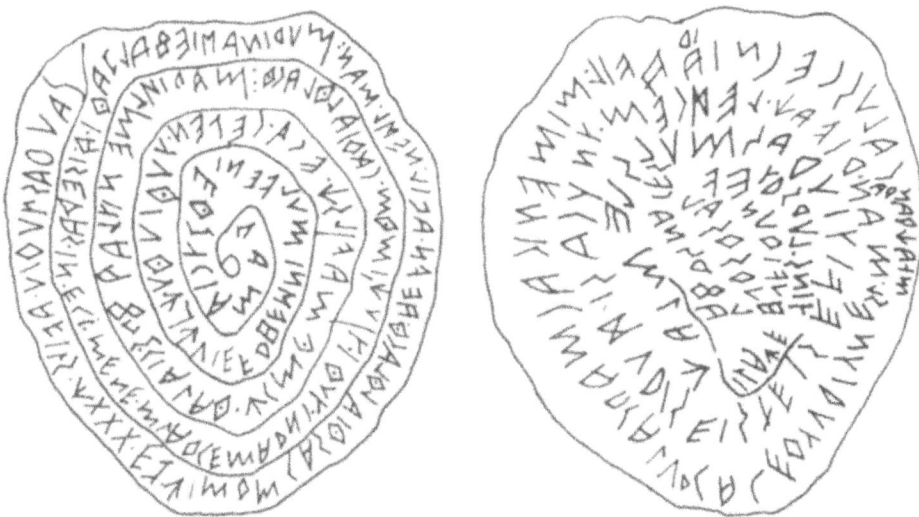

3.3. Reconstruction drawing of the Magliano lead tablet (from Heba Magliano in the Sabine territory): evocation of chthonic deities. Mid-fifth century. Florence, Museo Archeologico Nazionale, Soprintendenza Archeologica per la Toscana Firenze.

less, it confirms the important role of writing in religious life, for which it fixes the rites and defines the acts. These sacred texts are somehow authenticated or guaranteed by writing. At the beginning of the preserved text of the *liber linteus* one reads: *zichri*, "must be written." The expression *zichunce*, "has been written," occurs with an almost identical function on the Capua Tablet and the Perugia Cippus. It thus appears that the ritual is actually fixed mainly by writing.

The structure of these texts differs only slightly from that of the liturgical calendars or the "Iguvine Tablets," a famous list of the Umbrian religious festivals of Gubbio. The latter is written in Umbrian, and for this reason it is much more comprehensible. Also similar are the Roman ritual of the Arval Brethren and the religious laws related by Cato. Comparison with these texts allows us to propose a more concrete interpretation for the rules of Etruscan ritual.

The prescriptions most often inscribed in the *libri rituales* probably differed little from those contained in these rare documents. They deal primarily with one essential act: sacrifice.

### SACRIFICES

The rite most frequently mentioned in the *libri rituales* is the sacrifice. One verb is frequently used to prescribe it: *nuntheri*, "one must sacrifice." The actual word for sacrifice seems to be *nunthen*, which appears almost twenty times in the text of the *liber linteus*. The performance of the sacrificial rites is strictly fixed and differs in several ways from that which we know from the Greek world.

# Sacrificial and Funerary Rites

3.4. Relief from Perugia on the circular base of a funerary monument, probably sculpted by an artisan from Chiusi: priests and a scene of sacrifice. Beginning of the fifth century. Perugia, Museo Archeologico Nazionale.

3.5. "Campana" plaque from Caere: painted terracotta, originally part of the decoration of a sanctuary or house: an altar and an incense burner are visible. Sixth century. Paris, Musée du Louvre.

Everything begins with a procession. Every participant, whether priest or family member, brings something necessary for the sacrifice, offerings as well as implements. Many depictions of sacrifice no doubt show us only private acts, taking place within the family or in a funerary context. A travertine base,[9] probably carved by a Chiusine artist, depicts priests carrying the curved *lituus*, other bearers of insignia, women, and children. They approach an altar where the fire is prepared and above which clouds are forming (fig. 3.4).

A painted terracotta plaque from Caere[10] shows a man in a short tunic standing in front of a burning altar on which an incense burner (*thymiaterion*) has been placed. He seems to be praying or preparing himself for a sacrifice (fig. 3.5). Another scene on a relief from Chiusi (fig. 3.6) shows the sacrificants and people leading and trying to calm the victim, a bull. They face an altar on which an incense burner sits and a fire is already lit.[11] On a mirror from Praeneste, a musician plays the *aulos*, the double oboe, while a priest, who is probably the sacrificant, pours a libation above the flame. The victim, a goat, is being caressed and reassured at the foot of the altar by an aide with the features of a Silenus (fig. 3.7). Sileni are often present in sacrifice scenes as well, and it is not clear whether their presence alludes to a cult of Dionysus or to one of nature more generally.

These are clear allusions to the necessity that the sacrificial victims "consent" (or pretend to). An animal that recoiled or bellowed could not be sacrificed, nor could an animal with a defect. The Romans called the preliminary examination of the victim *probatio*. In Greece the sacrificial knife was hidden inside a basket of barley, the *kanoun*, apparently so that the violence of the act would be masked as long as possible. This practice did not exist in Etruria, where the sacrificial instruments are quite visible. The knife, the single-bladed axe, and the libation vessel even appear on certain coins.[12]

In the Capua ritual, the April sacrifice to Letham involves a whole series of rites performed by priests. It seems that they first brought lesser offerings, then led out the victims in the manner prescribed in the Greek ritual. The calendar of the Attic deme Ercheia stipulates that it is necessary, in certain ceremonies, to sacrifice a ewe

# Sacrificial and Funerary Rites

3.6. Scene of sacrifice; fragment of a sarcophagus or cinerary urn. Relief from Chiusi, beginning of the fifth century. On the altar, a blazing fire and an incense burner are visible. Paris, Musée du Louvre.

"that is not pregnant," and in others, a victim "with a black fleece."[13] It seems that stipulations of the same kind applied in Etruscan sacrifices, and the Capua ritual appears to give examples. Unfortunately they are impossible to translate with certainty. As in Greece, certain parts of the victim, often the skin or sometimes a thigh, were reserved for the participants, the personnel of the sanctuary, or the most important priests.

In some cases the sacrifice could be an offering of bread or cake or a simple libation. The word *vinum* appears frequently in the *liber linteus*, suggesting that many of the sacrifices were merely liquid offerings. It seems, however, that the rules sometimes forbade the use of wine. Nonetheless, some altars of clearly funerary function were hollowed out expressly for libations, and an altar at Populonia even bears a fragmentary inscription that mentions wine in a jug. It must be wine, too, that a bearded man, accompanied by a young *aulos*-player, offers to a female, either the deceased or a goddess, in the Tomb of the Baron (fig. 3.8).

*Human Sacrifices?*
Should we, as is usually done, interpret as a human sacrifice the scene on a sarcophagus of Tuscania[14] in which two busts appear on an altar? It may instead be a scene of a massacre in a consecrated place. Human sacrifice was not unknown in Rome during grave crises, and it is very possible that the Etruscan ritual books, like the Sibylline Books, had provided for these sacrifices. Aulus Gellius' comment (5.12.12) that the slaughter of a goat to Veiovis[15] was to be performed *humano ritu*, by the

Sacrificial and Funerary Rites

3.7. Mirror from Palestrina with a scene of sacrifice: note the obligatory presence of the musician and the gesture of the sacrificial aide who calms the future victim. Fifth century. Florence, Museo Archeologico Nazionale, Soprintendenza Archeologica per la Toscana Firenze.

human ritual, suggests that this was a substitute animal, meant to bring the deceased a kind of immortality (see *infra*, "Heroization and the *Di Animales*"). An event that historians generally interpret as a war crime, the massacre of 307 Roman prisoners at Tarquinia in 358 (Livy, 7.15.10ff.), might be considered a sacrificial act intended to heroicize Etruscan victims of the war against Rome. The popularity of the theme of the slaughter of Trojan prisoners on the pyre of Patroclus[16] might lead one to think that the efficacy of such an act was generally accepted. Ultimately this painting, the only possible reference to a real, not mythical, human sacrifice, is unfortunately not very explicit.

Depictions of sacrifice scenes are often very simplified: the participants are limited

## Sacrificial and Funerary Rites

3.8. Tarquinia, Tomb of the Baron: offering (libation?) to a god or a deceased woman; here, too, the music seems indispensable. End of the sixth century.

in number, and the *aulos*-player, although indispensable, is often forgotten. Besides, the most archaic illustrations place very odd sacrificants in the scene: Sileni and satyrs, who impart a Dionysiac atmosphere, or at least evoke the savage character of the sacrificial act. One finds such characters on a mirror from Praeneste (see fig. 3.7), a bronze relief from Bomarzo, and a black-figure amphora in Dresden, for example.[17]

It is more difficult to perceive the real function of the sacrifices depicted in the reliefs or stipulated in the calendars. The Etruscans (and to a lesser degree the Greeks) distinguished two types of victims. As we have seen (chapter 2), the haruspices consulted or interrogated one type, which the Latin language designates by the term *hostiae consultatoriae*. They offered an opportunity to know the divine will. The others, used to satisfy cult obligations and to honor the gods, were rather curiously named *hostiae animales*. Each of these sacrificed victims, in dying, freed a soul, and these souls, through complex funerary rites that were influenced by Orphic-Pythagorean cults of Magna Graecia, brought life again to the dead, who could thus escape the common fate and acquire the status of *di animales*, a kind of immortality. The majority of funerary sacrifices must have had this function, at least after the end of the Archaic period, and the altars that one finds in the necropoleis of Tarquinia and Caere or on the terraces of the tombs at San Giuliano and Castel d'Asso probably

Sacrificial and Funerary Rites

3.9. Amphora of the Micali Painter depicting a religious procession, a *pompa* with dancers and Sileni. From Vulci, end of the sixth century. The British Museum.

served for rituals of this kind. These were rites of heroization which we shall discuss later.

*Processions*
Sacrificial processions are seldom illustrated and nowhere described. This is not the case for the great parades traditionally called *pompae,* which we know both from descriptions and from illustrations.

Who are these women, magnificently dressed in their long, finely pleated tunics, their heads crowned with a diadem and partly covered by a fold of their long cloaks, who, holding a palm in their veiled hands, walk in procession, two by two, to the beat of a musician? We encounter them on several monuments from Chiusi[18] of the early fifth century and on a lost urn from Volterra, but a famous amphora attributed to the Micali Painter depicts them best.[19] On this remarkable, often-studied vase (fig. 3.9)[20] runs a long procession, which we should probably put into the category of funeral ceremonies. It is a veritable *pompa,* often compared to the procession for the games that took place in Rome in 499, as described by Dionysius of Halicarnassus (*Ant. Rom.* 7.72–73). We see a succession of dancing Sileni, veiled women, other dancers

## Sacrificial and Funerary Rites

who play the castanets called *crotales*, and two important personages carrying the insignia of their rank. The painter could not have depicted the entire procession described by Dionysius, especially since he assigned a large part of the vase to the funeral games. We are not shown the participants in the rest of the procession, but there must have been musicians, *aulos-* and *cithara*-players, whom the same bas-reliefs of Chiusi depict marching backward to guide the procession of women. Finally, Dionysius mentions bearers of incense burners (*thymiateria*) and divine images, which were placed on the altar where the sacrifices initiating the games took place.

The most important sacrifices, whether for public or private ceremonies, probably followed ritual processions that were fixed or stipulated by the sacred texts. A passage of the *liber linteus* may name these ceremonies when it lists, in terms that we cannot translate with certitude, the acts that must be performed in honor of Letham on the Ides of April.

### FOUNDATION RITES

In the *libri rituales* we also find prescriptions regarding the ritual founding of cities. According to Festus (258 L), everything that concerns the city was stipulated in the Etruscan books:

> The rites that one should follow to found cities, the manner of consecrating altars and temples, of making walls inviolable, the legal function of the urban gates, the system for organizing tribes, centuries, and curiae, the system for forming and organizing armies . . .

But the variety of the subjects listed in this simple text also reveals their limits. The rites mentioned in this passage have clearly been collected at a late period in order to establish, by means of a false antiquity arbitrarily dated to the Etruscans, their sacred and hence untouchable character. This theoretical reworking owes much to the Greek cities of the East as well as to the founding of Roman colonies.

Although everything that concerns the organization of the city seems to stem from an *a posteriori* justification, the antiquity of the foundation rites as they were practiced cannot be doubted. They fit easily into the general concepts of spatial organization discussed above (chapter 1), and their form is in accordance with those of divination and sacrificial procedures. That they were widely practiced is confirmed by the orientation of sanctuaries,[21] urban axes, and even tombs. Cities founded *etrusco ritu*, according to this secular rite, were more prestigious and more sacred than those that could not claim such an origin.

The first rite to be performed, naturally, was auguration, the taking of the auspices. Rome's traditional founding is preserved in all the accounts.[22] It began with the observation of the flight of birds, which confirmed the identity of the founder and the choice of site. This consultation of the divine world required an observation spot rigorously oriented toward the south and a *templum* whose projection on the ground served as the orientation point for every urban development.

## Sacrificial and Funerary Rites

Next came the rites of orientation and the laying out of the site. The latter were described or prescribed in the *libri rituales*. The sighting tool, the *groma*, was borrowed from Greece, transformed in Etruria, and bequeathed by the Etruscan surveyors to the Latin *gromatici;* its very name came into Latin through Etruscan. Its method of use is well known, and it gave a strict orientation to the urban fabric. The streets and avenues of Marzabotto testify to its use (see fig. 1.10), as does the layout of Capua. The requirement that every city have three streets and three gates probably originates from examples of this kind. It is possible, however, that this technique of surveying and orientation is rather late and that the rules that govern it date at the earliest to the second half of the sixth century. They may have originated both in the Etruscan Po valley and in Etruscan Campania.

Finally, the circuit of the city was traced out. The founding rite is strictly stipulated. It is described in detail by Plutarch (*Rom.* 11) and must certainly be of Etruscan origin:

> The founder places a bronze plowshare on his plow, harnesses a bull and a cow to it, then guides them as he cuts a deep furrow along the circular line that has been traced. Men follow him who have the task of throwing to the inside the clods that the plowshare turns up and not letting any remain on the outside. . . . At the places where he wants to set a gate, he pulls back the plowshare, lifts the plow and leaves an interval. Thus did they consider the whole wall sacred with the exception of the gates.

A marble plaque from the beginning of the first century A.C. depicts this unusual task[23] as it was performed by Roman magistrates for the foundation, *etrusco ritu*, of the Roman colony of Aquileia. It is perhaps possible to identify this same activity in the famous bronze group of a plowman and his team from Arezzo.[24] He wears a hat similar to that of certain priests (fig. 3.10).

The ritual books probably specified the conditions for the founding and consecration of cult places and certainly for the orientation of temples. If one studies the variations in these orientations at the same site, one can often detect changes in the attribution of cult places. But the tradition requiring a city to have three temples—to honor a triad—seems too Romanizing. It must have originated at the time of the founding of Roman colonies in Etruscan territory.

It is difficult to determine what in the "Etruscan rite" is really Etruscan and not a later attachment. It is certain, on the other hand, that very strict rules of a quasi-religious nature governed all urban changes. It is customary to attribute to Hippodamus of Miletus the invention of the orthogonal plan, which, in fact, appeared from the beginning of the sixth century in the cities of the Greek West; but the city plans of central Italy are certainly Etruscan and derive from the science of measuring the world that was fixed by the *libri rituales*.

The consecration, the ritual founding, the truly religious creation of buildings within a space ordered by divine laws, renders them untouchable. Any destruction would have been a sacrilege, a strike against the consecrated order, unless certain

# Sacrificial and Funerary Rites

3.10. The Arezzo plowman: is this a scene of agriculture or of the foundation of a city? Around 400 B.C. Rome, Museo Naz. di Villa Giulia.

rules, symmetrical to those of the foundation, were respected. The ritual destruction of the Murlo complex[25] and the religious burial of the debris from the building, about 530, are evidence that there were very strict religious procedures of "defoundation." The same rites persisted for a long time. They were used at Bolsena for the destruction of the sanctuary of Fufluns/Dionysus/Bacchus.[26] Thus every act involved in establishing or removing a cult place was done according to a fixed ritual and was probably prescribed in the books of the *etrusca disciplina*.

FUNERAL CEREMONIES

*Prothesis*
No text exists that describes the ceremonies associated with death. We particularly regret the lack of texts preserving rites that might illuminate the passage to the Etruscan Afterworld. On the other hand, the rites of death have often been depicted. The most commonly illustrated ritual is the laying out of the corpse, which the Greeks called *prothesis* (fig. 3.11). Here again practices differ from what we know in Greece. Under a tent with flaps open to allow a view through to a grove of shrubs, the body has been arranged on a bed of state, elevated on several mattresses, and partially covered with a heavy cloth. Sometimes, the scene takes place under a columnar portico. The women of the family lament or offer perfumes. The men, toward the foot of the bed, make gestures of grief, their hands to their foreheads. Sometimes a child is lifted up to the dead person's face. Often an *aulos*-player, mounted on a stool, plays a music that one imagines to be strident and violent.

Sacrificial and Funerary Rites

3.11. The dead person lying in state (*prothesis*) under a tent: relief on a hollow base from Chiusi. Beginning of the fifth century. Copenhagen, Ny Carlsberg Glyptothek.

3.12. Dance of lamentation on a funerary relief from Chiusi. Beginning of the fifth century. Copenhagen, Ny Carlsberg Glyptothek.

*Lamentations*

Dances of lamentation encircle the scene. Women in heavy cloaks, their hair unbound, raise their hands to scratch their faces, then their fists to their chests in a movement regulated like a ballet (fig. 3.12). In this scene the displays of sorrow seem restrained, and the other mourners limit themselves to greeting the dead with raised hands. The burial and the cremation are never represented: no pyre is ever shown, even in the regions of northern Etruria where cremation was common. When Etruscan artists depict the Homeric theme of the funeral of Patroclus, they simplify or suppress the image of the pyre altogether. The *ekphora,* the funeral procession to carry out the corpse, is rarely pictured, although this theme is frequently represented on Greek ceramics.[27] The disappearance of the corpse is, as it were, kept secret. Instead the funerary repertoire offers detailed and pleasing depictions of the rituals that follow.

*Banquets*

The funeral banquet was clearly the preferred theme of artists, at least until the last quarter of the fifth century. It is important to distinguish, however, between the scenes of ordinary gatherings of men reclining, listening to a musician, and being served drinks, and the actual funeral banquets, complete with richly dressed women, songs of praise to the dead, and the necessary athletic and equestrian games taking place nearby.

Sacrificial and Funerary Rites

3.13. Tarquinia, Tomb of the Funeral Bed. The banquet *kline* is occupied by two cones bearing garlands and crowns: images of the dead? Mid-fifth century. Modern rendering from the beginning of the twentieth century. Copenhagen, Ny Carlsberg Glyptothek.

For the latter, some depictions seem to offer more information. The paintings of the Tarquinian Tomba della Scrofa Nera[28] (about 460) show one of these funeral banquets where the women do not drink, but hold eggs, symbols of life, or crowns of flowers, symbols of protection. The men maintain a serious attitude, even while they are playing *kottabos*; and a young woman, accompanying herself on a lyre, sings a poem that must have a connection with the ritual depicted.

In the famous Tomb of the Triclinium, many banqueters stretch out empty hands. They seem neither to drink nor to eat, but to mime a banquet, as if the rite were less about food than about gestures.

In the Tarquinian Tomb of the Funeral Bed, the painter has represented the whole scene[29] as it actually occurred. Under a fabric pavilion, banqueting couches have been arranged for all the mourners, but the people gather around a monumental bed, a sumptuous *kline* covered with a mattress and costly fabrics. On this bed are two cones of draped fabric, crowned at their base with garlands, as the hats of banqueters would be. According to one theory, this is a *lectisternium*, a bed bearing sacred images, where the Dioscuri were worshipped, and it thus symbolizes a banquet for the class of knights. This interpretation is tenuous, however. The cones of fabric are not the headgear of the gods, and the whole scene is bathed in a funerary atmosphere (fig. 3.13).

## Sacrificial and Funerary Rites

Are these two cones the headwear of dignitaries or religious symbols? It is difficult to determine, but certainly these images symbolically replace the "kings" of the banquet. For them the musician plays and the servants offer food and drink. The funeral banquet is being celebrated around the emblematic representations of two absent personages: the dead husband and wife, we think. Beyond this fabric pavilion are the offering procession and the athletic and equestrian games that accompany the ceremony. The dead were probably believed to preside over the banquet that was taking place around their symbolic presence and over the games that took place before their *kline*. All funerary meals and banquets, all athletic and equestrian games, were probably celebrated this way, around the symbols of the dead. Most other depictions leave out the image of the empty *kline* that symbolized the presence of the dead.

### Dances

Servants, musicians, dancers, athletes, and horsemen all crowd into these banquet scenes. The reliefs of Chiusi and the paintings of Tarquinia vie with each other to depict them. First come the offering bearers, who bring vessels for serving or drinking or, like the little servants on contemporary Attic funerary stelae, carry boxes with the lids open. On a sarcophagus from Vulci,[30] servants bring the dead their personal objects: for the woman, a cista and candelabra, feminine and domestic objects; for the man, masculine objects and magisterial insignia. It is difficult to know with certainty who actually participated in these activities. While the servants and offering bearers are obviously subordinate figures, one cannot say the same for the male and female dancers. They are dressed like the masters reclining at the banquet, and with infinite elegance they cross and meet each other in laurel groves where birds fly (fig. 3.14). Are these household servants, dependents, inferiors dressed in a manner "too beautiful for slaves," as Theodorus said (*Diod. Sic.* V. 40), or are they relatives, members of the clan (*genos*), participants in the banquet who have momentarily left it to dance a spirited dance of reanimation? The musicians who accompany them and sometimes dance with them do not always seem to be servants, and the space where the spontaneous dance takes place begins near the banquet and appears to be an extension of it.

### Funeral Games

The most spectacular of the funeral rites were certainly those which, because of an apparent resemblance to the Greek sporting events called *agones,* and for lack of an Etruscan word to designate them, we call "games."[31] These were not "games" in the modern sense, nor *agones* in the Greek sense, but daring contests that developed into a spectacle. From the painted tombs of the late sixth century to the Chiusi reliefs, from the representations on black-figure vases from workshops at Vulci to the cinerary urns of Capua, the Etruscan iconography everywhere abounds in images of games, almost all in a funerary context. The Murlo scenes of horse races (see chapter 5), although not at all in a funerary context, seem to be an expression of youth and,

## Sacrificial and Funerary Rites

3.14. The dance of reanimation during or after the funeral banquet, taking place in the open air, in a field planted with laurel trees. Tarquinia, Tomb of the Triclinium. Mid-fifth century. Rendering by C. Ruspi. Rome, Deutsches Archäologisches Institut.

like the majority of Greek games, are probably merely heroic *agones* that originated in funeral rituals.

After the burial and probably after the banquet and dances (it is difficult to determine the order of the rites), the funeral games took place. Some contests appear similar to those in the Greek games: the foot race, jumping with weights, javelin throwing, discus, and wrestling. One notices immediately, though, that the illustrators insist on depicting certain peculiarities in these contests—for example, wrestlers being tossed head over heels over their adversaries.

The preferred contest, however, the queen of sports, is boxing. It is extremely rare in Greek representations but it is depicted in all Etruscan games in spite of, or perhaps because of, its brutality. The violence of the blows is shown with realism. The artists stress the blood flowing from the face of the defeated, as in the Tarquinian Tomb of the Funeral Bed. Next come the horse races. These very dangerous contests,

## Sacrificial and Funerary Rites

called *kalpe*, involve acrobatics performed alternately on the horse and beside it. Last are the three-horse chariot races (*trigae*), run at break-neck speed. The illustrators of these delight in the most serious and spectacular accidents.

In addition to these often dangerous and bloody competitions, other physical "contests" are highlighted that are not of a sporting nature, but are violent and dangerous. In one illustration, a climber mounts the length of an oblique perch and performs a dangerous leap; in another, two masked characters, wearing tight cords around their necks, pull with all their might, to strangle their adversary; in another, a man with his head bound in a sack defends himself with a club against a dog led by a masked character named *Phersu*.[32] A relief-carved base from Chiusi, recently discovered,[33] shows this strange mixture of sports and knock-about spectacles, almost all of which are dangerous, bloody, and life-threatening.

The paintings of the Tomb of the Inscriptions in Tarquinia preserve the names of the participants in these funeral games and thus give information about their social status. The horsemen seem to be young men from the family of the deceased, but the wrestlers and boxers and the musician who accompanies them are certainly dependents, almost serfs. An anecdote tells of the tyrant-king of Veii, who became angry and interrupted the games at the sanctuary of Voltumna by taking away all the participants, "who were almost all his people" (Livy 5.1.4). It is thus probable that most of these "games" were merely professional demonstrations—performances, not *agones*. They served a religious purpose beyond that of mere spectacle. These "games" seem intended to revitalize the dead, to bring them, by the shedding of blood, a supplement to life.

These are a far cry from the games in the Greek stadium, but, on the other hand, they are rather close to the jousts commemorating the death of Anchises as Virgil describes them in Book 5 of the *Aeneid*. The libations and sacrifice at the tomb, the banquet, and last, the competitions—Virgil's account illustrates the order of the funeral rites.

In trying to understand the meaning and function of these rites, one is struck by their double character. On the one hand, they show an extreme vitality, activity, force, and dynamism. The dances and races that shake the earth, the din of the chariots racing at top speed, the power of the blows, and the courage required display a vitality that might be considered mimetic. On the other hand, the dangers of the acrobatics, the somersaults imitating the fatal fall of death, the trampled charioteers, the wrestlers trying to strangle each other, the bloody boxers, and the man blinded by the sack and bitten by the dog, a chthonian animal sacred to Calu and Aita, all seem to serve as a kind of payment, a tribute to the infernal world. Like the bloody combats of the Samnite funerals and Roman gladiatorial games, like the slaughter of the *hostiae animales*, these would give the dead, through the spilled blood, added life, perhaps a chance for an afterlife.

# Sacrificial and Funerary Rites

## FUNERARY CULTS

This is also the goal of the funerary cults, as numerous monuments indicate. Offering tables, hollowed out and often equipped with drainage channels, occur in association with tombs. They are primitive altars intended for libations, vegetal offerings like the Greek *panspermia*, and perhaps the sacrifice of small animals. An offering table extends out from the so-called Ara Guglielmi (fig. 3.15),[34] a small cubical monument with false doors carved on the sides, and, carved on the façade, the deceased standing between two columns. The dead man thus seems to be present at the sacrificial rites performed before his funerary altar. This is a distinctive case, however. Many other cippi, similar except that they lack figural decoration, must have had the same function.[35]

These cubic cippi with false doors are miniature reproductions of great aristocratic monuments of the sixth and fifth centuries. The necropoleis of Norchia, Blera, San Giuliano, and especially Castel d'Asso probably served as the models for them.[36] At

3.15. Guglielmi Altar, from Vulci: a stele in the form of a tomb. A door is carved on each of the four sides of this little monument. In front of the fourth one is a large flat place for setting offerings; the deceased is shown on the threshold, as if this place were his dwelling. Third century. Rome, Museo Naz. di Villa Giulia.

## Sacrificial and Funerary Rites

the top of monumental die-shaped tombs (*tombe a dado*) is a platform, accessible by a ramp or stairs, which was used for sacrificial ceremonies. These rites may have been annual and associated with others performed at the entrance to the *hypogaeum*, which is located under a portico at the base of the monument. Other funerary altars occur on the tops of the *tumuli* of Caere and the Archaic necropoleis of Tarquinia, and on the *meloni* (tumulus tombs) of Sodo, near Cortona. Small temples (*naiskoi*) also seem sometimes to have been built on these *tumuli*. We shall discuss later (chapter 5) the large aristocratic altar discovered in the necropolis of Grotta Porcina in the territory of Tarquinia.

The hollowed-out "libation altars" are generally believed to have served the cult of chthonic divinities, or of gods such as Tinia, who sometimes had this dimension in Etruria. They are not usually thought to have served the cult of the dead. This theory does not take into account, however, the natural slippage of practices over time, which eventually caused the cult of the chthonic gods to be confused with the cult of the dead.

### HEROIZATION AND THE *DI ANIMALES*

What was the function of these practices? We know that funerary cults in Greece were born from a sort of aristocratic need:[37] a need for the clan to find a mythic ancestor and establish a cult of its own identity. This might also be the function of the Etruscan aristocratic funerary cults, which left imposing monuments like the great die tombs at Castel d'Asso and Norchia, or the astounding Melone del Sodo II at Cortona of about 560 (fig. 3.16).[38] Against one side of this enormous conical monument at Cortona was a terrace, a place of funeral cult for the deceased of the princely family; its parapet and sculpture recall those of East Greek altars. It was reached by a monumental stairway flanked by two sculptural groups of a sphinx and a warrior in combat. It seems that similar terraces also existed at Tarquinia and Chiusi.[39]

Clearly, the whole ensemble of funerary celebrations—the banquets and games, the annual sacrifices and the commemorations that followed them, the buildings constructed to give permanence to the cult, and the painted or sculpted images—were believed to transform the deceased, to render him "greater and better," in a word, to make him a hero, called to a happy afterlife. This consequently also elevated the social and political rank of his descendants. The funerary cult heroicized the dead, and heroization bolstered an aristocracy proud of its origins.

The primary aim of these rites, which was probably stated in the revealed texts or their scholarly exegeses, was life in the Afterworld. When the power of the aristocracy became less secure, a larger stratum of the population, without the character or the status of a "middle" class, took up some of these rites. When Orphic-Pythagorean influences from Magna Graecia and new concepts of the afterlife spread into Etruria, cultic practices that were once purely aristocratic began to appear in urban contexts, even in relatively modest burials. At this same time the rites, which

## Sacrificial and Funerary Rites

3.16. Melone del Sodo II, Cortona, the stairway of the tumulus, around 560.

were now simplified and no longer exclusive to the families of the *principes*, became purely religious. They no longer heroicized, but simply promised an afterlife to the dead, who thus became *di animales*. The late theory mentioned by Arnobius (2.62) and expressed in the *libri acheruntici* does not contradict the archaic practice. On the contrary, it is evidence that the ancient aristocratic rites had spread outside their original context, and it attests to a belief in an afterlife in the world beyond.

CHAPTER 4

# The Afterworld

Can one discuss the Etruscan Afterworld without getting lost in overinterpretation of the sources? No written document sheds any light, and it is often difficult to judge the meaning of the figural representations[1] from the images of the deceased, the nature of the offerings presented to them, and the furnishings and architecture of the tombs.

### HINTHIAL: SHADE OR SOUL?

The only solid evidence is epigraphic: the word *hinthial*[2] (or *hinthie, hinthiu, hinthu*) occurs rather frequently, sometimes accompanied by a proper name in the genitive. Many of these inscriptions identify images of the deceased. In the François Tomb at Vulci,[3] which dates from the second half of the fourth century, the famous scene of the sacrifice of Trojan prisoners takes place before the eyes of a standing character, pale, clothed in a blue cloak. He is clearly the beneficiary of the offerings. The figure is labeled *hinthial patrucles,* which can only be translated as "the shade (or soul) of Patroclus" (fig. 4.1). The same uncertainty clouds other inscriptions: is it the shade or the soul of Tiresias who is depicted on a mirror from Vulci and in the Tomba dell'Orco at Tarquinia (as *hinthial teriasals*)?[4] Is it the shade of Turmuca *(hinthia turmucas)*—that is, of *Aturmuca*, Andromache[5]—that one sees on the late fourth-century crater from Vulci, or is it her soul? Interpretations vary, but there is general agreement that the oldest occurrences mean "shade," and the more recent ones, "soul." This is, however, only a hypothesis that presupposes an evolution of the concept under Greek influence.

The distinction is nonetheless important. The former translation would correspond to the Homeric Greek notion of the *eidolon:* "phantom," "shade"; the latter would translate the concept of *psyche*. On a relatively late engraved mirror,[6] a young woman, who is certainly the Psyche of Greek myth, is labeled *hinthial*.[7] It thus seems probable that the same word served to denote the appearance of a dead person and the late Greek personification of the soul. The notion of the soul is probably not foreign

# The Afterworld

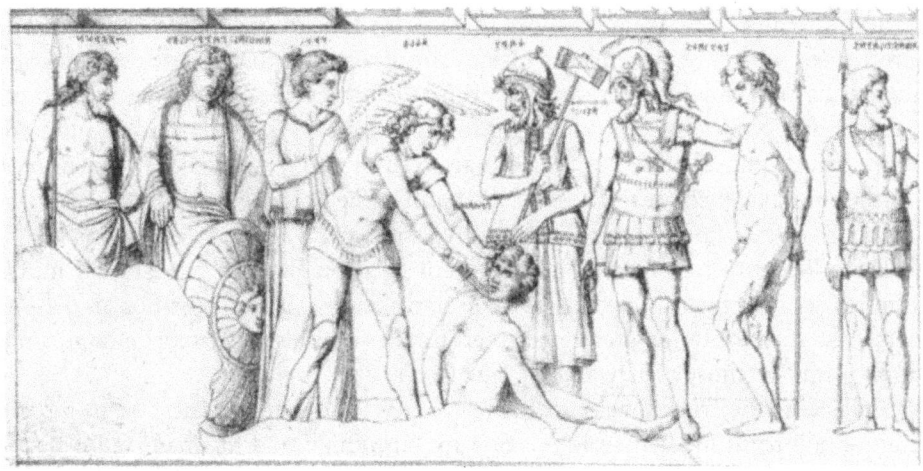

4.1. François Tomb, Vulci. Trojan prisoners slaughtered by Achilles before the shade of Patroclus, in the presence of Agamemnon, Charu(n), and Vanth. Around 330. Drawing after N. Ortis. Rome, Villa Albani.

to the Etruscan concept of humanity, at least from the middle of the fourth century, when the inscriptions that we have cited are most frequent. Although this word came to denote the soul, that part of the personality that survives physical death, its original meaning denoted a concept that was probably not very different. The Archaic shade already had certain characteristics of what came to be defined as the soul.

### THE DWELLING OF THE SHADE

Funerary offerings are common from the Villanovan period on. They suggest that some concept of the afterlife existed. Toward the end of this obscure period, the funerary rites discussed above became fixed: the lamentation and praise of the dead, revitalization in the banquet, the dances of reanimation. All occurred at the place of inhumation or cremation. On the hut urns of Tarquinia[8] appear the first depictions of "assemblies of men" seated face to face, gravely exchanging praises of the dead. We find them toward the end of the sixth century in the paintings at Caere and on the reliefs of Chiusi. Lamentation scenes occur on cinerary urns, which in southern Etruria took the form of huts. The urn was a dwelling, a veritable habitat for the dead, a miniature image of the house of the living.[9]

In the early seventh century, when the *principes*, the powerful aristocrats of Caere, Cortona, Tarquinia, Chiusi, or San Giuliano, began to build or carve out their monumental tombs,[10] whose extraordinary tumuli cover the necropoleis of most cities, they created, not simple niches, but a veritable architecture. Let us consider only one example: Tumulus II, called the Tomb of the Hut,[11] in the Banditaccia necropolis at Caere. Four tombs were created over the course of four to five generations. The

## The Afterworld

earliest resembles a thatched-roof hut in its structure and decoration. Real beds, the furniture of the living, were placed inside. The other three tombs of the same family imitate the plan of noble houses of their time. On either side of the *dromos*, or access corridor, are two rooms corresponding to those that typically flanked a house entrance. The dromos leads to a richly decorated central room, which in turn opens onto a back room, reserved for the head of the family. The openings imitate the windows and doors of real houses, such as those hypothesized from the excavations at Acquarossa. The furniture was cut in place out of the rock. The most recent tomb in this tumulus adopted the complex plan of late sixth-century aristocratic houses. All the elements of the interior architecture—columns, capitals, pilasters, ceilings, door jambs—imitate those of a dwelling of the living.

Tombs cut from rock that was of poor quality for carving details had to rely on tromp-l'oeil painting. This was the case in Tarquinia[12] and for many tombs elsewhere, principally at Caere, where painting was probably chosen for economy. Windows, pilasters, beams, even furniture and accessories were painted on the walls and ceilings to evoke funerary chambers in homes.

Let us briefly consider a motif that occurs repeatedly in the painted tombs: the false door.[13] It is always depicted closed, but with illusionistic detail. It is often Doric, with jambs slanted inward and its lintel protruding on each side. At Caere or Vulci, the projection of the lintel has an elegant hooked form. Sometimes it is carved in relief, as in the Tomb of the Charontes at Tarquinia. These are interior doors like those in a vestibule, opening to other rooms. This motif has been variously interpreted. Some believe it is the door of the tomb, viewed from the exterior; others, the door to the Afterworld. To others still, it is merely a tromp-l'oeil device marking a place where a family that wanted to enlarge the tomb would carve access to new chamber. Whatever their function, these false doors are merely a detail in an illusionistic architecture. The fact that two grieving men in the Tomb of the Augurs at Tarquinia make gestures of lamentation in front of a closed door leads one to suppose that the dead person was believed to be behind it. It seems to us that this is a private, interior house door and, at the same time, a private access to another world.

Thus the tomb has become a house: the dwelling of the dead, of their shades, of whatever survives of them. Now it is time for the inhabitants of the tomb to make an appearance.

### THE DEAD DEPICTED

At the same time that the first hut urns appeared in southern Etruria, a need to individualize the dead took form.[14]

The lid of a mid-seventh-century biconical ossuary from Montescudaio, near Volterra, bears a scene of a dead man attending a funerary banquet. This ossuary, though still Villanovan in style, carries an image of the dead man on the very container of his ashes. At the same time, in the Chiusi region, people began to make a

# The Afterworld

4.2. Ossuary from the former Paolozzi collection from Chiusi: the deceased magically surrounded by a dance of lamentation. Seventh century. Chiusi, Museo Archeologico Nazionale.

type of anthropomorphic cinerary vase, for which we use the inadequate but accepted term *canopic urn*.[15] These were at first simple biconical vases with bowl-shaped covers that were decorated with two eyes and a mouth. After that, the cinerary urn evolved rapidly: the head emerged; the face was modeled; the arms, which appear at the sides of the urn in place of the handles, were first attached to the shoulder of the vase, then partially detached, and, finally, formed separately. The sculptor delineated certain physical traits or details of clothing,[16] not to create a portrait in the proper sense of the term,[17] but to affirm the deceased's individuality. Next to evolve were terracotta urns with a standing statuette on their lid (fig. 4.2). The costume shows the importance of the personage. Dancers, arranged in a circle on the lid, surround him with their lamentations.

In fifth-century Chiusi, the long tradition of representing the dead individual leads to the production of personalized funerary receptacles carved from the soft local stone. These show the deceased seated or semireclining, attended by a genie from the Afterworld, probably Vanth.[18] Elsewhere this urge to personalize the urn or ossuary produces a kind of standardization. In Cerveteri, for example, potters created

## The Afterworld

4.3. One of two "couple" sarcophagi from Caere. Is the reclining couple participating in a funeral banquet? End of the sixth century. Paris, Louvre.

the magnificent "couples" groups (fig. 4.3),[19] as well as a whole series of urns and ossuaries, noticeably less beautiful, but comparable. Following suit, the later sarcophagi of Vulci and Tarquinia depict the deceased, sometimes banqueting, sometimes reclining in a position of repose, while the sculptors of Chiusi strive to fix in terracotta, in works of very high quality, the features of the wealthy dead like Seianti Hanunia Tlesnasa (fig. 4.4)[20] or Larthia Seianti.[21]

Why did they enclose the remains of the dead person in a vessel that carried his image? Was it a substitute for the dead body? Was it considered the physical envelope for that which does not die, the *hinthial*? None of these monuments was intended to be seen: the ossuaries called *canopi* were buried in narrow trenches; the other depictions were walled up in the chambers of tombs that resembled houses. Was the deceased, through his material image, believed to be living in the funerary chamber, which has become a house, or in the trench, where offerings of food were

# The Afterworld

4.4. Sarcophagus of Seianti Hanunia Tlesnasa. An idealized portrait: the deceased is clearly shown younger than she was when she died. Painted terracotta, from Chiusi. Third century. London, British Museum.

set out for him? In the Greek Archaic period, the dead were given offerings as if they were actually sojourning in their burial place. They were magically evoked in front of the tomb. Etruscan practices suggest a belief in an afterlife in the tomb: the funerary vessel, which sometimes yields food remains, the small perfume vases that retain the odor of their unguents, the furniture, first real and then made of stone, the interior decoration, cut from the tufa or painted on the walls, the plan of the tombs imitating that of the houses, and finally, the door, closed on the funerary chamber and saluted by grieving men (fig. 4.5). The individualized image of the deceased further suggests that this afterlife was personal.

### THE JOURNEY TO THE AFTERWORLD

At the same time, however, some of these same monuments—the sarcophagi, for example—show images of a journey, the departure of the deceased from the place of burial. While sculptors at Chiusi are modeling their last canopi to substitute for the cremated mortal bodies, a sculptor at Vulci is carving the famous "seahorse" group.[22] In it, a young man rides a seahorse whose undulating form evokes the swell of the sea. It was placed at the entrance to a funerary monument, so it must certainly allude

## The Afterworld

4.5. Tarquinia, Tomb of the Augurs. A *tanasar* (see chapter 7) in front of the door to the tomb or the Afterworld: is he gesturing in salutation or reciting a funerary prayer? Around 520.

to a sea journey toward a mythical destination. A little later, on tomb walls at Tarquinia, artists painted other mystical mounts. On the pediment above the entrance to the Tomb of the Bulls (around 530), a young man, perhaps an adolescent, rides a hippocamp toward an island (fig. 4.6). He is followed by a sea dog held, rather curiously, on a leash. A similar scene on the partially destroyed right side repeats him heraldically. In the same tomb, on the pediment of the rear chamber, two hippocamps swim toward each other. This theme of the rider on the hippocamp occurs also on several Etruscan black-figure amphorae intended for the tomb.[23] Hippocamps appear alone in the Bartoccini Tomb, in the tomb called Stefana, and in the tombs of the Tritons, the Baron, the Topolino, and the Painted Vases; they date to between the last third of the sixth and the first half of the fifth century.

These images are not simple allusions to the sea. Painters used dolphins to evoke that element, as in the Tomb of the Lionesses. It is highly probable that the hippocamps on the urns, and particularly those on the sarcophagi of following centuries, served the function in Etruscan imagery of *psychopompoi*, guides for the dead. Later, sea centaurs and aquatic dragons, hybrid beings from the world of Nethuns, came to share the task. These representations show death as a voyage toward an island Afterworld. The *hinthial* rides the sea monsters across the sea (or ocean) toward a land where he will dwell.

# The Afterworld

4.6. Tarquinia, Tomb of the Bulls. A young man rides a hippocamp toward an island (the Afterworld?). End of the sixth century.

Thus, on one hand, the funerary rites practiced at the tomb, the food offerings, the grave goods, the tomb architecture, and the individualized depictions that substitute for the body arise from a belief in an afterlife in the tomb. On the other, the images of a journey beyond the waters suggest that another belief, perhaps originating in Magna Graecia, has superimposed itself on the first. It did not cause the earlier rites to disappear or the beliefs to be excluded altogether, but it added the image of death as a sojourn on a distant western island.[24]

*Routes and Guides*
The images just mentioned seem to be the first allusions to a journey, a voyage, that the shade or the soul takes after death. These scenes multiply rapidly from the fourth century on, and their nature varies. Usually the journey proceeds from right to left, the direction in which most Etruscan texts are read. Often the journey is made over land. The dead person, dressed comfortably as if for a long and dangerous trip, plods along in a horse-drawn covered wagon *(carpentum)* or trots in a two-horse chariot. Sometimes he rides on horseback. Often he walks. One sees him advance and advance again along interminable routes that lead to the world beyond. A small hooded figure sometimes precedes him. Vanth lights his way with her torch. The hideous *Charu(n)*, holding a mallet, accompanies him. He traverses arid expanses that lack any recognizable features. He encounters only shapeless rocks, serpents, or disturbing snake-footed creatures. Sometimes one senses that the trip will turn into a voyage: the hippocamps and sea monsters become more numerous; a hooded female in a tightly wrapped cloak straddles a *ketos*, a dragonlike sea monster, as on an urn from

# The Afterworld

4.7. Tarquinia, Tomb of the Blue Demons. The last stages before embarkation on the ship to the Afterworld: an Etruscan transposition of an idea from Magna Graecia. Fourth century.

Volterra;[25] a rider approaches a shore and must mount (or battle) a sea monster;[26] a dead person is led to a ship that is being menaced by a snake-footed creature;[27] finally, a sea-going ship waits at the end of a long route strewn with pitfalls (fig. 4.7).[28] Sometimes one of these hideous *psychopompoi* carries the rudder of a ship,[29] like a pilot or helmsman identified by his instrument.

This is the road that leads the dead toward their resting place. One part of the route is over land, another part over the sea. The deceased person does not merely cross a marsh or river. It is a sea monster or a ship of the high seas that will bring him to the other shore, not the flat-bottomed barge poled by the ferryman of Acheron. The Etruscan Afterworld thus does not correspond to the traditionally accepted geography of the Greek Underworld, in which the infernal regions lie beyond a subterranean river. Instead, it resembles that mystical topography, formulated in Greece and the West, which evoked an occidental archipelago of the blessed, an Afterworld beyond the ocean, in the sector belonging to the netherworld's gods.

*Demons*
Completely anachronistic interpretations have often been applied to these scenes: interpretations that betray a total incomprehension of the Etruscan Afterworld. Scholars have seen tormenting demons, satanic beings that torture souls in a mediaeval-like hell (figs. 4.8, 4.9). Several Italian painters at the end of the Middle Ages and the beginning of the Renaissance copied[30] or reused certain disquieting figures from Etruscan iconography. This led some excellent scholars, in a curious mental lapse, to delirious reconstructions of what they actually called hell. For example, telamons, figures of giants that served as pilasters or columns, like the karyatids of the Erechtheum, held up a painted architrave in a tomb that is now lost. Some imagined them to be the damned, condemned to be flayed eternally by an infernal tormenter.[31] Images of Vanth, young females holding torches to guide the dead, were interpreted as horrible Furies who burn the damned; and Charu(n), who often brandishes an enormous mallet, became a character from a nightmare, an executioner who strikes

## The Afterworld

4.8. Tarquinia, Tomb of the Aninas. Charu(n), holding his mallet, to the left of the door. Middle of the third century.

4.9. Tarquinia, Tomb of the Aninas. Vanth, holding her torch, guards the door of the tomb. Middle of the third century.

the mortal blow or torments those who fall under his fire-encircled sway. We must reread these images in a more reasonable or less dramatic manner: their meaning is quite different.

As we see in countless depictions, the great voyage to the Beyond can be accomplished only with the aid of *psychopompoi*, "demons" or genies whose task is to bring the dead to his new world. In the famous painting in the François Tomb at Vulci, the pretty young Vanth stands behind the Trojan prisoners who are being slaughtered for the pyre of Patroclus,[32] and awaits the last sigh of the dying. One finds her again every time death is near. She is represented at the edges of all the scenes showing the laying out of the dead, a silent witness.

She is usually not alone. There are several of these feminine genies, winged or not, who lead the dead. These young women are dressed in short skirts, as is convenient for those who must move quickly, and shod in boots appropriate for a terrain full of pitfalls. Sometimes they have wings, symbols of both their supernatural character and their speed. Almost with affection, they guide the shade or soul, whose pace is slow and uncertain. They put their hand on his shoulder, and light his way with their

## The Afterworld

torches. They are neither Furies nor Erinyes pursuing vengeance, but guides and illuminators of a route to the world of the dead. It is true that some of them carry swords, but that is to defend themselves against menacing beings, usually snake-footed monsters. Several carry enormous door keys. We may call them *Culsu*,[33] the word for a person in charge of a door.

Often the man about to die is attended by a much more disturbing creature, ugly and repulsive. His flesh is spotted or solidly blue or green, a sign of decomposition. He has a hideous face, a hooked nose, pointed ears like an animal, hair in disarray or writhing with serpents, and frightening, protruding eyes. He is usually dressed in a short tunic like that worn by artisans and household slaves: this is the livery of the servants of the Afterworld. One of the servants of Aita in the Tomba dell'Orco wears the same tunic. In every scene where the name of this sinister character, Charu(n),[34] is written, he is depicted carrying a huge mallet. Other frightening and similarly dressed characters sometimes accompany him. They brandish serpents or hold a pair of tongs; they may carry a sword, a boat's rudder, or enormous keys. In spite of their frightening appearance, these characters often aid the traveler. One pushes the chariot or pulls the horses; another encourages the walker, clears the road, and threatens the snake-footed creatures with his mallet. Like the Vanth figures, with which they are often symmetrically posed in funerary representations, these demons can appear two, three, or even four times in the same scene, but with different attributes.[35]

Like the female genie, then, Charu(n) is multiple. Every time we encounter one of these repulsive characters in an identifiable place, it is in front of a door: the gate to a city or the door to a house. The keys, the tongs, and the mallet enable him to open

4.10. Tarquinia, Tomb 5636. Charu(n) and Vanth, the door to the Afterworld, and the deceased bidding farewell to the living or greeting the shades of his parents. Second century.

# The Afterworld

the passage.[36] The key has an obvious use. The function of the mallet has long been obscure, but let us bear in mind that the large gates of cities were blocked from inside by heavy bars that the doorkeepers slid into place with great blows of a mallet and fixed with inside bolts that had to be removed with special tongs. Thus these Charu(n) figures, who have only a distant connection with the Greek Charon, must have been the gatekeepers of the Afterworld, holders of tools for opening and closing the gates of the city of the dead (fig. 4.10).

## THE CITY OF THE DEAD

The half-open gate in the city wall, toward which the frightful mallet-bearer leads the dead, as on the Bruschi sarcophagus (fig. 4.11), marks the end of the journey. All the depictions that we know stop at this point. They show nothing beyond. Was the journey all that the Etruscans knew?

In fact, the scenes of departure of the dead, the farewell to the living, the journey with Vanth or Charu(n), and the reunion with predeceased relatives all seem to follow a story or a doctrine that was defined and precise. Everything proceeds according to an agreed and repetitive scheme, a scenario described countless times. We are tempted to believe that this was all contained in the *libri acheruntici*, but no fragment of them remains. Like the Egyptian Book of the Dead, they would have described the itinerary to the city of the dead with its traps and pitfalls; and like the other books revealed to the Etruscans, they probably stipulated the rites and codified the procedures that accompanied each step. They did not describe the world of the infernal gods any more than the other books described a celestial pantheon, but they provided the means to reach their domain. This is only a hypothesis, however, and it rests solely on this inability or refusal to depict the home of the dead.

4.11. Tarquinia, Bruschi sarcophagus. The final stage of the journey to the city of the dead under the direction of Charu(n) and Vanth. The gate of the city is partly open. Third century. Tarquinia, Museo Nazionale.

# The Afterworld

*Chez* Aita

Some important exceptions that should be mentioned, however. Three tombs of the fourth century actually seem to bring us into the realm of Aita and Phersipnai, the Etruscan Hades and Persephone.

In the right-hand chamber of the Golini I Tomb at Orvieto, an unusual banquet is taking place. On the right wall, the master and another banqueter recline luxuriously on a rich *kline* with a phiale or cup in their hands, while an *aulos*-player and a citharode entertain them. This scene is today almost destroyed. The painting on the adjacent wall to the left, however, represents a unique couple. Aita and his wife, Phersipnai, are seated on a throne in a composition reminiscent of Greek cult images, particularly the terracotta ex-voto plaques of Italian Locri. The richly dressed goddess, shown in a three-quarters view to the left, turns toward her husband, who is depicted in right profile. Aita's head is covered with the skin of a wolf or a dog-wolf, and in his right hand he holds a long scepter entwined with a serpent. The divine couple is separated from the mortal banquet only by a serving table. Two servants busy themselves around the table, which holds a large krater and an incense burner.[37] We meet the same puzzling scene in the newly discovered Sarteano tomb (see note 35).

These paintings seem to place the mortals and the gods at the same meal, illuminated by the same candelabras, attended by the same servants. The gods, however, do not eat or drink. So are the gods of the dead being entertained among mortals, or are the deceased dining *chez Aita*? Are we among the living or the dead here? There is another interpretation: that the artist wanted to show the gods physically present at the funeral banquet because libations and sacrifices ritually associated them there. Similarly, on the sarcophagus of Torre San Severo, the wolf-cloaked master of the Afterworld and his wife appear in the background of a scene in which Achilles slaughters the Trojan prisoners (see fig. 8.7). Given these different possibilities, it is not at all certain that this banquet is set in the Afterworld.

The paintings of the Tarquinian Tomba dell'Orco pose another problem. The tomb initially belonged to the Murinna[38] and Velcha families, but it was enlarged by joining an older tomb with a slightly more recent one through a new third chamber. The connecting chamber is not relevant here. The walls of the first tomb are covered with typical scenes of an open-air funeral banquet amid groves of laurel. But into this funeral celebration slips the disquieting figure of Charu(n) carrying his mallet. In this chamber, then, we are still in the world of the living, or at least not yet in the world of the dead. Only the figure of the pyschopomp doorkeeper indicates that, for one person at least, the great journey has begun.

The second chamber has a completely different atmosphere. To be sure, a Charu(n) carrying a mallet appears on the right wall and perhaps again on the back wall, but it is clear that we have now arrived among the shades or souls. Here is the "shade of Tiresias" *(hinthial teriasals)*. Agamemnon, Achilles, Ulysses, and Ajax are nothing more than shreds of flaking paint, but from old drawings we know they are here. On

# The Afterworld

4.12. Tarquinia, Tomb of Orcus. Aita and Phersipnai enthroned in Hades. End of the third century.

another wall, Sisyphus, Heracles, and Cerberus are also only partially preserved, while Pirithoos and Theseus are still clearly visible. At Theseus' left stands the terrifying silhouette of a demon named Tuchulcha, who is similar to Charu(n). All surround the divine couple, Aita and Phersipnai (fig. 4.12), who are enthroned on the back wall in a sort of rocky cavern guarded by the triple-bodied Geryon. Now we are surely in the realm of the dead, and, like Aeneas or Dante, we encounter the heroes of myth. The chthonic rulers with their sumptuous gold vessels seem to be acting as hosts for the deceased members of the Murinna family, who are rubbing elbows with the epic heroes. But only the names and the demon figures are Etruscan: this Afterworld comes directly from Greek literature and not from Etruscan concepts. Furthermore, behind the figure of Tiresias, tiny human silhouettes frolic in the reeds. These are the *animulae*, freed from the weight of living bodies. They too have been borrowed straight from contemporary Greek mystical doctrines.

The exception thus only confirms the rule: the Etruscan Afterworld is unknowable, and it is not depicted here. The scene in the Tomba dell'Orco illustrates the Greek Underworld. The artists have created a kind of imaginary cultural world where Etruscan heroes encounter those of the literature that served as their model.

## The Afterworld

Through it they claim a prestigious Greek ancestry or display political opposition to the Romans.[39] When the Etruscans depict the Greek Afterlife, it is to justify their historical stature, while the somber domain of the shades beyond the half-open doors remains unknowable, impossible to depict. The silhouette of a female genie slips through; a male gatekeeper arrives with his mallet; the hooded dead approach this opaque door. Only the difficult road that leads to it is illustrated or described in texts. Only the journey has ritual prescriptions.

### Virgil and the Etruscan Afterworld

Echoes of the *libri acheruntici* may still have been heard in Virgil's time. Book 6 of the *Aeneid* is largely dedicated to Aeneas' visit to the world of the dead. One part of the dark route (vv. 268–384) leads to Cocytus, where the ferryman's boat awaits. This passage is often compared to the Eleusinian initiation, but it recalls even more the scenes on sarcophagi and in the Tomb of the Blue Demons (see fig. 4.7).[40] Besides personifications of evils and deadly passions, which are probably a Stoic borrowing, Aeneas encounters monstrous, hybrid creatures: centaurs, a chimaera, gorgons, harpies, a triple-bodied shade in which we recognize Geryon from the Tomba dell'Orco, and the Lernean hydra, together with Scylla. These two sea monsters are among the figures most often depicted on sarcophagi, and Scylla becomes one of the most common motifs on late-period urns. In depictions of the journey to the City of the Dead, the guides chase or threaten snake-footed creatures, also hybrids. Aeneas crosses this world with his sword in his hand, as do the dead and those who lead them, Vanth and Charu(n). Finally, having crossed the "circles" of the edge of the world, Aeneas comes to two walled cities. The first is the City of the Damned. Its immense iron door is guarded by Tisiphone, her robe girded up. When interrogated she responds: "The divine laws forbid a man to cross this threshold" (6.548). A little farther on, the ramparts of City of the Blessed loom:

> I perceive the walls that came from the Cyclops' forge, and before us the arched gate where it is prescribed that we should leave this offering. (6.637)

The poet has, under the influence of the Greek thought of his time, delivered punishments and rewards and distinguished a hell from a paradise, but he has placed them behind city walls closed by powerful gates. The entrance to the first of these cities is guarded by an inflexible woman very similar to the one depicted at the tomb entrance on some late-period urns (fig. 4.13). For the poet, this city is inaccessible and unknowable. Such was the world of the dead for the Etruscans.

We do not expect from Virgil, and still less from Dante, a description of the Etruscan Afterworld, but some major elements that we have observed in the art occur also in the poets' work. These are probably the last echoes of the itineraries beyond the tomb.

# The Afterworld

4.13. Cinerary urn from Chiusi. The gate is guarded by a female genie of the Afterworld. Third century. Palermo, Museo Archeologico Regionale "A. Salinas."

CONTACTS WITH THE AFTERWORLD

Calling up the dead, and the rites and sacrifices necessary to establish communication with the world below, occupy part of Book 6 of the *Aeneid*. The belief that the living could have a relationship with the world of the dead was common in Greece. One form of Greek divination was based on evoking the dead, especially those who had been prophets when they were alive. What was the practice in Etruria?

One of the most commonly performed sacrifices elevated souls to the status of *di animales*. The ancient authors tried to name and characterize the divinities who had been mortals. Interpretations are a bit varied, but the late sources always cite two rather vaguely defined groups of deities. The Penates are the most often mentioned. Among the four categories in this group, there were three pairs of Penates corresponding to the three realms of the world and the gods that ruled them: Jupiter/Tinia, Neptune/Nethuns, and Pluto/Aita. The fourth group of Penates consisted of "mortals."[41] These would have been the *di animales*, persons who had, through the appropriate rites, gained immortality. Was the cult of the Penates a means to weave a rapport with the dead? It is difficult to determine the nature of this relationship. The sacrifices and libations were not meant to call up the dead; this cult was not for divination. The sacrifices were believed to placate the gods and prevent the dead from bothering the living. This cult was probably of Etruscan origin, but it is known to us only through very late sources.

Due to a curious contamination, the Lares of the crossroads (*Lares compitales*), whose cult at Rome celebrated the festival of the Compitalia, and the Lares of the roads *(Lares viales)* were considered souls of the dead people who had become gods.[42]

## The Afterworld

This is certainly an error, but it was rooted in the Roman tradition that Tarquin had offered human sacrifices to the Lares of the crossroads. The fact that it was originally human sacrifices that elevated human souls to the status of *di animales* is probably the cause of this confusion. The attribution of the cult to Tarquin broadly indicates an Etruscan origin. The name of the Lares is Etruscan, but what else? Their plural character relates them to other deities whom we observe in the Etruscan divine universe. But did the cult of the Lares Compitales, which was probably a Roman borrowing of Etruscan rites, permit contact with the dead? Did the late practices attested at Rome resemble their distant Etruscan models?

A whole series of cinerary urns, mostly from Perugia,[43] depict a mythical or symbolic episode that may imply a direct relationship between the living and the dead. At the center of this scene is a wellhead from which a wolf or wolf-headed monster emerges. Sometimes this animal looks more like a horse; sometimes it is a man cloaked in a wolf skin, like Aita in the Golini and dell'Orco tombs. This monster or man with animal attributes attacks a kneeling figure who is already in the posture of submission. He takes possession of the man by seizing him in his claws, or putting his paw on his arm, shoulder, or head. To the right of this group, a standing man, perhaps a hoplite, unsheathes a sword and threatens the monster. Sometimes, too, a small man tries to capture the monster by passing a rope around his neck.[44] A third figure, standing behind the well, pours a libation from a phiale onto the dog-headed attacker. Vanth is in the background, as she is present at the death of every man: immobile but ready to guide the one who must leave.

This scene is so bizarre that it has given rise to many interpretations. Brunn and Körte identified it as King Porsenna[45] evoking the monster Volta, but the details of the scene do not support that reading. Besides, it is difficult to imagine a funerary significance for that story. A more apt suggestion is that it illustrates the episode from the *Odyssey*, in which Ulysses consults the shades about Elpenor's fate and tries to appease him as he returns to the Underworld (Servius, *Ad Aen.* 6.107). It is thus a scene of necromancy. This divinatory practice, however, does not seem to have been used in Etruria, so this interpretation, too, is unconvincing.

Nonetheless, the latter theory does stress the most important fact: that any communication with the "world below" inspires revulsion and terror and requires a ritual defense. The monster that emerges from the lower world is both man and dog (or wolf); in this he is comparable to Aita/Hades. Another chthonic divinity, Calu, is known from inscriptions. He was offered statuettes of dogs, and dogs were also sacrificed to him. Calu is perhaps only Aita himself before he received an Etruscanized Greek name. The supernatural creature that comes out of the well must be the bearer of death, or death himself. The man he grasps is going to die, as the presence of Vanth suggests. This is an intrusion of the world of the dead into that of the living. It is terrifying, like the passage to the Afterworld. Neither the sword, as powerless as that of Aeneas on the road to Hades, nor the rope around the monster's neck will turn away

## The Afterworld

the threat. The only effective act is the purifying or appeasing libation. The figure who pours it wears a *pileus* and, by his gesture as much as by his headgear, is marked as a priest.

Is this an illustration of an unknown myth? Is it only symbolic? Does it accurately depict the Etruscans' fear of the world below? In any case, this image suggests that every death temporarily opens up a passage to the world of Aita. And the terror that this contact inspires is empty; a religious act, a libation, would render it harmless. If this scene illustrates it accurately, the Etruscans' relationship with the world below was marked by prudence and ritual piety.

### A LONG EVOLUTION

It would be wrong to imagine that the Etruscan Afterworld was always conceived and depicted in the same way or fixed in the canonical books, or that the idea of a world beyond the tomb never changed from the way it was first described. We suspect that, for several centuries, the place of the afterlife was believed to be the place of burial. The first sea rider suggesting an Afterworld across the sea dates to the beginning of the sixth century. The first mention of a cult to Vanth is a little earlier yet, at the hinge of the seventh and sixth centuries, on a Vulcian aryballos from Marsiliana.[46] It reads: "I am the beautiful offering to Vanth." A late sixth-century sherd attributed to Oltos in the Louvre bears a dedication to Charu(n).[47] In other words, the psychopomp genies—guides, ferrymen, gatekeepers—seem to be already in place at the end of the Archaic period, well before they were depicted. On the other hand, if Calu is known as early, Aita appears only toward the middle of the sixth century, when he takes on the traits of Hades. Phersipnai scarcely existed before she was named.

The Etruscan Afterworld seems to have been formed from a series of influences. It became fixed with the assimilation of ideas borrowed probably from Western Greece. These beliefs came out of Orphism and Pythagoreanism, with some details from Stoicism. It is not even certain that the basic belief in the *di animales* was really ancient. In spite of this odd formation, however, the Afterworld, as the Etruscans conceived it and as the *libri acheruntici,* whose redaction was probably late, no doubt described it, showed a sure originality. Through the work of Virgil and Dante, though unconsciously, it has strongly affected the imagination of all of western Europe.

CHAPTER 5

# Sanctuaries

Sanctuaries must not be confused with temples. The latter are only a part of the former, albeit the largest and most visible part. In Greece and later in Rome, in fact, many sanctuaries did not even have temples.

A sanctuary is a space dedicated to a deity. It is enclosed, or at least bounded, clearly marked off by visible signs such as cippi. At Bolsena, one of these boundary stones was inscribed with a dedication to Selvans, the god of boundaries and limits.[1] Often a masonry wall surrounded the god's domain, as at the famous Portonaccio Sanctuary at Veii (fig. 5.1),[2] at the sanctuaries of Celle and Sassi Caduti at Falerii, and in Caere's cosmopolitan port sanctuary of Pyrgi, which was encircled by a beautiful wall of *opus quadratum*. At Fiesole, the earlier enclosure, which predated that of the Hellenistic-period temple, was built in polygonal masonry. In rural sanctuaries, mere dry stones would have served, as at Pozzarello in the territory of Bolsena or in Caere's seaside sanctuary of Punta della Vipera.

Thus, some sanctuaries did not include temples, but all were bounded or enclosed. These domains closely resembled Greek *temene*. The preservation of the enclosure walls is often too fragmentary to permit study or identification, so our knowledge of them is very incomplete. The walls were breached by one or more gates, some monumental, others defensive in function. At Pyrgi, the sanctuary was entered through an enormous *propylon* that resembled a city gate.

The internal organization of this space devoted to the gods resembled that of the urban fabric. City plans became geometric from the sixth century on, and the divine enclosure, whatever its size, came to be inscribed into that orthogonal scheme. The sacred domain was thus an integral part of the urban community. The sanctuary does not always have a temple, but it must have an altar. It also sometimes includes a raised terrace with complex moldings on its walls, a podium, which seems to have served as an "open" temple. Here, in fact, the physical representation of the god was found. Originally this image was not figurative, but was probably just a simple stone, a sign

# Sanctuaries

5.1. The Portonaccio Sanctuary at Veii: view of the altar.

or symbol, though, as we shall see, it became increasingly anthropomorphic. The cult image was also indispensable to the functioning of the altar.

Ancient authors called this primitive sacred space a *sacellum* and believed that its origin was earlier than that of the temple.[3] Its essential elements were the altar[4] and the podium, a sort of divine dwelling, very common in the sanctuaries of Etruria. In the most developed and elaborate cult places, the podium serves as a foundation for the Tuscan temple and will later form the base of the Roman temple.

Thus from the simplest rural sanctuaries to the most complex civic or pan-Etruscan cult places, the form seems immutable. The differences are merely linked to the sanctuaries' functions, and these were strictly dependent on their location.

## LOCATION

Etruria has many cult places whose geographic positions tell us much about the cults' functions.[5]

To the modern observer, urban sanctuaries are the most noticeable. Here, as in Greece, we expect to find them mostly on heights, on acropoleis. One of the characteristics of urbanism in Etruria, unlike that in Greece, however, is that the inhabited centers of the historical period do not seem to have grown out of settlements that were important in the second millennium. They appear instead to cluster around a nucleus that was unremarkable in size and rarely situated in a defensive position. The "princely" Bronze Age dwellings, which are often very modest, and the cults linked

# Sanctuaries

to them, did not give rise to major sanctuaries. There is no equivalent in Etruria for the Erechtheum or the sanctuary at Eleusis, which had been powerful princely residences during the Mycenaean period before they became, in historic Athens, essential cult places for the city. Also, although all Etruscan urban centers possess sanctuaries, many of great size, the cult sites do not appear to be especially old. Very ancient sanctuaries are often found outside the city proper, on sites that could not have been inhabited beyond the Iron Age. In fact, only a few ancient settlements actually developed into cities, and thus the memory of past grandeur was not important in the choice of a cult location.

The largest cities of Etruria did possess sanctuaries of considerable size. Servius, in a late gloss (*Ad Aen.* 1.422), claims that every city should have three temples, just as it had three gates and three streets. This late mention of an alleged rule in the *etrusca disciplina* also states that these buildings should be dedicated to Jupiter, Juno, and Minerva. This so obviously evokes the Roman Temple of Jupiter Optimus Maximus that we are tempted to think that the tripartite division attributed to the Tuscan temple by Vitruvius (*De arch.* 4) was probably based on a Roman model and dates from the early third century, when Rome ruled southern Etruria. But Servius' comment, as late as it is, clearly reveals that the number and the size of the temples were important criteria in distinguishing a large city from a modest settlement.

The most common location for a sanctuary is thus the city itself, and we shall discuss the impact of these urban cults on the political and civic plan. The relationship between the sanctuary and the urban nucleus confirms the tight connection between religion and politics. The vicissitudes of one affected the other. There could be many sacred zones in the city. They are commonly fixed in three positions: on the highest point, on the edge of the largest *piazza*, and near the gates. The function of the sanctuary was often not specific to the city, and it evolved continually.

The outskirts of cities were also locations for important sanctuaries. They could be distributed along roads or within necropoleis; they could be located at distinctive points such as meeting places, crossroads, bridges, or fords; or they could be set within a family "fief," an ancient village belonging to a *genos,* and served as aristocratic sanctuaries.

In the open countryside, around places that sparked the imagination—on a hilltop, along a water course, at the shore of a lake, on the edge of a forest, beside a majestic tree, at points struck by lightning—were situated very ancient cults that were rarely incorporated into the organized, coherent religious systems. These rural sanctuaries, although we understand them poorly, were very popular, and they give us such diverse information that it is difficult to generalize about the religion of the countryside. Some of these rural sanctuaries are known from their large votive deposits, which evolved over the centuries and thus are very instructive.

Also outside the city walls were two other very different types of sanctuaries. Port sanctuaries, located near landing beaches and commercial wharves, welcomed the

# Sanctuaries

sailors who frequented the ports as well as the foreign merchants who sometimes lived there, and from this they acquired a cosmopolitan character. Probably because the different ports attracted specialized clienteles, some temples display a specifically "national" character, here Punic, elsewhere Greek. Inland sanctuaries on the frontiers between the *nomen etruscum* and other peoples similarly shed light on the various phenomena of contact. These port and border sanctuaries are important for the evidence they give, not only about commercial relationships, but also, particularly for this study, about religious interactions among the peoples of the Mediterranean.

The second type of important extramural sanctuary is that which historical tradition calls *federal*—that is, pan-Etruscan. While the literary allusions to these sanctuaries are numerous, precise facts are rare, and archaeological evidence almost totally lacking. Thus the questions that this subject raises will occupy us more than the answers.

## URBAN CULTS AND SANCTUARIES

Urban sanctuaries belong to three well-defined groups: sanctuaries of the acropolis, of the agora or forum (that is, the urban center), and of the gates.

The detached hill of the Piazza d'Armi was once the acropolis of Veii. It is located at least 100 meters south of the hill occupied by the city. At the center of a rather dense, orthogonally gridded monumental space was a temple, part of whose decoration is preserved. This building with two cellae, oriented east-west, did not fit into the geometric plan of the acropolis, as if the temple's plan antedated the urban grid. The low-relief terracotta plaques that adorned the structure depict processions of foot soldiers, horsemen, and heroes in chariots:[6] a repertory of military and civic motifs with obvious aristocratic references. Do they illustrate a triumphal ceremony, a parade, a battle commemoration, or simply the city in arms?

At the very end of the sixth century, this building seems to lose its importance. Was it still used? The city's center of religious activity had shifted northward, to a plateau some 500 meters away, where a tufa foundation indicates that a large temple once existed. This must be the famous temple of Uni/Juno,[7] whom the Roman conqueror of Veii evoked in 396, as Livy tells us (5.21–22).[8] Was the supplanted temple on the acropolis dedicated to the same deity? Was the shift in the religious geography related to a change in the city's political regime?

This example of an acropolis sanctuary stripped of its primacy is not unusual. Vulci's acropolis, dominating a meander of the Fiora and facing the necropolis of Cavalupo, comprised an Archaic temple whose placement at the strongest point of the city denotes its civic function. The great fourth-century urban temple, however, whose plan we shall study, rises from the center of the plateau and is integrated into the urban fabric.

The same thing occurs at Tarquinia and Roselle. Only cities that are almost without pasts, that are constructed *ex nihilo* like Marzabotto[9] or Falerii, did not

## Sanctuaries

5.2. Tarquinia: ruins of the urban temple called Ara della Regina, southeast corner. Sixth to third century.

experience this shifting of the civic cult from the acropolis to the center of the city, where the major temple was usually located. In Marzabotto and Falerii, the initial acropolis temples were contemporary with the "agora temples" of older cities, and their integration into the city is evidence of a homogeneous political and religious development. This may explain their permanence.

The most expressive example of an urban sanctuary is at Tarquinia, the Ara della Regina (figs. 5.2, 5.3).[10] It sheds light on how a large religious building erected in the center of a city functioned and developed. The terrace on which this building stands, 77 meters long and 36 wide, oriented toward the east, levels the slope of the terrain. It looms above the city and dominates the outlying settlements. This sacred area resulted from the transformation and enlargement of an Archaic sanctuary, which probably lay outside the sixth-century city and became incorporated into the fourth-century settlement.[11] The temple erected on the terrace has a 100-foot-wide podium, a "*hekatompedon*"; its form is Tuscan (see chapter 6), with a wide porch supported on four columns, a wall enclosing the three other sides, a central cella with three niches, and two small rooms *(adyta* or *opisthodomoi?)* whose function is not certain. The roof was widely extended to protect the side walls. The later plan of the mid-third century did away with the rooms at the back of the building, but repeated the tripartition of the central cella. It thus seems that three cult images were worshipped in this place.

To whom was the sanctuary dedicated? There is no written documentation, and the decoration of the open pediment, to which the elegant team of two winged horses

## Sanctuaries

5.3. Tarquinia: relief plan of the Ara della Regina.

belongs (fig. 5.4), does not give us precise information. Its votive deposit, too, gives us only meager data. In the deposit was a shaft, now broken, from a weapon that had been offered in the sanctuary. It bears the inscription *artum*[es]: "to *Artumes*"—that is, Artemis. Who could have been the other gods in the triad? It has been suggested that Artumes was honored in this sanctuary under three forms, like Diana at Nemi. This is only a hypothesis, but it nonetheless coincides with what we know about the plural character of Etruscan gods. Also on the terrace, a small, clearly sacred space, out of alignment with the plan of the building, is evidence of a very venerable cult that antedated the existing building. Would this be, as M. Torelli has proposed,[12] the spot where Tages was believed to have emerged from his furrow? A third theory, with no archaeological proof, suggests that this sacred domain was a federal sanctuary before that function fell to Fanum Voltumnae. We shall revisit these questions when we discuss that type of sanctuary.

Can the Belvedere sanctuary at Orvieto (fig. 5.5) be considered urban? Established on the northern extremity of the plateau, in an area where the buildings have been poorly excavated and thus seem quite unimportant, it might appear marginal. But it was built at the beginning, and redecorated at the end, of the fifth century by terracotta sculptors influenced by the school of Pheidias. It could well be the major sanctuary of this opulent city.

5.4. Tarquinia, Ara della Regina: pediment decoration—horses of the chariot of the dawn. Tarquinia, Museo Archeologico Nazionale.

5.5. Orvieto (Volsinii), plan of the Belvedere Temple. Fifth century.

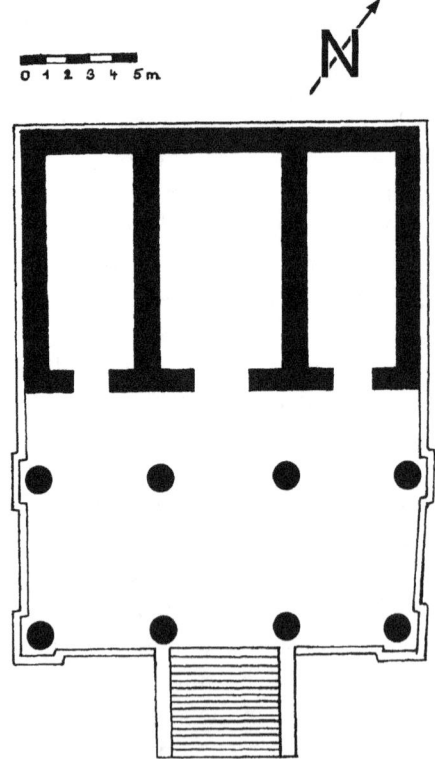

## Sanctuaries

5.6. Marzabotto, urban sanctuary: podium of the great altar. Sixth to fifth century.

Here again substructures support the high podium of the temple, which is poorly restored. In front of the temple extends a *temenos* encircled by a large wall, while behind it is a subterranean room that was part of the sanctuary. Throughout the whole town are found several altars with a drilled central channel, like those intended for sacrifices to the chthonic gods.[13] Other stone blocks, roughly pyramidal, with a central hole, are known elsewhere in the Volsinian territory (Bolsena, Bagnoregio, and other sacred places in Orvieto). On these "libation altars" appears the inscription *tinscvil*, "to Tinia."[14] A small vase found in the votive deposit also bears an inscription: *tinia calusna*.[15] Calu is a subterranean god belonging to the world of the dead. The adjective *calusna*, applied to Tinia, forms the equivalent of the Greek *Zeus Chthonios* (infernal or funerary Zeus), and was perhaps another name for Aita. Thus the "dimension" of Tinia honored by this offering was chthonic and perhaps even funerary. The *hypogaeum* behind the temple was probably connected specifically with this cult. Thus, it is Tinia, the most important god of the Etruscan pantheon, who is at home here. The lateral cellae of the temple, narrower than the main axial room, suggest that the cult of a triad was organized around him. But one could equally well imagine that this sanctuary sheltered Tinia in three dwellings for his three functions, which are indicated by the three sections of the Piacenza liver[16] and the references of Martianus Capella.

On the acropolis of Marzabotto (fig. 5.6) stand two temples and two square

## Sanctuaries

terraces, which probably functioned as altars. The major sanctuary of the city was perhaps one of the two temples. These buildings are situated on a leveled area in the northwest zone about 10 meters above the plateau where the settlement was founded. They are in perfect alignment with the general orientation of the city plan, but shifted along a diagonal. This placement seems to result from the need to display two façades at the same time to the whole city. But a recently discovered building, resembling Temple B at Pyrgi, and probably dedicated to Tinia, is perfectly integrated into the fabric of the city center and may also have been an important temple for the area of political activity.

The best preserved of these, Temple C, had three cellae of unequal size, but it is impossible to identify the god or gods that reigned there. A terrace/altar beside it contains a well and a basin for receiving water; these suggest that its function was curative. This cult, the heir of a similar, much more ancient practice attested on the adjacent hill, was probably reestablished in the sacred zone when the new city was founded, and it was situated immediately beside the major sanctuary. This illustrates how the more ancient cults became integrated into the religious life of communities founded later.

Like churches in mediaeval cities or in papal Rome, Etruscan sanctuaries were placed in front of city gates, at points of passage and contact with the nonurbanized world. At Vulci, there is a sanctuary of Hercle in front of the passage through the east gate. At Tarquinia, the sanctuary of Thufltha (whose place in the sky is near Tin and is sometimes worshipped with Śuri; see chapter 9) stands beside the northwest gate. The Macchia Grande sanctuary at Veii is situated at the approach to the northeast gate.

At Arezzo it is certain, in spite of the difficulty posed by the continuous occupation of the site since antiquity, that the main city gates were linked to sanctuaries. Their function was related to their position. The temples of San Lorenzo, San Bartolomeo, and Catona are positioned at gates, while others, sometimes larger, are some distance out. These three sanctuaries possibly served to mark the city limits. An Etruscan phrase, attested in inscriptions, has been associated with them: *tular rasnal*,[17] "limits of the city-state." The placement of these sanctuaries at city gates confirms what we know from the foundation rites: that the gates had a sacred nature. The votive deposits at gate sanctuaries are seldom rich, but they attest to the antiquity of the cult.

### PERIURBAN CULTS AND SANCTUARIES

Just outside the city one encounters sacred enclosures, temples, altars, and cultic installations of quite varied character.

Sanctuaries linked to necropoleis take on widely diverse forms. One of the most remarkable is the Cannicella necropolis sanctuary at Orvieto. Situated on the east of the plateau at least 15 meters from the foot of the cliff, the sanctuary was increas-

## Sanctuaries

ingly hemmed in, from the last quarter of the sixth century, by a dense crowd of tombs, one on top of the other, as if the families of the deceased had particularly wanted their tombs to be close to this cult place. Its disorder contrasts with the regularity of the Crocifisso del Tufo cemetery. At La Cannicella, a spring flowed from the cliff, and the water was immediately channeled into vats and basins, which seem to have played a large role in the cult. Some scholars have hypothesized that they were used for ritual wine production; Dionysus/Bacchus would have been important here. But the Greek marble cult statue, known by the probably inappropriate name of "Venus of Cannicella," indicates another deity and a different cult orientation (see fig. 8.4). She is a nude woman with evident breasts,[18] but she does not correspond exactly to either Vea/Demeter[19] or Turan/Aphrodite. Although she is a goddess of female fertility, she is tightly connected with the world of the dead. Unusual terracotta antefixes or appliqués, dating to the late fifth century, come from this sacred area. They depict a double male-female face, perhaps the sovereign couple of the Afterworld, Aita and Phersipnai. This identification would confirm the funerary character of the sanctuary. This sacred enclosure of ancient Volsinii must have housed a community cult. Even if it was under the control of a single aristocratic family—which we do not know—it served a religious function for a very diverse society whose tombs cluster around it.

It was not the same, however, for all funerary sanctuaries. Many originated and remained strictly associated with an aristocratic family. Whether formed around the family tumulus or even on it, as at Cortona,[20] or situated within a group of family-owned tombs, as at Chiusi,[21] funerary sanctuaries were often attached to the cult of the hero/founder of an aristocratic group. One of these is located between Blera and Norchia, in an area made rich by commerce, first with Caere, then with Tarquinia. At Grotta Porcina, a truly monumental sacrificial area was used for rites that served only one *genos*.[22]

These sanctuaries linked to aristocratic tombs occur in the majority of Archaic necropoleis. They became veritable family sanctuaries. Here the ritual was identified with familial piety, the place of burial with the *heroon* of the founder, and the funerary cult with a cementing of aristocratic society. It is probably for this purpose that permanent structures were built. On several Archaic bas-reliefs from Chiusi, some funerary scenes take place under a building that looks like a temple;[23] others, around a monumental altar. Many small but telling clues point to the existence of private funerary sanctuaries, all of which seem to have had an aristocratic function.

Several ritual inscriptions confirm this appropriation of a cult by a family. The Capua Tablet furnishes the surest proof. It states that certain specifically directed acts and sacrifices should be performed by members of certain *gene*, such as the Velthur clan for the rites of June,[24] or by certain social groups, such as colleges of priests or political communities. We have inscriptions that mention the gods of these family cults: *Uni Ursmnei* (Juno of the Ursmnei family), *Uni Curtunei* (of the Curtuna

## Sanctuaries

family), and *Kavtha Achuia*, a deity of the Achu family.[25] This practice is not unique in the ancient Mediterranean world. In Greece and Rome certain priestly families were attached to specific cults—for example, those of Eleusis or of the Ara Maxima in Rome. Furthermore, in Etruria some cults that appear to serve the whole city-state were in reality dominated by a single family.

At Arezzo, the so-called Sanctuary of the Chimaera is situated outside the city walls, not far from the ancient settlement, along the main route to Fiesole. The excavations conducted in 1954 do not add much to our knowledge of it, but the discovery that occurred on November 15, 1553, near the gate of San Lorentino was clearly indicative of an important sanctuary. Cosimo dei Medici ordered transported to Florence, besides the famous Chimaera (see fig. 7.8), "numerous bronze statuettes that had been found at the same place and which represented children, birds and animals." It was a votive deposit in which the quality of the offerings varied greatly, from modest figurines to the sumptuous bronze sculptural group depicting the Chimaera with Pegasus and Bellerophon. Discussions in the *Comune d'Arezzo* (the City Council) of 1553 mention "figurines of children" that appear to resemble those found in nearby Cortona.[26] The latter date to the second century and seem to have been offered by a sort of *"grande bourgeoisie."* This suggests that the Arezzo sanctuary had a long period of activity ending in a late "democratization" of the cult.

But the Chimaera group evokes the image of the sanctuary before the anti-aristocratic revolution of 302, which reversed the power of the city's great noble families, and in particular that of the Cilnii, ancestors of Maecenas. Certainly one of the great aristocratic families, perhaps even the *genos* of the Cilnii themselves, dedicated this expensive group, and it is possible that the name of the donor was engraved on one of the Chimaera's paws: the one that was broken, perhaps for that very reason. The theme of the hero-horseman conquering the monster, common in Etruria in the late fifth and early fourth centuries, is strongly aristocratic, as it had been in Greece. It is hard to imagine that a family wealthy enough to commission such an elegant group from artists in Chiusi or northern Etruria[27] did not exercise or gain authority over the sanctuary itself. Thus at least until the uprising of 302, the sanctuary of the Chimaera must have been an aristocratic family domain, strictly dependent on the wealth of a single family.

Such was probably the status of many periurban sanctuaries erected on the lands of the great *gene*. They were bound to these families all the more strictly because the sacred "laws" (calendars, rituals, and revealed texts), whether in written or oral form, were jealously guarded by members of the same families.

Some of these sanctuaries, however, located within view of a city but not in an outlying village, escaped their socially limited function and developed to become important, multifaceted cult places. They took advantage of their proximity to the city, but drew independence from their exterior location. Often a water source or a strik-

## Sanctuaries

ing natural site, which, if it were far from the city would have inspired only a rural *sacellum* at best, in this location became the occasion for an important sanctuary.

The Temple of Uni/Juno Curite on the site of Celle at Falerii, and that of Turms/Mercury at Sassi Caduti, are both linked to running water, as is the famous Portonaccio Temple at Veii. In all cases, the channels, basins, wells, and tanks affirm the importance of water. But it is difficult to determine the actual role of this element. Was it the reason for the location of the sanctuary, or was water only given this importance later? Did it have mantic or curative powers? Did its use change over time? The votive deposits do not permit us satisfactorily to pin down the evolution of its function. On the other hand, at Marzabotto, it is certain that the sanctuary "of the waters" had a curative function since the Archaic period, although this is an isolated example. There must also have been an Archaic sanctuary on the site of Chianciano, which today is still dedicated to medical care. Since the Archaic period, it is certain, water sanctuaries had a curative function.

In the park of Chianciano Terme, near the Sillene spring, still a thermal spa today,[28] stood a temple where it is very likely that a cult of the moon was practiced since the end of the sixth century.[29] The site was ultimately Christianized with the construction of a sanctuary to Saint Michael. The ancient building was probably just a large covered space, since no trace of masonry has been found.[30] The offerings in this water sanctuary were sumptuous, as evidenced by the fragments of a bronze two-horse chariot and the remains of a male statue, perhaps of Aplu.

The large structure at Fucoli,[31] which dates from the middle of the second century B.C., is the most impressive of the sanctuaries built over thermal springs. The dimensions of the partly reconstructed pediment suggest that this had been the largest temple in all Etruria. Excavations have exposed a large, partially sunken *piazza* and yielded furnishings of a richness that attests to the sanctuary's importance. The remains of a large bronze lamp, similar in type to that of Cortona but much larger, almost 1.6 meters in diameter, evoke the luxury of the place. Similar lamps occur only in Second Style Pompeiian paintings. The Fucoli lamp would have held a bronze statue in its center. As at Sillene, a human burial, found here in association with inhumed animal victims, may reveal foundation rites of disturbing strangeness.

The sacred complex was probably deliberately destroyed. It is almost impossible today to reconstruct the organization of the sanctuary. The associated votive deposits are not securely identified, and the anatomical ex-votos from the area are relatively few and of uncertain provenance. Only a few column drums and a part of the pedimental decoration have survived from this enormous sanctuary, and it is very difficult to imagine how it looked.

The terracotta decoration, though fragmentary, is some of the most remarkable of the Hellenistic period. The closed pediment was decorated with high terracotta reliefs whose meaning still escapes us, but whose imagery—Heraclean, Dionysiac, and

# Sanctuaries

5.7. Fucoli: acroterion in the form of a winged female spirit, from the right corner of the pediment. Painted terracotta. Mid-second century. Chianciano Terme, Museo Civico delle Acque.

oriental—is intriguing. The sculptural group is strongly influenced by Pergamene techniques and was probably executed by coroplasts trained in the Greek East, yet it is infused with the taste of the local Etruscan patrons. The refinement of its execution and the elegance of its composition are seductive. The raking sima is decorated with a delightful relief of a marine *thiasos* in which nude children ride dolphins and sea horses. The fully preserved acroterion from the right corner of the pediment is a magnificent winged female, nude except for jewels and sandals. Like a follower of Dionysus, she holds a kantharos in her left hand (fig. 5.7). Below, male figures, clothed like orientals in soft trousers and tunics with wet, clinging folds, are set in a rocky landscape near a male who is seated on a throne and faces the center of the pediment. The latter, very Greek and supremely calm, resembles a god, perhaps Zeus. A beautiful half-overturned krater lies among the rocks.

Several heads (one of which has been stolen) also came from the pediment. One of these heads wears a Phrygian bonnet and probably belonged to one of the figures in eastern costume. Another is of a young, beardless man. A third, whose twisted beard and neck torsion clearly proclaim their Pergamene origins, wears a lion skin; this must be Heracles. Another head, also with contorted hair, belonged to a more static figure.

The mythological theme depicted in this vast group is almost impossible to reconstruct. The fragment from the right side of the pediment is all that remains, and the

## Sanctuaries

scene on it is quite fragmentary. There is no inscription to identify the god to whom the temple was dedicated. Hercle/Heracles is possible,[32] but questionable. Was the head stolen during the excavations that of Aplu/Apollo? If so, it would be tempting to connect the purifying role of the waters with the god of healing. The theme of a pediment, however, does not necessarily have a direct relationship to the god worshipped in the temple. The krater, the kantharos, and the depiction of the marine *thiasos* might also point to Fufluns/Dionysus, whose cult is so widespread in northern Etruria in the second century.[33] Here, still, the clues are tenuous.

F.-H. Massa-Pairault hypothesizes[34] that the imagery of the pediment illustrates the complex myth of Laomedon, punished by Heracles and perhaps by the Argonauts (Diodorus Siculus, 4.49). The theme would thus carry a political message, celebrating the alliance between Rome and Chiusi by recalling how Priam, the ancestor of Rome, was placed on the throne of Troy by Heracles, ancestor of the Etruscans. Though seductive, this reading of the fragments of the Fucoli pediment is too fragile. Once again, it is wisest to state our ignorance. The immediate proximity of a thermal spring suggests that the sanctuary probably had curative functions, and perhaps, as often accompanies them, a mantic role.

The great Portonaccio Sanctuary at Veii was the type of periurban sacred zone whose religious role extended beyond the narrow framework of the city. It was situated on a natural terrace at the foot of the plateau of Veii and bordered the route leading to the Tiber. It was positioned at a crossroads, a suitable place for meeting, markets, or commerce. This very important religious complex consisted of a triangular enclosure pierced by two entrances, a large temple of the Tuscan order, a vast basin, a well, a monumental altar, a *bothros* (sacrificial pit), and, in the eastern part of the *temenos*, porticoes and various service buildings.[35] The complex was richly decorated: excavations have revealed splendid acroterial statues. It had replaced, around 500, an earlier sanctuary that was noticeably more modest but occupied a larger *temenos*. The functions of this sanctuary are known to us only from the archaeological elements—the structures and votive objects. As to the gods who were honored here, the iconography, the dedicatory inscriptions, and allusions in the ancient historiographers allow us to make a tentative identification.

The votive objects and structures allow us to define certain aspects of the cult. The great basin and its subsidiaries, as well as the anatomical ex-votos, suggest a curative function, and the presence of Apollo (and his mother, Leto) among the large terracotta acroteria confirms the later sanctuary's health-giving role in the Archaic period. Farther to the east, around the monumental altar and near the *bothros*, were found inscriptions designating Menrva/Athena in an oracular role. Turan/Aphrodite and Aritimi/Artemis also had cults here, although their functions are not clear. The latter is depicted on one of the large acroteria. Myths of Hercle, too, mingle with those of Aplu on the roof sculptures at Portonaccio. We are led to conclude that the sanctuary was home to various gods, and that its nature was at once uranian and

## Sanctuaries

chthonian, masculine and feminine, mantic and curative. The logical and restrictive categories through which we are accustomed to view Greek religion seem out of place here. The sanctuary is multiform, and it is difficult to imagine which gods occupied the temple's three cellae.

Not only Veiians worshipped here, although there has been found a dedication by a certain Tolumnius, perhaps a relative of Lars Tolumnius, king of Veii, who, according to Livy (4.17), was killed by Cornelius Cossus in 437 or 426 during a battle for the Cremera valley. The inscriptions also preserve names that are known from Caere, Tarquinia, and Vulci. The Portonaccio Sanctuary's influence thus extended beyond Veii to the whole of Etruria. Its pan-Etruscan calling was well suited to its location outside the city walls and to its plurality of cults honoring very diverse gods. The identification of these gods has given rise to an abundant bibliography full of contradictory opinions. Portonaccio was more than the sanctuary of a single god or of a mere triad. It was a sacred area where, as often in Etruria, the divine world showed its surprisingly complex face—surprising even to its contemporaries! This plural character, very marked here, was probably also found in a number of other suburban *temene*.

### RURAL CULTS AND VOTIVE DEPOSITS

In the middle or on the edges of forests, in the open countryside, at the border of a city's territory, at the crossing of a water course, at the meeting point of two natural regions such as a plain and a mountain, at the summit of a mountain visible from a great distance, other sanctuaries arose whose role is not always easy to evaluate. Little excavated, many of them have left us only the contents of their votive deposits. The architectural vestiges are of little importance, but the cults established in these places were considerable. At the summit of Mount Soracte, in Faliscan territory, tradition mentions a cult to Apollo. On this site, today occupied by a church, only a few Etruscan ex-votos confirm Pliny's information. This is the case for the majority of rural sanctuaries.

If we exclude the rather particular case of the aristocratic funerary enclosures that abound in rural necropoleis, as at Blera, at San Giuliano, and to a lesser extent at Grotta Porcina,[36] we can state that many rural sanctuaries are found in places of passage, places of rupture, or borders.

A border sanctuary occurs at Grasceta dei Cavallari in the middle of the Tolfa mountains, in the area of contact between the territory of Tarquinia and that of Caere. Others, at Sovana and Pieve a Socana, mark the confines of the territories of Chiusi, Vulci, and Roselle. Still others in the frontier zones of Campania or of northern or eastern Etruria confirm the ubiquity of sacred places at the limits of Etruscan habitation.

In the territory of Sovana, on the embankment of a little brook now named Picciolana, a rectangular cult space cut into the tufa is bordered by a sort of trench in which

## Sanctuaries

a large number of locally produced ex-votos were deposited. These objects are characteristic of rural societies[37] but completely foreign to the Late Etruscan aesthetic.

The little sanctuary of Grasceta dei Cavallari, initially in the territory of Caere, consists of a rectangular enclosure bordered by porticoes of wooden pillars and a central *naiskos*. The votive deposit is most revealing. Mass-produced anatomical ex-votos are found in great quantity in all the sanctuaries of Italy, but while the ones from Grasceta are similar to those of the same functions found elsewhere, they are executed with such awkwardness that they betray a total absence of Hellenistic aesthetic models. It is clear that worshippers from two very different social strata frequented this place, and the second category, rural or foreign, interests us more. Here again, it is impossible to identify a specific god, and the architectural remains do not suggest a triad.

The little sanctuary at Punta della Vipera, near the sea, is very different. Menrva was honored there, at a beautiful altar erected for her in the fourth century. Worshippers first offered depictions of the goddess and then, as they did everywhere from the end of the fourth century, anatomical ex-votos. An Archaic inscription on lead mentions rites that are attested elsewhere (for example, at Capua). These rites suggest that the original functions of this sanctuary were fecundity and fertility, and, later, healing. The coastal fishermen offered their fishhooks, perhaps in the hope that the goddess would favor their activities. The most remarkable activity practiced there—which completes this tableau—is divination. The mantic function was probably important.

A poorly defined sacred space near the sources of the Arno[38] must be a countryside sanctuary. It stands beside the high road from Bidente and marks a pass through the Apennines toward the coastal Adriatic plain and the site of Ravenna. There, at the foot of a mountain, on the shore of the small lake of Falterona,[39] between the end of the sixth century and the beginning of the first, worshippers from everywhere came or passed, and made an offering to its deity—sometimes a very poor statuette, sometimes a splendid bronze by a recognized Greek hand, sometimes a weapon, a cuirass, or an anatomical ex-voto. Not only did the sick come in search of a cure, but also soldiers, legions of them, who offered their weapons and probably invoked a warrior Hercle as their military god. Curiously, this Hercle, who seems to have been the god of the site, is here associated with the water of the lake, perhaps even with running water. One must recall his "aquatic" labors: his battle against Acheloos, his use of water to clean the Augean stables, and his draining of the Stymphalian lake. There are also depictions of Hercle on a goatskin raft.[40] Stylistic analysis of some 600 bronzes that came out of the mud of the lake, but are now in London or Paris, indicate that the worshippers came from Chiusi, Caere or Campania, Volterra, and Magna Graecia.

Of the sanctuary's architectural traces we know nothing. Should our ignorance be blamed on the 1838 pillaging that was called an excavation, or were its structures so slight that they left no traces? Hellenistic Greek depictions, and especially the copies of them made by decorative painters at Pompeii and Herculaneum, have shown us

## Sanctuaries

many of these minuscule enclosures, *temene* sketched out in a few details, trees hung with ribbons (*taeniae*), garlands, crowns, *oscilla* (hanging discs) and various offerings. In the Tarquinian Tomb of Hunting and Fishing, the decoration of the first room, less famous than that which gave its name to the monument, shows one of these sacred places, certainly a "country sanctuary." Its trees, covered with offerings, hung with *taeniae* and garlands, mirrors and *oscilla*, frame the thundering dances of a reanimation ritual.[41]

The famous bronze votive statues from Monteguragazza (or, better, Monte Acuto Ragazza), today in the Museum of Bologna—some of a very high artistic level, others quite modest—were offered in a tiny $4 \times 4$–meter sanctuary that included an altar and a well. This rural cult place of an unknown deity is on a route that passes near the valleys of the Reno and the Setta; the variety of its votive offerings suggests a complex usage, frequently by travelers.

Another rural sanctuary known to us only from its votive deposit is that of Brolio, south of Arezzo, along the valley of the Chiana.[42] Forty-seven bronze offerings survey the life of the sanctuary, to which worshippers from all over Etruria, from the end of the seventh century to the beginning of the fifth, brought their gifts. Hunters who tracked the hare or the deer, travelers from southern Etruria or from nearby Arezzo, soldiers, perhaps Greek mercenaries in the service of local *lucumones* (nobles or *principes*), visitors from primitive Rome, women of high society, and the rich donors who dedicated a griffin-head protome cauldron made on Samos—all made their way into this sanctuary. It is quite far from any large city, and the small settlement on the hill of Brolio cannot justify a deposit like this. This countryside sanctuary was important only because it was situated at the border of two territories, Chiusi to the south and Arezzo to the north. When the expansion of Chiusi on the plain of the Chiana pushed back the "frontier" of its actual territory, the deposits here became fewer and poorer, and the sacred place returned to its original role as a small local sanctuary.

Such were these consecrated places on arteries of travel and contact, at the edges of Etruscan territories. They resemble the later "ports" of the Alps or the Pyrénées. The cults that arose here were eclectic and responded to diverse needs.

### CULTS OF CONTACT AND PORT SANCTUARIES

Strabo (5.2.8) mentions the sanctuary of Pyrgi, which he believed was dedicated to Eileithyia and founded by the Pelasgians. Pseudo-Aristotle (*Oec.* II. 1349b), on the other hand, speaks of a sanctuary of Leucothea. The destruction and pillage of Pyrgi's sacred enclosure by the Syracusans in 384 reveal the importance that the Greeks themselves attributed to this place. Diodorus Siculus (XV, 14.3–4) estimated that the temples' treasure amounted to the enormous sum of 1,000 minted gold talents, 500 of minted silver, and more than 1,000 other uncoined silver talents! This is probably an enormous exaggeration. The discovery of this sanctuary in 1956 by M. Pallottino and the excavations that followed have been significant for Etruscan research. They

## Sanctuaries

have brought to light two temples and their decoration as well as many documents, including the famous dedicatory "gold plaques" (see figs. 1.7, 5.8). More recent work to the south of the great enclosure has revealed a sector attributed by Aelianus to Apollo. Here was found an offering inscription to Śuri and Cautha.[43] The mantic character of the former god and the solar dimension of the latter are certain, so the connection of both of them with Apollo, as Aelianus mentions, is legitimate. In addition, this sanctuary included a *bothros*, which can be considered a partially chthonic element. Elsewhere Śuri is known to have a chthonic quality.[44]

The great sanctuary of Pyrgi certainly existed from the beginning of the sixth century.[45] At first its structures were modest, as we know from the fragments of terracotta decoration and the course of the road to the sanctuary. It was situated slightly to the south of the later Roman settlement, almost on the beach, and at its apogee the great complex must have presented an imposing aspect toward the waterfront. The absence of bedrock at the site necessitated the construction of a powerful masonry foundation to create a level surface for large-scale building. The sacred domain has the form of a large trapezoid, 80 meters by more than 75. It is oriented toward the southwest, like the grid of the Archaic settlement, and is divided into two distinct, equal spaces, each occupied by a temple.

About 510, the first large building, the south temple or Temple B, was begun. A text commemorating the foundation—if not an important offering or a later development[46]—was inscribed in Etruscan on two gold plaques and in Punic on a third (fig. 5.8). It states that the site was consecrated to Uni/Astarte, and that Thefarie Velianas, "ruler over Caere," in thanks for the goddess's favor, dedicated a gift to her.[47] While this peripteral temple—which must have resembled the Greek temples of Sicily—was going up, about twenty small cellae and a whole series of small altars were built along the sea to the south of the *temenos*. The small *cellae* were perhaps the chambers for the goddess's "sacred servants," the *hierodules*, who, as at Acrocorinth or Eryx, practiced sacred prostitution, according to one interpretation (perhaps an overinterpretation) of an ancient text.[48]

About 460 a second temple was built, parallel to the first and immediately to its north. This doubled the surface area of the large sacred domain. This second building, Temple A, is not quite as tall as the first and a little wider. Its form is Tuscan, with a wide, deep portico and three interior cellae. Its decoration, part of which has been found, illustrates the myth of the Seven against Thebes. The choice of that motif proves the very Hellenized character of the local culture, but its interpretation remains relatively obscure because scholars have been looking, perhaps mistakenly, for a strictly political reading (see chapter 6).

The large square altar between these two temples was actually a *bothros* with a vertical channel for communication with the chthonian world. Two symmetrical wells on either side of the façade of the second temple also had some religious function.

Sanctuaries

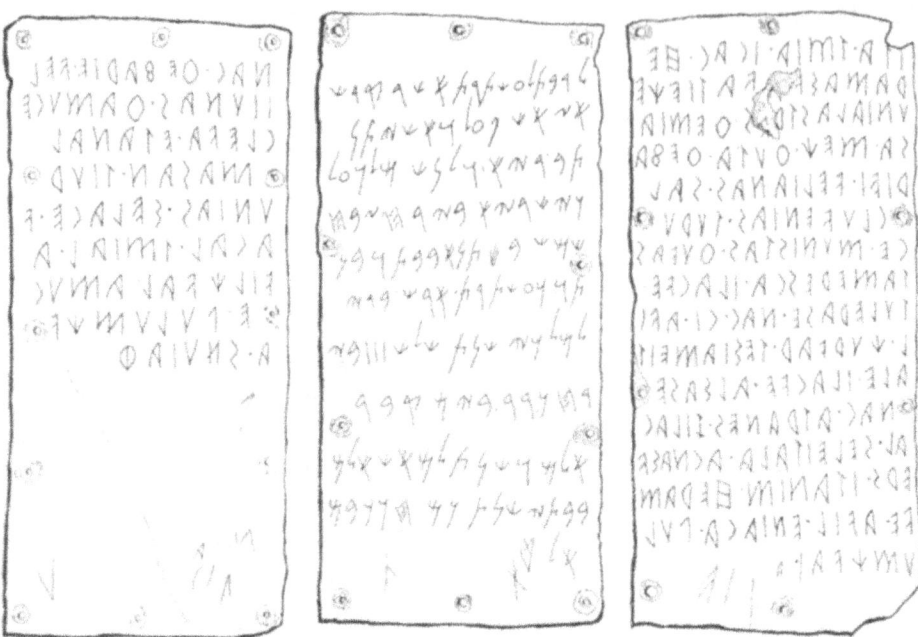

5.8. Sanctuary of Pyrgi (Caere): the "Pyrgi tablets," text commemorating a dedication. Gold leaves with inscription in Etruscan and Punic. Beginning of the fifth century or very end of the sixth. Rome, Museo Naz. di Villa Giulia.

The complexity of the Pyrgi sanctuary defines it as a particular type of sacred area. Founded at a port site, it was important for one specific category of foreigners, the Punics, authors of the inscription on the gold plaque. They traded or even lived at the site, probably under the terms of a treaty that was the ancestor or prototype of the one said to have been established in 509 by the nascent Roman Republic.

The deity worshipped in Temple A is called by some Ino or Leucothea, by others Mater Matuta. She is in effect the Etruscan Thesan. The goddess of Temple B is named Uni in Etruscan, Astarte in Punic. This plurality of names illustrates the complex but irreducible character of the Etruscan deity, in whom each worshipper recognizes the goddess that is most familiar to him or her. Some religious practices in this sanctuary were relatively rare but attested in the Punic world, including, perhaps, sacred prostitution, which was known at Eryx and in a number of other Phoenician sanctuaries. This sacred space was open to contacts with the Greek Mediterranean, too: it adopted Siciliote architectural forms and Theban iconographic themes in the pedimental sculpture; it lived according to the vicissitudes of Syracusan politics and agreements with the Carthaginian thalassocracy. The religious functions of the complex were so linked to the activities of the port that they did not outlive it.

Just to the south, the neighboring sanctuary consecrated to Apollo and to the corresponding Etruscan deities, Śuri and Cautha, was much more modest and had to

## Sanctuaries

satisfy the Greeks of the port enclave. Here the political authority does not seem to have played as important a role. This type of cult area, somewhat comparable to that at Gravisca, was probably more common in the ports than were the great *temene* remembered in tradition.

Here we are a long way from the rural sanctuaries. This port religion, both product and proof of contacts with other cultures, illustrates the open character of a city like Caere at its apogee. All the foreign borrowings of this port sanctuary, however, become strongly Etruscanized, as the locally made votive offerings indicate.

Slightly different conditions prevailed in Gravisca, the port of Tarquinia. Founded about 600, it appears to have been frequented principally by Greek merchants.[49] Its first religious structure, built some twenty years later, was a sanctuary to Turan/Aphrodite. She was soon joined by Uni/Hera and Vea/Demeter, who received offerings mostly of Greek origin. A cult to Adonis is also attested there, tenuously.[50] Throughout the sixth century, Greek travelers or resident merchants frequented the site, to the point where it became a veritable Greek sanctuary in Etruscan territory. Samians, Ephesians, Milesians, and Ionians from all the cities flourishing at that time, merchants who also frequented Naucratis, where their names are also attested, came to worship the three major divinities: Aphrodite, protectress of sailors and merchants; Hera, the most often honored; and Demeter.[51] When Persian pressure restricted, then definitively stopped, the commerce of these oriental cities, merchants from Aegina took over. They worshipped Apollo. An Attic kantharos of the 520s was offered to him by a certain Euarchos, who wrote in the Aeginetan alphabet, and a marble anchor was dedicated by the famous Sostratos,[52] whose legendary wealth may have been acquired in part through the importation of Greek ceramics into Etruria. So far, the sanctuary seems to have been visited only by foreigners.

Around 470 the situation changed. The Greek sanctuary was reorganized, renovated, and clothed in imposing façades along the main route. The *naiskos* of Aphrodite became that of Turan, and a courtyard with altars was created behind it. Vea in her turn was granted an open-air sanctuary: in its paved courtyard were erected two altars, one of which was circular and similar to that of the Thesmophoria. Uni, too, received a courtyard with two altars, and space was made at the center of this sacred area for a huge parallelepiped coffer for the cult of Atunis/Adonis.[53] This transformation of a Greek *emporion* sanctuary into an Etruscan one is very interesting. Here Greek cults molted into indigenous cults. The rich offerings of the merchants were replaced by modest votives, which, over the years, became anatomical, often linked with female fertility. Thus, curiously, a civic cult of Greek gods, frequented by Ionian merchants, was transformed for private local worship like that in the rest of Italy. The Greek sacred place was absorbed into the undifferentiated religious atmosphere of late Etruria.

The fate of the foreign elements in cults located in port sanctuaries varied according to the conditions of the cults' foundation. At Pyrgi, when the foreign elements were introduced under the direct authority of the "king of Caere" the dominant

## Sanctuaries

character of the cult remained Etruscan, but the many Punic borrowings survived even after the peoples who had brought them had left the scene. When, as happened at Gravisca, the cult developed within a Greek *emporion*, when a kind of "concession" was granted first to Ionian, then to Aeginetan practices, the initial participation of the indigenous Etruscans was minimal. As the Greek presence shrank, these sanctuaries were profoundly modified, although they retained their individual deities and were not transformed into triad temples. The cult practices, however, became homogenized rather quickly, and they slowly lost their initial Greek character to follow the standardized evolution of the majority of Etruscan cults.

### "FEDERAL" CULTS AND SANCTUARIES

The subject of "federal" cults has stirred endless controversy, all of it based on tenuous and often questionable evidence. Here it will be useful to organize what is merely an amalgam of uncertainties.

Livy's history contains several references to a sanctuary where the Twelve Peoples of Etruria met (4.23, 4.25, 4.61, 5.17, 6.2), but they are not conclusive evidence for the existence of an actual *federal* sanctuary or of a *federation* that had its seat there. The first reference dates to 434:

> The capture of Fidenae caused great alarm in Etruria, especially in the towns of Veii and Falerii—the former from dread of a similar fate, and the latter from the uneasy consciousness of having supported Fidenae when the war started, even though in the second outbreak she had stood aside. Accordingly when these two communities obtained the consent of the Twelve Peoples for the *concilium Etruriae* to meet at the temple of Voltumna, the Senate in Rome expected a serious uprising. (4.23)

This is not proof of a federation and still less of a federal sanctuary, but only of the convocation of the *concilium*, authorized by the "Twelve Peoples." The later references are no more explicit. The next year:

> War plans were discussed in the councils of the Volscians and Aequians, and also in Etruria at the shrine of Voltumna. (4.25)

This is still not proof of a federal sanctuary. It is the same throughout Livy's history. The only possible reference to an actual supra-civic sanctuary concerns the festivals and games at which the "king" of Veii drew the hostility of the peoples of Etruria:

> He in effect had become hateful to this people by his pride and his wealth, by interrupting, sacrilegiously in a fit of anger, the solemn games because the Twelve Peoples had designated another for the office of priest. (5.1)

It is generally believed that these games took place at the Fanum Voltumnae. This is quite probable, but in reality the precise location is not indicated in this reference, or anywhere else.[54]

## Sanctuaries

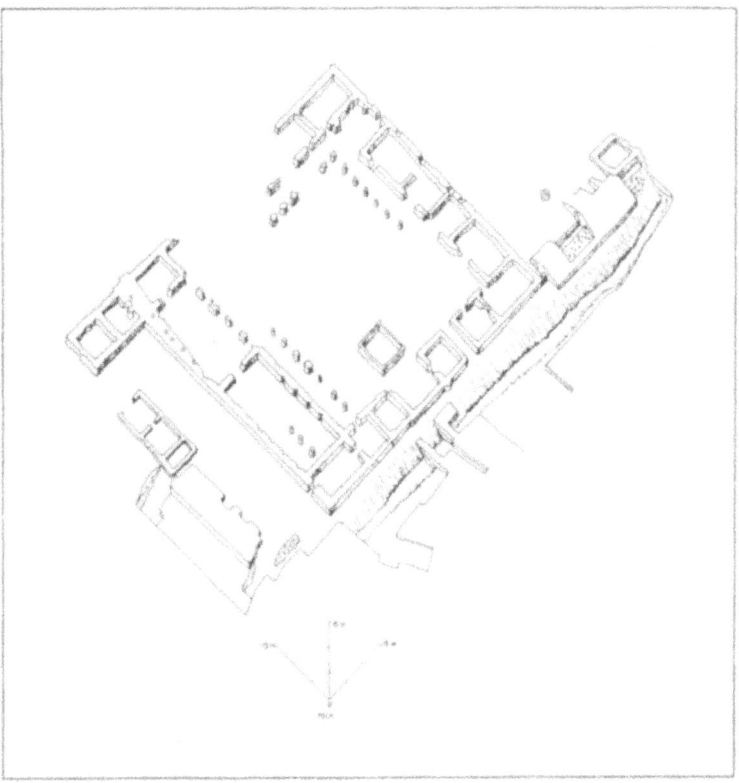

5.9. Plan of the Murlo complex, second building. Beginning of the sixth century.

It thus seems an overinterpretation to conclude that there was a federal sanctuary, conceived, built, and managed as such. The account of the capture of Volsinii and the sack of the Fanum Voltumnae mentions the sanctuary's wealth, but not its federal function. Situated in the territory of Volsinii,[55] this prestigious sanctuary, from the last third of the fifth century, had an importance, wealth, and central geographic location that destined it to serve as the setting for the pan-Etruscan games. The priest/magistrate who organized and presided over the games, the person whom the inscriptions call *zilath mechlrasnal*,[56] was perhaps the *sacerdos totius Etruriae* mentioned by Livy. At these occasional and exceptional meetings of the "Twelve Peoples," issues of common interest were certainly raised, just as in the pan-Hellenic sanctuaries, particularly Olympia in the fourth century. But the sanctuary of Voltumna has not been identified, although it has been sometimes equated with the Belvedere Temple or, most recently and with high probability, with the Campo della Fiera.[57]

The Volsinian *fanum*, whose first mention dates back only to 434, probably did not always have this function as a pan-Etruscan sanctuary. The possible federative role of the Montetosto complex, near Caere, has been mentioned (chapter 2). It must have

## Sanctuaries

5.10. One of the seated acroterial figures from the second building at Murlo. Antiquarium di Murlo.

been a place for assembly and games, perhaps those games prescribed by the Pythia.[58] It has also been suggested that the Tarquinian Ara della Regina temple had served the same function in the mid-sixth century before the Volsinian sanctuary supplanted it. This hypothesis would imply that Voltumna—actually Velthumena, the "principal god (*princeps*) of the Etruscans" according to Varro—was not the exclusive god of the pan-Etruscan festivals and games, but that Artumes, the goddess of the Tarquinian sanctuary, had once held that role on occasion.

If this was the case, it must have been difficult to situate these games at Tarquinia, in southern Etruria, without *de facto* excluding the cities of northern Etruria. The "residence" of Murlo (fig. 5.9), according to the hypothesis of its first excavator,[59] could have been the seat of a northern "league," in competition with that of the south. We know this "league" existed, at least for a brief period, as a symmachy, a de-

## Sanctuaries

fensive alliance (Dionysius of Halicarnassus, *Ant. Rom.* 3.51). The large-scale building at Murlo, at once a sanctuary and a palace, could have hosted games and festivals that brought the northern cities together. The terracotta plaques that decorated the "residence"—depicting horse races, banquets, and assemblies of high-ranking people—argue in favor of activity of this kind (fig. 5.10), but no archaeological or formal textual proof has yet confirmed this seductive hypothesis.

We thus cannot assume the existence of Etruscan federal sanctuaries comparable to the well-known Greek religious centers that have wrongly been viewed as their exact models. The festivals and gatherings too often described as federal seem to have existed only at a much less organized level.

The considerable variety of Etruscan and Etrusco-Italic sanctuaries, whose locations, structures, and functions form complex and coherent wholes, does not permit us to speak, as we once did, of the Etruscan temple as a fixed and abstract concept. This diversity has led us to suspect a variety of cults, a disparity among the worshippers, and a complex articulation of divine functions. There is no less variety in the buildings themselves, which reflect the complexity and evolution of Etruscan religious practices.

CHAPTER 6

# The Buildings

THE ALTAR

The altar is the only indispensable monument in a sanctuary.[1] Altars are quite varied, however, in both size and form, and we should not spend more time on them than is necessary. The altars that have come down to us are rigorously similar to those depicted in the artistic sources. Only the constructed altars, as a rule, are shown in Etruscan art, and from these representations it is clear that the Etruscans knew the difference between Greek and Etruscan types. Scenes of the capture of Troy, and other scenes from Greek epic illustrated by Etruscan ceramic painters, show Greek altars, generally of an Ionian type.[2] These are frontally accessible by a flight of steps and are decorated with stylistically appropriate motifs. The altars depicted in Etruscan religious or mythical settings are immediately distinguishable from the Greek ones by their profiles and moldings.[3] The painted terracotta "Campana plaques," now in the Louvre, offer a good illustration (see fig. 3.5).[4]

A second type of altar appears on the reliefs of late-period (third- and second-century) urns. These show noticeable particularities: they are generally much smaller (fig. 6.1), sometimes round, and fitted with much more discrete moldings. They are often decorated with garlands and crowns. Statues sometimes adorn them, or small obelisks (usually three, closely related to Phoenician "betyls" or *betyli*: sacred stones).[5] These are almost certainly funerary. Etrusco-Campanian black-figure vases usually depict such altars.[6]

The actual altars differ little from their depictions. Behind the apse of the church of Pieve a Socana rests the lower part of a beautiful third-century altar.[7] Its profile is close to that of the temple altar at Fiesole (fig. 6.2), which is later, as well as to much older examples, such as that of the *lapis niger* in the Roman Forum and those at Lavinium.[8] The shape of these altars varies with their dimensions. The more modest ones are rectangular, while the larger take the form of a U (fig. 6.3). The altar of the Portonaccio Temple at Veii, for example, had this form, as did the vast terrace at Marzabotto called Zone D, which actually functioned as a monumental altar.

6.1. Urn of *Ceicna Fetiu*, from Volterra: Pelops sacrifices the charioteer Myrtilos, who sabotaged the wheel of Oenomaus' chariot. Note the form of the sacrificial altar. Florence, Museo Archeologico Nazionale, Soprintendenza Archeologica per la Toscana Firenze.

6.2. Altar of the Hellenistic temple at Fiesole. The molding is characteristic. Fiesole *in situ*. Third century.

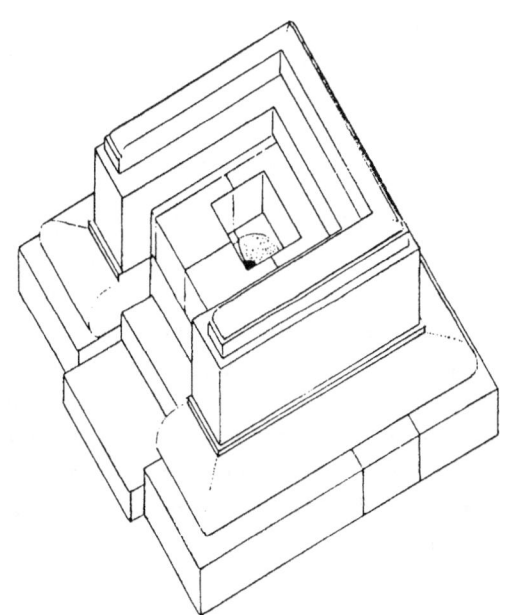

6.3. Altar of Punta della Vipera in the shape of a U (axonometric drawing). The form is of Greek origin.

The Buildings

Other altars were intended for chthonic offerings and funerary sacrifices and therefore take the form of *bothroi*. It is noteworthy that several of these altars, pierced by a channel of communication with the world below, were dedicated to Tinia, who in these cases probably had the attributes of Zeus Chthonios. Several examples at Orvieto and Bolsena are of this type. A *bothros* altar also occurs near Temple B at Pyrgi, and another at Santa Marinella. These are constants; in effect, this chthonic dimension is rarely absent from a sanctuary, of whatever kind.

Finally, we must mention, if only in passing, those funerary altars that occur by necessity in necropoleis, on the peaks of die-shaped tombs (*tombe a dado*), at the entrances to porticoes, or cut into the bedrock in the middle of areas used for funerary spectacles and games. Some are cylindrical, like that at Grotta Porcina in the territory of Tarquinia, and the one in the southern zone at Pyrgi, mentioned just above.

### THE TEMPLE

Vitruvius, the best-known theoretician of ancient architecture, wrote his *De architectura* during the reign of the emperor Augustus. What he called the Tuscan order (*ratio tuscanica*) was then still alive (4.7.1–3). The Temple of Jupiter Optimus Maximus on the Capitoline, rebuilt in stone, nonetheless retained the forms of its Archaic predecessor. It illustrates how the *ratio tuscanica* was born from a rationalization of the architecture of the Etruscans and ultimately became a model for most of Italy and the provinces. The haruspices, consulted on the rebuilding of the temple after the Capitoline fire of 83 B.C., confirmed the extremely conservative nature of religious architecture. Their response in effect was: "The gods do not want the old form to be changed" (Tacitus, *Hist.* 4.53).

Actually, the proportions and decorations of this order, as Vitruvius' treatise defines them, are purely theoretical and rather artificial. Nonetheless they are indispensable for us in restoring the appearance of buildings of which only vestiges remain.[9] Archaeology usually only yields the plan of the foundations and some terracotta decorations. From them it is difficult to imagine how the complete building would have looked. Whenever material facts have come to us in sufficient number, however, they generally confirm Vitruvius' principles. A study of the actual monuments, the object of this chapter, will permit us to add nuance to Vitruvius' descriptions, to note, here too, the astonishing variety in the examples that have come down to us, and to sketch their evolution. Let us bear in mind, however, that the most ancient temples are usually called Etrusco-Italic, while Tuscan is a term only applied to the Romanized "Vitruvian" form with three cellae.[10]

*The First Buildings*
Miniature models of temples or of small sanctuaries, *naiskoi* or *heroa*, illustrate the smallest and probably most ancient sacred buildings of Etruria.[11] These representations in terracotta or soft stone display an appreciable realism in their detail.

## The Buildings

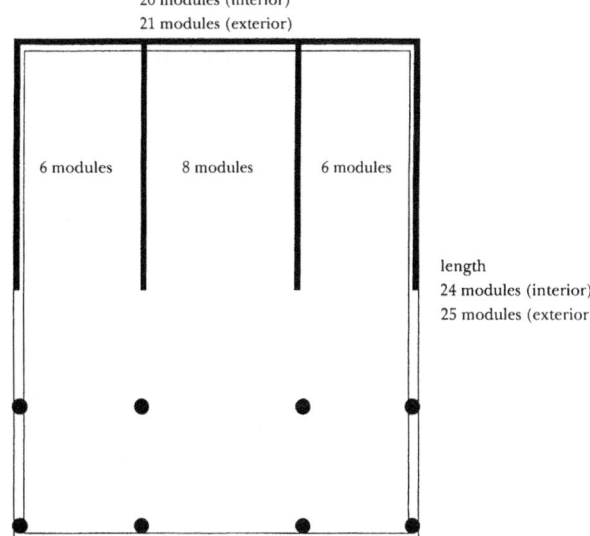

6.4a. Terracotta model of a distyle temple, from Satricum. Rome, Museo Naz. di Villa Giulia.

6.4b. Plan of the Etruscan temple according to Vitruvius. After H. Knell.

It is remarkable and a bit surprising that these primitive models are all very similar to those of contemporary Greece. They invariably consist of a single elongated room, which sometimes ends in an apse. Its entrance is later protected by a porch *in antis* or by a projecting roof supported on two columns (fig. 6.4a–b). This is the form of the *oikos*, the first house of the early Orientalizing period. This house seems merely to be a geometricization, a regularization, of the oblong hut that preceded it and existed contemporaneously with it.

For a rather long period, from the ninth to the end of the eighth century, southern Etruria and Latium used cinerary urns, made of terracotta or sometimes sheet bronze (fig. 6.5),[12] in the form of huts. These urns often carry geometric or geometricizing decoration consisting of little comb-made parallel marks, identical to the ornamentation that develops on Villanovan urns. The designs made by these marks, however, are generally considered specific to the house. They have been compared to the painted decoration on the walls of the houses at Acquarossa. Several of these motifs,[13] particularly those that depict figures dancing, walking, praying, or seated face to face, have a place in religious or heroicizing iconography.

These hut urns follow houses in evolving toward a rectangular plan. The architecture of the earliest tombs, with the conservatism proper to funerary art, echoes the evolution of the house with a delay of one or two generations. A comparison of house plans of the early Orientalizing period with plans of late Orientalizing tombs shows this phenomenon well.[14] The Campana Tomb of Veii, the Tomb of the Ship, and the

## The Buildings

6.5. Hut urn in sheet bronze: residence of a "chief," the probable model for the first temples. Eighth century. Rome, Museo Naz. di Villa Giulia.

Tomb of the Painted Animals illustrate the evolution toward a house type consisting of an elongated apsidal room.

The first known religious buildings exactly follow the pattern of the "house," the Archaic *oikos*. At Piazza d'Armi at Veii, on the site of a Villanovan habitation, a sanctuary of rectangular plan opens toward the southwest. Its form is very simple: the cella, 18 meters long and a little more than 6 meters wide, opens directly to the exterior through one of its short sides. The roof beam was supported in the center by two pillars. The framework of the roof was protected by relief-decorated terracotta revetment plaques that were twice "modernized."

Another very similar building was discovered at Bolsena, at the site of Poggio Casetta. The modesty of the structure, which does not rest on a podium, contrasts with the vast extent of the *temenos*. But when the architectural elements of this small temple were still too poor to demand a privileged axis of view from the city, the urban grid was already made to conform perfectly to its orientation, as it leaned its blind apse against the wall of the *temenos*. It seems that the most primitive of these buildings already dictated the organizing principles of the urban fabric.

Some ex-voto temple models from the seventh and sixth centuries echo the plan of the *oikos*. A typical example from Velletri is now in the Villa Giulia Museum (see fig. 6.4a–b).[15] The length of the miniature is proportionately shorter than that of the original temple, and the façade is exaggerated by a sort of projecting pediment. A roof resting on two columns shelters the narrow porch on its façade. This type of building certainly resulted from a geometricization of the oval hut. Its interior arrangement must have consisted of a linear suite of rooms, similar to those in Caeretan tombs.[16] All seem to have derived from houses of the mid-Orientalizing period, which were themselves merely derivations of Greek houses *a thalamos*—that is, with an inner chamber. The latter appeared during the eighth century in the Greek colonies of the West: for example, at Pithecusae.

# The Buildings

## *The New Models of the Seventh Century*

But we very quickly see great changes. The early seventh-century settlements, still largely influenced by Greek domestic architecture, produced a new structure. The elongated buildings from this time on had a portico, but on one of the long sides. The interior space was divided into groups of rooms on either side of a central, transversal space, from which the atrium no doubt eventually developed. This type of private dwelling—the most illustrative example is a house at Acquarossa[17]—gave birth to a type of chamber tomb that was very distinctive and widely used, particularly at Caere.[18] At the same time, Greek architectural production slowly defined the form that would become the Greek temple. At Argos and Thermon toward the end of the seventh century, peripteral buildings were erected that gave a monumental new value to the column. It is both from this local substratum and from Greek models that the canonical structure of the Etruscan temple developed.

## *Vitruvius' Models*

It is possible to obtain a plan and an elevation of the architect's theoretical model by transcribing his text into graphic form.

The first defining element of the building is the plan. Its Archaic rectangular form gradually evolved toward square. From the aristocratic house type it borrowed the interior division into three rooms or three parallel spaces. Under Greek influence its façade developed a columnar portico. The proportion of length to width, as Vitruvius sets it, is 6:5. This relationship is not observed everywhere, but it seems to correspond in a general way to the *templum*, the almost square and strictly oriented space in which celestial phenomena were observed. The plan creates a total opposition between the anterior part (*pars antica*) and the posterior part (*pars postica*), whose surface areas are in theory equal. While the front half is completely open, both on the façade and on the sides, the rear half is completely closed by lateral walls, a back wall, and a structural front that is only penetrated through a few simple doors (fig. 6.6). The temple plan can sometimes show only one narrow open façade, supported by two columns between the antae (*distyle in antis*). Later, probably under the influence of Greek architecture, it can have a portico completely supported on columns (*prostyle*); or the line of columns can be extended along the sides up to the back wall (*peripteros sine postico*). It is extremely rare for the temple to be completely surrounded by columns (*peripteros*). If it is, it never has a false rear porch (*opisthodomos*). The building is strictly frontal: it is inaccessible both from behind, often because it is built up against the *temenos* wall, and on the sides, but it opens up completely through its unique façade. This frontality stimulated an urbanism of axial perspectives, which the cities of the west later inherited.

The elevation is equally original. Conceived as a *templum* or *auguraculum*, the building is often elevated and oriented toward the south. A high podium with a large

## The Buildings

6.6. Model of the Tuscan temple, following Vitruvius. Rome, Università "la Sapienza," Istituto Archeologico.

stairway extending from its frontal face raises the structure and makes the three other sides inaccessible. It suggests a desire to mark the superhuman character of the place. The high position with frontal access reinforces the axiality of the building and situates it to preside over urban developments on either side of it. The walls of the podium are not vertical, but are adorned with complex, often deep moldings,[19] whose plastic values create strong contrasts of light and shade. Two masses of masonry with the same moldings frame the frontal stairway and complete its monumental aspect.

*Architectural Decoration and Its Function*
The decoration of the building was also very distinctive. There must have been stone architectural decorations, such as those on the tomb pediments at Blera and Norchia (fig. 6.7), as well as some metallic ornaments. But the sculptures in limestone long ago disappeared into the lime kilns,[20] and the gilded bronze acroteria that Pliny the Elder (*HN* 35.154) saw on Tuscan temples in Rome were melted down in metallurgists' crucibles, so that almost nothing remains except the terracotta decorations. They were light (relative to other building materials), inexpensive and easy to make, and ideal for the wooden structures of Etrusco-Italic temples. Etruscan coroplasts became masters in this technique and pushed it to an unequaled level.

## The Buildings

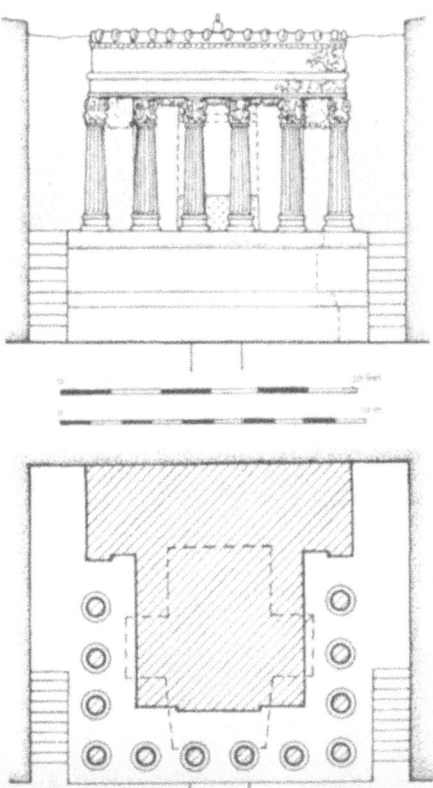

6.7. Rock-cut tombs in the necropolis of Norchia. These may have served as the formal model for Etruscan stone buildings.

Painted (fig. 6.8) or modeled terracotta plaques had long been used as decoration by Greek builders: at Corinth, which is thought to have invented the technique; in the cities of Asia and on the Hellenized borders of Ionia, as at Larissa on the Hermos or at Parzalii in Lycia; and naturally in the Greek West, particularly at Gela, which had even built its *thesauros* at Olympia out of this material. But the wooden structure of the Etrusco-Italic temple is inherited directly from the prehistoric hut. It is this heritage, more than an alleged lack of stone, that explains the choice of terracotta and justifies the entire aesthetic of this architecture. The wooden structure also creates the "airiness" of the building. The considerable space between the columns, made possible by relatively light materials borne on wooden architraves, ultimately produced the arrangement that Vitruvius calls "aerostyle." It inspired the Renaissance architect Giuliano da San Gallo to imitate it in the portico of the Medici villa at Poggio a Caiano.[21] It also influenced Andrea Palladio.

Vitruvius details various elements of this wooden structure, and even conveys the technical construction vocabulary. It was necessary to protect the wooden framework from the rain and bad weather, and the terracotta revetment provided shelter from

## The Buildings

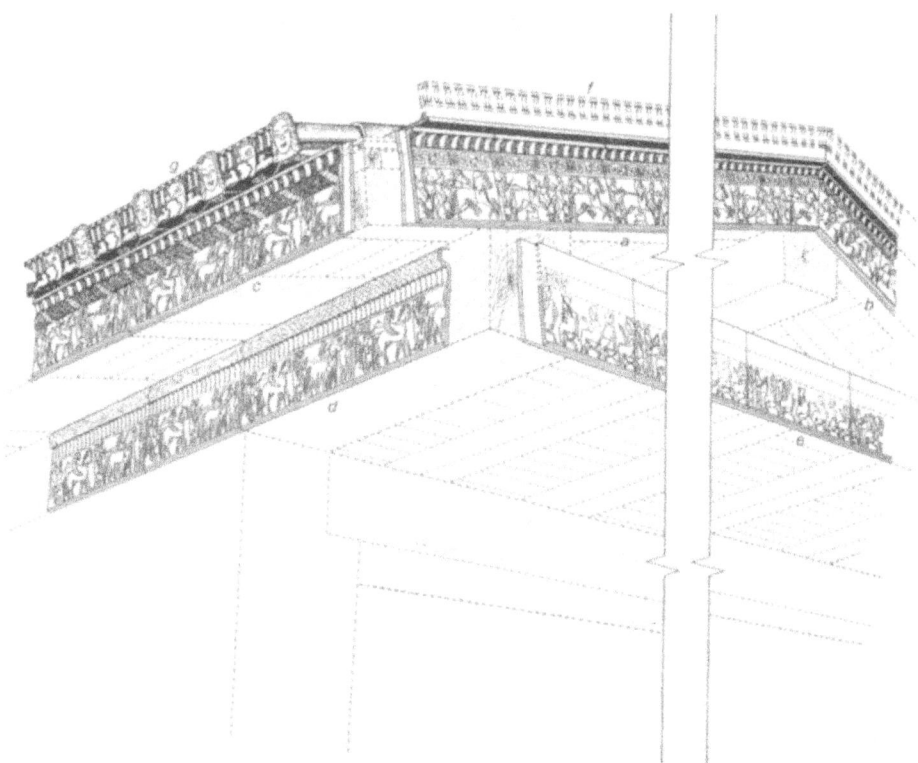

6.8. Decoration of the temple of Velletri, Tempio delle Stimatte (Temple of the Stigmata). Reconstruction of the arrangement of the terracotta revetment plaques. End of the sixth century.

the worst of it. This is a godsend for the archaeologist and the historian: a perishable architecture that was covered by an almost indestructible material. The molded frieze plaques run the length of the façade architraves (*trabes compactiles*), which are composed of several beams in an open construction:

> On the columns will be placed wooden beams joined together . . . , but in such a way that there is between each beam a distance of two fingers, because if they touch each other . . . they will rot. (*De arch.* 3.7: *de ratione etrusca*)

Other plaques cover the lateral architraves and the *mutuli*, the flat blocks below the cornice. Still others cover the rafters *(cantherii)* of the façade. Above them runs a narrow border, the *sima*, which masks the edge of the flat roof tiles. The ends of the lines of curved tiles are hidden by decorative vertical plaques: the antefixes. At the angles of the pediments and on the main roof beam (*columen*), sculptures of varying size, the acroteria, stand erect against the sky. The extremities of the major beams, the *columen* and the *mutuli*, project under the roof and would have been exposed if they

## The Buildings

6.9a. Model of a temple with an open pediment: the *antepagmentum* and *muluti* are visible. From Nemi. Rome, Museo Naz. di Villa Giulia.

6.9b. Small temple of Alatri, reconstructed in Rome in the gardens of the Villa Giulia. Rome, Museo Naz. Di Villa Giulia.

had not been protected by terracotta plaques. These decorated elements are called the *antepagmentum*. The entire pedimental space remains open (fig. 6.9a–b), however, which permits air to circulate. This arrangement recalls the triangular opening under the roof beam depicted on hut urns.

At the turn of the third to the second century, some pediments that had been adorned only with *antepagmenta* received a remodeling of their decoration, which now filled the entire space and transformed the open pediment into a practically closed one. Was this change stimulated by Asiatic Greek architecture? This phenomenon has been linked to the arrival of artists after the Battle of Magnesia on the Meander in 190. Another possible influence may have been the diffusion of rock-cut[22] and rock-built tombs, of which there are many examples in Vulci and Tarquinia.

Characteristic of these buildings is the periodic renovation of all or some of their revetment and the replacement of decorative plaques in poor condition. The ritual burial of broken pieces and changed elements preserves the history of the building. The progressive modifications to the decoration reflect changes in taste or, more significantly, in the religious or political climate.

These religious structures, which for convenience we have called Etruscan because they essentially originated in this geographic area, in fact extended well beyond it. Temples with these same characteristics were built in Rome during the Monarchy, particularly under the Tarquins, who erected and decorated the Temple of Jupiter Optimus Maximus on the Capitoline,[23] and under Servius Tullius, who built the Temple of Fortuna and Mater Matuta[24] along the Vicus Jugarius, near the bank of the Tiber. The Temple of Jupiter served as the model for the *capitolia* of the Latin and Roman colonies—in particular, for Cosa,[25] founded in 273 by the Romans in the midst of

## The Buildings

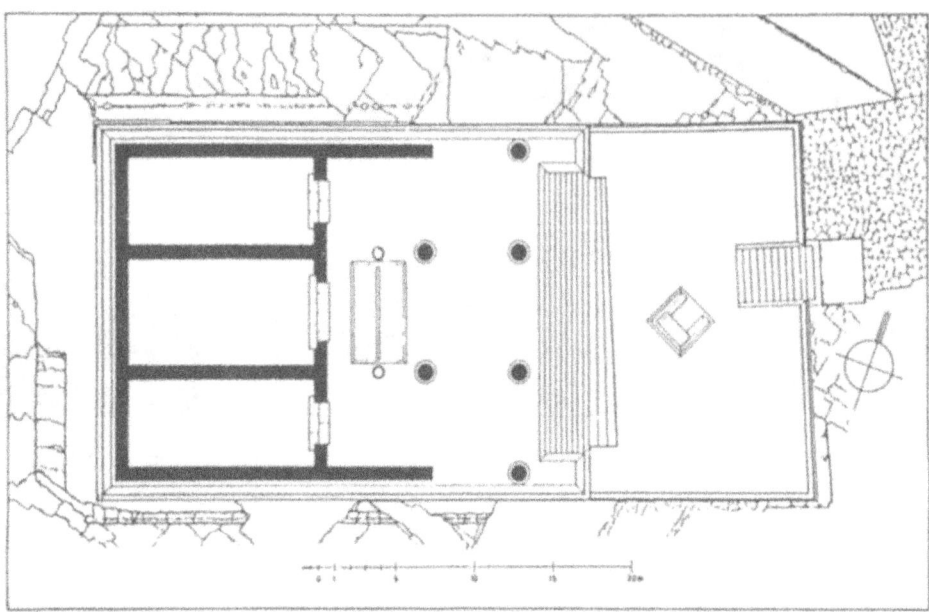

6.10. The Capitolium of the Roman colony of Cosa. 273 B.C. This building of the Roman colony adopts and perpetuates Etruscan norms. Reconstruction F. Brown.

Etruscan territory. Its "Tuscan" temples do not derive from a local tradition but from a Roman political model, even though they are clearly descended from Etruscan forms (fig. 6.10). Under similar conditions the same architectural choice was made in 177 for the colony of Luni.[26] Other temples, equally derived from the Etruscan model, are found elsewhere on the peninsula, especially among the peoples of interior and southern Italy who did not adopt Greek patterns. For example, the Samnites chose this model for their great theater/temple complex at Pietrabbondante, and the Daunians also used it at Ordona.

We shall now discuss a few specific temples that, through their plan, the stages of their modifications, or their decorative program, illustrate aspects of Etruscan religious history.

### The Temple of Satricum

One well-known site displays a continuous evolution in plan and illustrates changes in modes of construction: the strongly Etruscanized Temple of the Mater Matuta at Satricum (fig. 6.11).[27] The first cult building was a simple oval hut, 7 meters long, oriented to the southwest. A *sacellum* replaced it around 640. The latter was a small rectangular structure with no portico and very simple decoration. The orientation had changed to face due west.

Surrounding the foundations of this building and oriented in the same direction,

## The Buildings

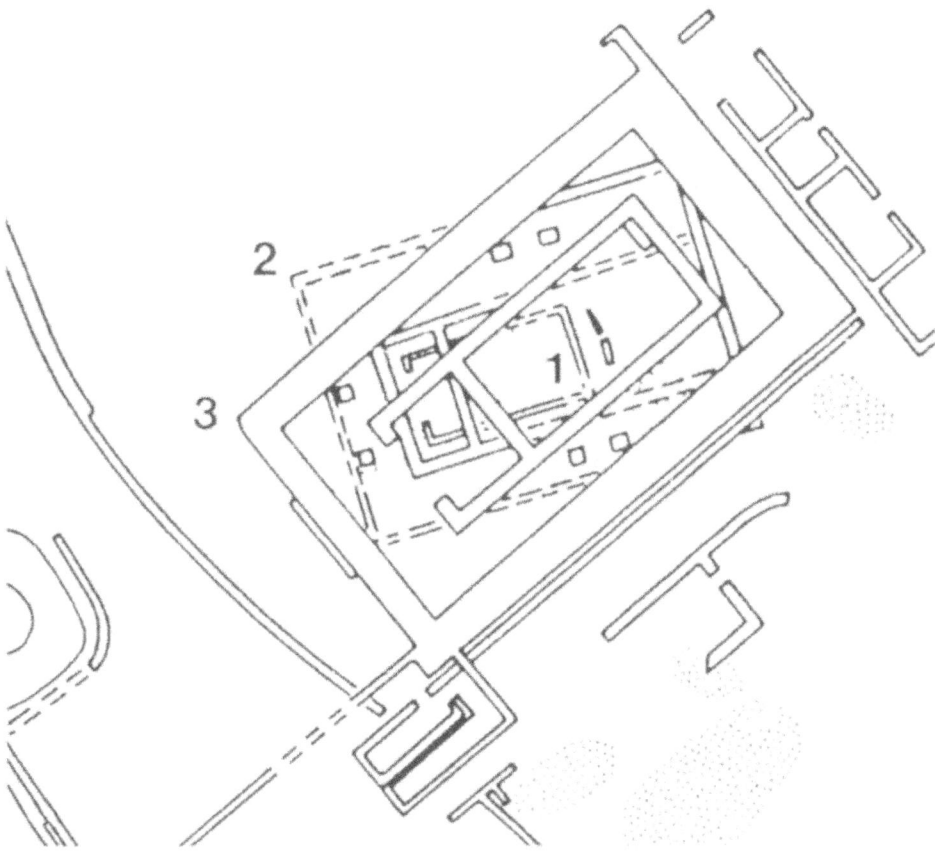

6.11. Plan of the temples of Le Ferriere at Satricum: superpositions and enlargements. Phase 1: c. 640; phase 2: 540s; phase 3: c. 480.

a much more elaborate temple was erected in the 540s. Laborers, particularly coroplasts, from a workshop in southern Etruria came to work there and not only decorated it but very probably constructed it.[28] This monumental structure may be compared to the almost contemporary temple in the area of Sant'Omobono in Rome, which Servius Tullius dedicated to Fortuna and Mater Matuta. The Satrican temple, conveniently called Temple I, consisted of a *pronaos* and a deep *naos*, and it was partially surrounded by columns: four on the façade, eight on the long sides. The rear was blind and consisted of a simple straight wall. In this form the temple was pseudoperipteral, what Vitruvius calls *peripteros sine postico*.

But the work did not stop there. Around 480, under the influence of Campania, which was deeply Hellenized but strongly affected by two centuries of Etruscan presence, a second temple was built in place of the first. The orientation changed again and returned to the axis of the primitive hut, toward the southwest. This time south-

## The Buildings

6.12. North sanctuary of Pyrgi, plan.

ern workshops were opened on the site. The clay of the terracotta molds used for making the temple's decoration proves that even the tools came from Campania. The temple became fully peripteral (*cum postico*). It looks Greek, at least in its plan, even if it was mostly Campanian, and it was the forerunner of considerably later buildings, such as the great temple at Vulci.[29] The astonishing series of acroterial statues on the roof, which depict the battle of the gods and giants,[30] could perhaps be understood as a condemnation of disorder and hubris, but it is difficult to know precisely what they meant to say. The aesthetic of this last building was directly inspired by Magna Graecia, and its theme conformed to the Greek attitudes of its time. Very probably, its construction had not only a moral finality, but also a political meaning, at a time when Etruscan influence had retreated north, and in an area where the Latin League was in open conflict with Rome.

## The Buildings

*The Temples of Pyrgi*

At the edge of the city of Caere, in contact with the port area, stood the sanctuary of Pyrgi (fig. 6.12), whose site and cult we have already discussed. Greek sources mention its tremendous wealth and its sack by Dionysius I in 384. A small sanctuary probably stood on the site before the construction of the two larger temples that concern us here. In fact, small antefixes from the middle of the sixth century have been found; these probably belonged to a building earlier than Temple A.

The construction of Temple B in the 510s shows the importance of the cult, and the dedication of the sanctuary or of a major offering by Thefarie Velianas to Uni/Astarte, shows the interest that the tyrant-king of Caere had in it: "because the goddess," the text tells us, "had shown him favor."[31] The choice of plan is unusual: it is a true peripteral temple with an elaborate porch supported by two rows of four columns (fig. 6.13). An open *pronaos* leads into a very small *naos*. This plan is similar to the temple at Satricum just discussed.

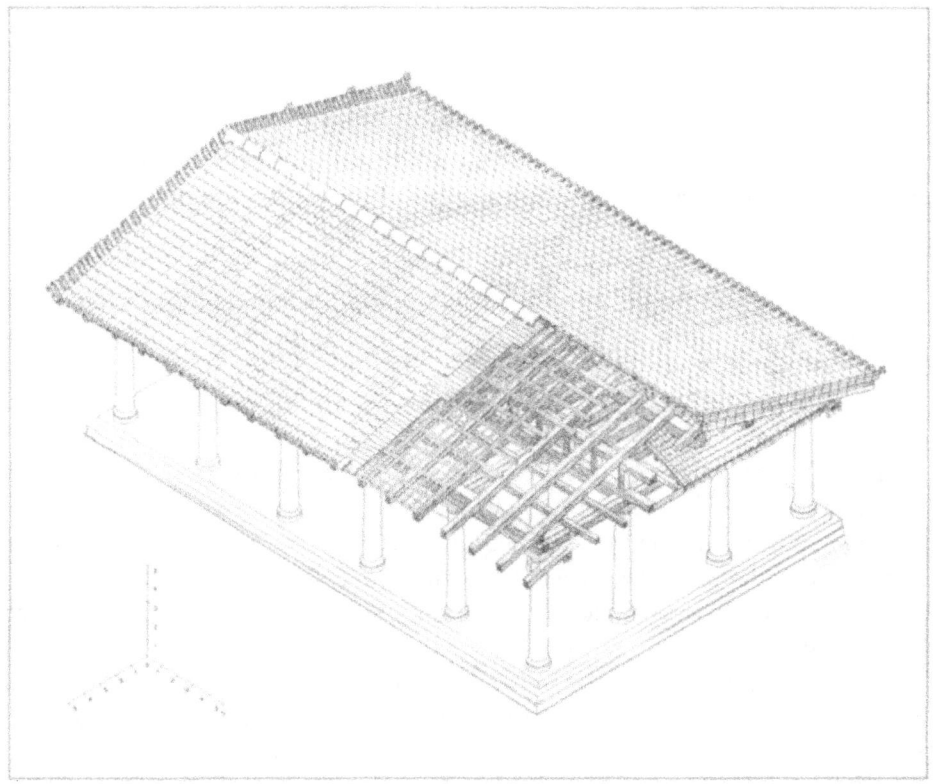

6.13. Pyrgi, peripteral Temple B: axonometric reconstruction. Around 510 B.C.

The Buildings

6.14. Dancer with a bird's head: a cult ceremony for a solar deity? Antefix from Temple B at Pyrgi. Around 510 B.C. Rome, Museo Naz. di Villa Giulia.

While its plan seems influenced by architecture of the Greek West, its elevation and decoration are truly Etruscan. Its theme is part of a religious and political program that was meant to satisfy the Carthaginians, who were probably co-founders of the temple, as the bilingual dedication suggests. Themes linked to the sun and probably to ritual dancing were mingled together. They were chosen to appeal to the mixed population of the *asylon* (the international zone of the harbor), whose culture was enriched by oriental influences. Antefixes have been found from annexed buildings and the small cellae said to be "of the hierodules." Some of these show a winged dancer with a bird's head;[32] others, a mistress of the horses (is this Thesan/Aurora?), or a winged dancer holding two phialai. All these figures clearly belong to the celestial sphere, and specifically to the sun (fig. 6.14).[33]

The pediment of the temple was completely Etruscan. It was open, and terracotta plaques covered the faces of its beams. Its themes seem to have been principally Heraclean: the battle with the Lernean hydra and a scene of harnessing, which has been interpreted as the episode with Diomedes' horses. This is a repertoire usually given specific meaning by the regimes of the "tyrants" who set themselves up as purifiers and reorganizers of the city.

Temple A, built several decades later, about 480–460, was Tuscan in plan, with a porch (*antica*) supported by two rows of four columns, and a *pars postica* divided into three spaces: a larger cella, flanked by two "wings," or two smaller cellae (fig. 6.15). Its plan is very closely related to that of the Temple of Castor and Pollux, inaugurated at Rome in 484. The most remarkable element is certainly the large plaque of the *antepagmentum* that covered the main roof beam at the back of the building (fig.

## The Buildings

6.15. Pyrgi, Tuscan Temple A: model. 480 to 460 B.C. Rome, Museo Naz. di Villa Giulia.

6.16). The relief illustrates two episodes, regrouped into a single scene, from the epic of the Seven against Thebes. At left, Athena, holding the ambrosia of immortality that she had intended for her protégé Tydeus, has changed her mind upon observing his scandalous behavior and appears to be leaving the battlefield. Zeus, in the center, opposes Capaneus, whose grimace of hatred is striking. Below, a wounded Melanippus lies on the ground, while Tydeus has fallen on him and is devouring his brain. The scene, composed of two superposed triangles, is shocking, filled with raging violence, terrifying. Did the political authorities of Caere, who chose this tragic theme of guilty excess, want thereby to condemn the hubris of some tyrant of Caere, or the growing menace of the rulers of Syracuse? Whatever the meaning or the date of this decoration, its message may be as much civic as religious. We must keep in mind, however, that such distinctions were meaningless in ancient Etruria.

### Etruscan Decoration and Roman Programs

There is more historiographic and archaeological evidence for Rome at the end of the sixth century, and it permits us to ask questions that elsewhere would find no

6.16. *Antepagmentum* of Temple A at Pyrgi: the Seven against Thebes. 480 to 460 B.C. Rome, Museo Naz. di Villa Giulia.

## The Buildings

answers. What decorative programs developed at Rome under the last Etruscan kings—or, rather, tyrants? Who were the artists who worked on them? What ends did they serve?

The most unusual area of construction is certainly that at the foot of the Palatine. Servius Tullius built a sanctuary to Fortuna and the Mater Matuta in the Forum Boarium and Forum Holitorium, in a *temenos* open to the port of Rome. There was already an early Archaic temple there, probably in the form of a hut, which dated to the middle of the seventh century. Servius Tullius built a small *distyle in antis* temple on a low podium (fig. 6.17). Under Tarquin the Proud, this building was finished or embellished, and much later, around the beginning of the Republic, the well-known twin temples were built on that same spot, but at a much higher level.

The building of Servius Tullius interests us here. Its two divinities were strongly linked. Around 540 the polychrome relief plaques that adorned the edges of the roof were produced by a workshop that also furnished, at about the same time and with tiny variations, decorative elements for a sanctuary at Velletri and for other buildings at Rome and Veii. It also made them, with some greater modifications, for temples at Pometia and Palestrina.

6.17. Plan and façade of the Tuscan temple at Sant'Omobono dedicated to the Mater Matuta. Rome, northern zone of the Forum Boarium. Sixth century.

# The Buildings

6.18. Terracotta plaque from the temple at Sant'Omobono: procession of chariots, gods, heroes, and personages of power. End of the sixth century. Rome, Antiquarium Comunale.

This workshop, which was probably itinerant but of Veiian origin, produced long repetitive friezes depicting solemn processions (fig. 6.18).[34] Among their common motifs are two females—probably two goddesses—riding in a chariot. Perhaps coming to meet them, another chariot transports the tyrant-king preceded by a herald. Also depicted are banquets, horse races, and cavalcades of young warriors, which recall the equestrian exercises of the *Lusus Troiae*, a celebration that took place every year at Rome and no doubt also in other cities of Italy.

Is it possible that these friezes, which are found on so many buildings, lack a precise meaning? Are they merely old aristocratic motifs, so often reused that they had long since lost their meaning? Why then would the artisans have modeled slight variations that allowed them to adapt the general design to local demand? Why do the specific insignia of the magistrates or attendants vary from one temple to another? This whole thematic program is at the same time religious and political. With minimal modifications, it is adapted to different places, to sanctuaries of different gods, and to the specific characteristics of different cities. The artisans transformed some details of the processions, races, and banquets in order to make them coincide with the local programs. Sometimes, as at Velletri, they depicted assemblies of gods and goddesses. The presence of these subtly varied decorations on so many buildings of similar structure is evidence for the deep relationship that existed between these sanctuaries. It also suggests that they served identical roles in the lives of their cities.

## The Buildings

6.19. Sant'Omobono: group of Hercules and an armed goddess, probably Minerva. Roof acroterion or a votive group? Sixth century. Rome, Antiquarium Comunale.

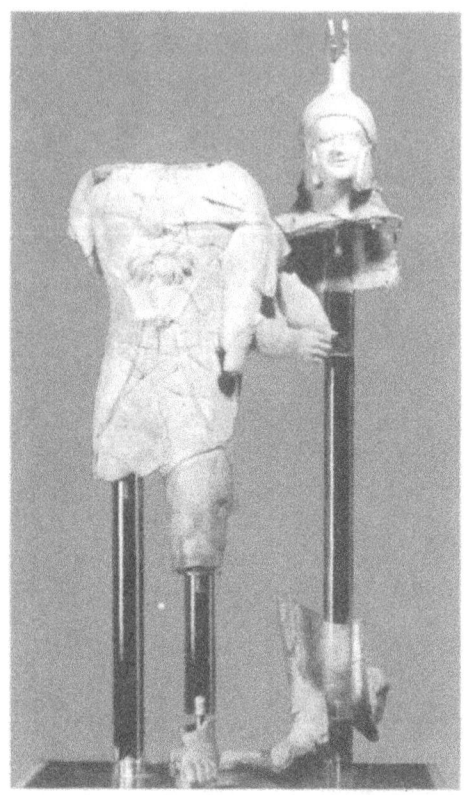

A splendid monumental acroterion (if it was not a princely or royal ex-voto) was made for the peak of this temple's pediment, probably by some coroplast trained in Greek Asia (fig. 6.19). It represents a standing Heracles, wearing a lion skin and a "Cypriote" cloak (i.e., one knotted at the belt). The hero is accompanied by a helmeted woman, whom we are tempted to call Athena.[35] A probably contemporary ex-voto, thematically almost identical but stylistically quite different, was found in the Temple of Menrva at Veii (Portonaccio).[36] Here Heracles is certainly in the arms of Athena, and this is probably his introduction to Olympus. These Heraclean themes, under the regime of Peisistratus in Athens or under the authority of Thefarie Velianas at Caere, expressed the ideology of the Late Archaic tyrants so well that these images are found everywhere they were in power.

But it is in the great Capitoline sanctuary, in the Temple of Jupiter Optimus Maximus, rather than in the somewhat suburban Temple of Fortuna and the Mater Matuta, that Etruscan architecture and large-scale sculpture triumphed. Tradition attributes the initiation of the work to Tarquinius Priscus and dates the temple's inauguration to the birth of the Republic in 509. The building remained approximately in its initial state up until 83 B.C. when a fire destroyed it completely. The building

## The Buildings

was gigantic: it measured more than 50 meters in width and 65 in length. The podium, of an impressive height, is still partially visible. The façade consisted of three rows of six columns, and a portico of six columns ran along the two sides. The back was a blank wall. It was thus *peripteros sine postico*, to use Vitruvius' categories. The *pars postica* consisted of three cellae, perfect for the cult of the Capitoline triad: Jupiter, Juno, and Minerva (fig. 6.20).

This canonically Etruscan building, commissioned by an Etruscan tyrant-king, was also decorated by Etruscan artists. In fact, tradition informs us that a sculptor of Veii, Vulca, was asked to create the terracotta cult statue of Jupiter. Did this Vulca, to whom a statue of Heracles is also attributed, really exist, or is this only a name that sounded Etruscan enough to satisfy Pliny the Elder (*HN* 35.157)? In any case, tradition also attributes the quadriga acroterion at the peak of the gable to a group of Veiian artists. The enormous scale of the building, the bold acroterial decoration, and the immense podium that elevated it further leave no doubt about Tarquin's intentions: to proclaim the power of Rome in the face of its Latin neighbors and perhaps to turn this prestigious temple into the seat of the Latin League, to the detriment of the federal sanctuary at Monte Albano.

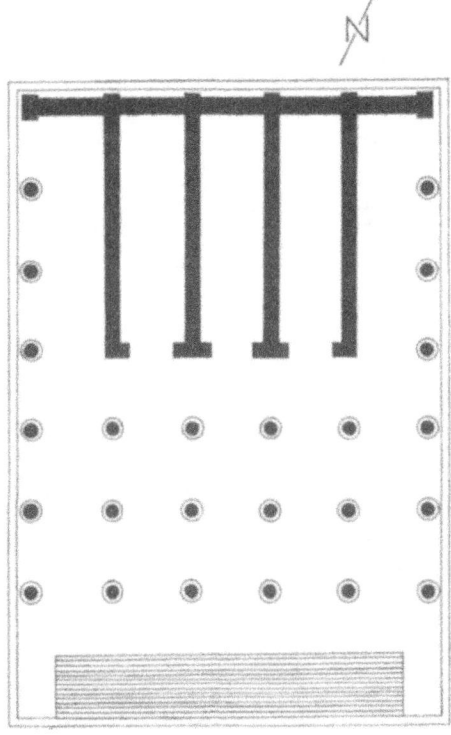

6.20. Probable plan of the Temple of Jupiter Optimus Maximus. End of the sixth century. Rome, Capitolium.

## The Buildings

The regimes of the tyrants, especially in the Archaic period, all waged a kind of architectural politics. From Samos under Polycrates to Agrigento under Theron, from the Athens of Peisistratus to the Rome of Servius Tullius or the Tarquins, all the religious choices of this late Archaic world were expressed in architectural programs of astonishing scope.

A desire for emulation must have inspired neighboring cities with all the more vigor because they were often rivals. The relations between Rome and Veii were not always strained, but the proximity of the two centers was probably not irrelevant to their intense construction activity.

### The Portonaccio Temple at Veii

Between 520 and 500, in an enclosure with other cults (see chapter 5), the great temple at Veii was consecrated to Menrva.[37] It is much more modest in size than the immense Roman structure, but it was a widely reproduced archetype. Its length and width are equal (18.5 m); its *pars postica*, divided into three cellae, was slightly more developed than the *pars antica*. The temple was conceived as a whole, and the decoration of the building that preceded it on the site[38] does not seem to have played any role in the new figural decoration (fig. 6.21). The figural program was expressed in the terracotta relief plaques that masked the wooden structure, in the pedimental

6.21. Hypothetical reconstruction of the acroteria on the peak of the Portonaccio Temple at Veii. Last decades of the sixth century.

## The Buildings

6.22. Turms/Hermes: large acroterial statue from the *columen* of the Portonaccio Temple at Veii. End of the sixth century. Rome, Museo Naz. di Villa Giulia.

sculpture, and especially in the large acroterial figures. A rather complex ideological reading has been proposed for the figures: it connects them with the exile of Tarquin or the ambitions of the king of Chiusi, Porsenna, and of the "king" or tyrant of Veii,[39] who exercised a power comparable to that of the last three kings of Rome. We shall concentrate on the themes depicted on the acroterial decorations. The arrangement of these large statues is unusual but not completely unparalleled. They are placed not merely at the extremities of the main roof beam (*columen*), but along its whole length. This configuration is also seen on little urns in the form of buildings and on the roofs at Murlo, where almost twenty statues stood against the sky.[40]

It is tempting to think that the architect of the temple also conceived the roof decoration, so that the theme of the *antepagmentum*, of which only a fragment remains, fits in with the whole. This pedimental fragment, depicting a horse with winged shoes, has been interpreted as an illustration of the combat between Bellerophon and the Chimaera,[41] but this hypothesis is tenuous. Only the large, mutilated acroterial statues remain sufficiently identifiable. Of the beautiful figure of Turms, only the head and shoulder are preserved (fig. 6.22), but the large statue of Aplu, which must have faced that of Hercle, has come down to us in satisfactory condition (fig. 6.23). Equally well preserved is Leto holding the infant Aplu, who may have just shot the serpent Pytho; this was the founding act of the oracle at Delphi (fig. 6.24). The last sculpture is a lively figure of Hercle capturing the Keryneian hind (fig. 6.25).

## The Buildings

6.23. Aplu/Apollo: large acroterial statue from the *columen* of the Portonaccio Temple at Veii. End of the sixth century. Rome, Museo Naz. di Villa Giulia.

6.24. Leto/Latona carrying the infant Apollo. Has the young god just killed the serpent Pytho? Acroterial statue from the *columen* of the Portonaccio Temple at Veii. End of the sixth century. Rome, Museo Naz. di Villa Giulia.

6.25. Heracles contending with Apollo over the Keryneian hind: acroterial statue from the Portonaccio Temple at Veii. End of the sixth century. Rome, Museo Naz. di Villa Giulia.

It is not easy to understand the overarching meaning of these images, which, oddly for a sanctuary dedicated to Menrva, all concern Apollo. Some suggest, based on the discovery of lots at the site (see chapter 2), that Menrva had a mantic function, and based on late-period ex-votos, a curative (*medica*) one as well. These two functions belonged to Apollo, but they were shared in later periods. It is still more difficult to find a place in this ensemble for Hercle capturing the hind of Artemis. He is under orders, but committing a sacrilege. Perhaps Pindar's suggestion in *Olympian Ode* 3.29ff.—a reconciliation of Heracles with Artemis (and consequently with Apollo) in the land of the Hyperboreans—explains his presence. Did the sanctuary of Menrva also make room for Apollo, her *synnaos*, her half-brother? We may simply have here two myths that illustrate the victory of order over disorder: Apollo vanquishing the serpent and opposing sacrilege. The decoding of these mythical allusions is quite dif-

## The Buildings

6.26. Podium and plan of the Belvedere Temple at Orvieto. Second half of the fifth century.

ficult, but it is clear that those who commissioned these works were profoundly Hellenized culturally, that artists of very high quality gave this cycle a religious and political coherence, and that the functions of Apollo are at the core of these themes.

### Tarquinia, Orvieto, Falerii

The great temple of Tarquinia, the Ara della Regina, was built during the first half of the fourth century to replace an Archaic building that had been decorated with terracotta plaques in the 520s. The new temple, oriented toward the southwest, was raised on a high podium and dominated the city (see chapter 5 and especially fig. 5.3). Access was by means of a ramp, which enhanced the monument's powerful impact (see fig. 5.2). The decoration changed considerably: the edges of the new temple's strongly projecting roof were decorated only with vegetal motifs—palmettes, *anthemia*—and the Silenus-head antefixes stood out against a halo of stylized florals.

The pediment of the building was open, as tradition demanded, and only the extremities of the beams, the *columen* and *mutuli*, were decorated. On the left-hand *mutulus* was the beautiful fragment depicting a team of two horses moving toward the left (see fig. 5.4). Another fragment, of a female figure clothed in a rich floral fabric, would have been placed on the right *mutulus*. This was probably a seated female deity. Who was in the chariot drawn by two winged horses? Probably the god worshipped in the central cella of the temple. Did Tinia already have a cult in this temple,

## The Buildings

6.27. Belvedere Temple at Orvieto, element of the second decorative phase of the pedimental decoration: old man (soothsayer or Nestor?). Beginning of the fourth century. Orvieto, Museo Claudio Faina.

6.28. Belvedere Temple at Orvieto, architectural terracotta from the second decorative phase: seated goddess. Beginning of the fourth century. Orvieto, Museo Claudio Faina.

or did he only make his appearance in the form of Jupiter, when Romanization transformed the plan of the original cella and installed the Capitoline triad? The presence of such a powerful god on a simple two-horse chariot is unthinkable, however. It must have been a female deity; Aurora/Thesan and Turan have been suggested.[42] The latter seems more likely, and would agree with the iconography of the cults at Pyrgi.

The Belvedere Temple at Orvieto (fig. 6.26) also stood in a dominant position that was further accentuated by a high podium. A staircase of twenty steps led up to the vast façade portico of eight columns in two rows (see fig. 5.5). The foundations preserve the trace of three cellae: but were they all cellae, thus implying the presence of a triad, or was there only a single cella with two wings? How were the large decorative figures of the pediment arranged? We think that the area occupied by the *antepagmentum* gradually became larger, but that the pediment remained open. Some of the figures from this pediment (figs. 6.27, 6.28), which are now in the Museo Faina, represent goddesses. One of them wears an animal skin, which was an attribute of Menrva and of deities who protected the dead.[43] A number of male figures, some nude, some dressed in a cuirass, are in a much better state of preservation. These

## The Buildings

could be deities, but they seem to illustrate some myth that we have difficulty decoding.[44]

The splendid sculptures of Falerii are dependent on the works of Praxiteles, Leochares, and Lysippus in spirit and aesthetic, but no doubt they borrow more from them than just the images. It is probable that the theme and the composition also came, either directly or by way of Magna Graecia, from now-lost Greek models. Both their form and their content seem to stem from currents that were not of local origin. Heroes, goddesses, and gods form a complex scene, perhaps an unidentified incident from the Homeric epic cycle. Its interpretation, to judge from the grandeur of the style, cannot be merely anecdotal. It was perhaps the return of the arms of Achilles.[45] The climate of heroic tension is strong here and is evidence that, by means of this Greek imagery, the masters of the Faliscan city attempted to appeal to their compatriots' emotions. Whether it was for a political or a religious reason, however, is unknown.

In any case, the thematic programs of Etruscan pediments changed profoundly. It seems that the scenes condemning hubris in reference to internal or external conflicts or to political regimes were replaced by an imagery that was more authentically religious, sometimes pathetic, and by stories that more directly concerned the sanctuary's deity.

### Temples with "Closed Pediments": Talamone, Civitalba

On the southeast slopes of the Talamonaccio promontory,[46] 15 kilometers north of Orbetello, stood a temple with four columns *sine postico*. It was about 29 meters long and 13 wide, in proportions that were originally 3:2 (fig. 6.29). Its antefixes, identical to some found at Orvieto, suggest that the temple was built in the second half of the

6.29. Model of a distyle temple with a full pediment depicting Dionysus and Ariadne. From Vulci. Third century. Rome, Museo Naz. di Villa Giulia.

## The Buildings

6.30. Talamonaccio, pediment of the temple at Talamone: the Seven against Thebes—assault and defeat of the Argive chiefs. At the center is Oedipus between his sons. Middle of second century. Florence, Museo Archeologico Nazionale.

fourth century. Several of these antefixes are in the form of busts of Hercle and Menrva. The building was probably dedicated to Tinia and Uni. Much later, around 150,[47] and for reasons that were certainly not merely aesthetic, the open pediment was transformed into a closed one, and the grand, well-known composition was commissioned. At the same time, the earlier roof antefixes were replaced by busts of Dionysus and Ariadne. The workshop that made the new decorative elements also worked at the same time for Temple D at Cosa. In the last decade of the second century, the temple was leveled to the ground and never rebuilt.

Framed by a particularly rich decorative molding, the mid-second-century pediment depicts a long episode from the epic tale of the Seven against Thebes (fig. 6.30). Oedipus is on his knees in the center. To his left, Queen Jocasta turns toward Eteocles, who is in agony. On the right, Polyneices expires in the arms of a companion. Above this composition the final act of the epic unfolds: Capaneus is again on his ladder, defying Zeus. On the left, Adrastus flees shamefully in his speeding chariot, trampling the wounded. On the right, Amphiaraos, surrounded by genies from the Afterworld, Vanth and perhaps Charu(n), rushes alive into the subterranean world with his galloping team. Other, very fragmentary figures may depict the other four protagonists of the expedition.

What were the meaning and the function of this large relief, which necessitated building a new wooden structure? The theme often occurs on urns from Volterra and Chiusi,[48] where it has been interpreted as a condemnation of civil strife. But could the same meaning apply to the large pediment, which predates them? The interpretation

# The Buildings

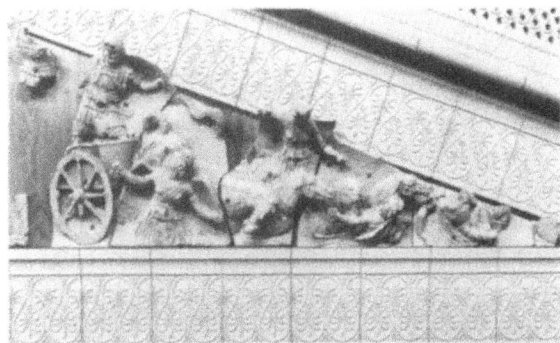

of this major scene should probably also accommodate the antefixes representing Dionysus and Ariadne.

The major theme of the Civitalba pediment[49] is Dionysus' discovery of the sleeping Ariadne, probably after a Pergamene model. While most of other scenes on this temple (on the friezes and one of the pediments) evoke the Gallic invasions and the gods helping to defeat them, the scene of Dionysus is too purely religious not to be directly related to the cults practiced in the temple.

More or less everywhere in Etruria, whether in the cities of the League or in the Roman colonies, between the first third of the second century and the Social Wars, temples adopted the Greek, then the Roman, closed pediment. The local authorities usually chose to have religious scenes depicted in these spaces: at Arezzo, Luni, Cosa, and possibly also at Chianciano[50] and Vulci, coroplasts influenced by models from Asia Minor gave Tuscan temples a more Hellenized look.

But even deeper transformations occurred beneath the surface. Whenever one of these temples reveals evidence of its earlier history, it suggests that a change of religious belief occurred during the second century. The innumerable terracottas in late-period votive deposits evoke a new kind of personal piety that asks the gods for cures or children. It seems that these temples and the deities that they sheltered blurred their own uniqueness and diversity to melt into a more uniform religious expression.

REMAINS

It would be wrong to think that all the temples throughout Etruria followed this same evolution. Many rural sanctuaries practically never changed at all. The Etruscans were content to maintain buildings by changing a few tiles here, a broken antefix there, and replacing them with more modern ones. The great programs, the bearers

## The Buildings

of religious, political, or ethical messages, the great constructions that reveal a competition between neighboring cities—all these vast complexes have left more traces than the modest rural or periurban structures where the rites most frequently took place. While the two temples at Pyrgi were going up, the little sanctuaries of Zone D got no larger, and the cult places of Gravisca remained in the state they had been in twenty years before.

The Sasso di Furbara[51] sanctuary, in the hinterland of Caere in the middle of the Tolfa mountains, hardly seems to have evolved at all. And in the Grasceta dei Cavallari sanctuary, situated in another isolated area of the same mountain range, one finds Hellenistic-period offerings so crude that they would be undatable without their ceramic context.

Some religious buildings almost totally escape the evolution that we have attempted to describe. The history that we have tried to trace is, as always, fragmentary and biased.

But the people who frequented these prestigious sanctuaries or forgotten chapels, the priests and cult auxiliaries who organized the festivals and sacrifices, their gestures, their acts, and their piety naturally varied over space and time.

CHAPTER 7

# Worshippers

HARUSPICES

A first-century B.C. marble plaque from Pesaro bearing an inscription in Latin and Etruscan gives us the word for haruspex:[1]

[L.CA]FATIUS.L.F.STE.HARUSPE[X]
    FULGURIATOR
*(C)afates Lr. Lr. netsvis trutnvt fronta(c)*

This inscription is often called "the Pesaro bilingual." In this text *frontac* is translated by *fulguriator*, "observer of lightning," and the whole expression *netsvis trutnvt* signifies a type of haruspex. The plaque comes from the borders of Umbria and dates to a late period, however, so that it is not certain that there has not been a modification in the terms. Nonetheless, the Etruscans must have had several categories of priests, because this one appears to be qualified for the observation of lightning, which could not have been the case for all of his colleagues. We find the same term *netsvis* again on an inscription from Chiusi, but its context is unfortunately less clear.

The haruspices are a little better known iconographically. In fact, it has become habitual to consider all figures who wear the *apex* haruspices. This head covering is a kind of beret with a raised central part at the top of the head. The fabric that covers it seems to be spiraled like a turban. One of the best depictions occurs on a mirror from Tuscania, dating from the beginning of the third century (see fig. 1.1);[2] here two barefoot characters wear this hat. On the left, a bearded man with a long cloak and cane wears it, not on his head, but on his shoulders behind his neck; it is probably held by a cord. On the right, a young beardless man, dressed in a large cloak held together by a curved fibula, wears the famous beret on his head. Having placed his left foot on a rock, he closely examines a liver that he holds in his left hand. The older man, Avl Tarchunus, looks attentively at the young man, Pava Tarchies, who extends the pyramidal lobe of the sheep's liver and seems about to proclaim the conclusions of his observations. This scene looks like a sort of lesson in haruspicy, or a test for the

## Worshippers

office. But what interests us most here, besides the pose of the consultant, is his costume. Its major elements are perfectly depicted: the distinctive hat with a cord at the neck, of which there are countless examples, and a cloak held together by a fibula, which indicates that it was not sewn.[3]

A small bronze votive statuette[4] from the middle of the fourth century gives us even more precise information about this costume (fig. 7.1). The hat is tied tightly under the chin, like the *apex* of the Roman flamen, who was required to resign his office if his hat fell off during a ceremony (Servius, *Ad Aen.* 10.270). One of the essential elements is certainly the fibula, whose type dates to the eighth century.[5] This fixes the original date of the ritual costume, and of this priesthood as well, or at least of the features that define it externally. This little statuette is a votive offering, as the inscription tells us:[6]

*tn turce vel sveitus*
This has been offered by *Vel Sveitus*.

Another statuette of a haruspex, somewhat similar, bears a dedication to Tinia:[7]

*temres alpan tinias*
From Temre, a sacred offering to Tinia.

A large number of other images of figures wearing this singular beret lack some of the characteristics that we have just observed. This hat, atrophied but recognizable, is the mark of the Roman *flamines*. On the obverse of a third-century coin (fig. 7.2),

7.1. The haruspex Vel Sveitus: votive bronze with dedication. Mid-fourth century. Vatican, Museo Gregoriano Etrusco.

7.2. Coin of Volsinii (Orvieto): priest wearing a pointed hat (*apex*) and, on the reverse, sacrificial instruments—the *makaira* (sacrificial knife) and *secespita* (axe). Third century. Paris, Bib. Nat., Cabinet des Médailles.

Worshippers

7.3. Priest wearing the characteristic hat. Preceded by an *aulos*-player, he carries a palm in his hand, wrapped in a fold of his cloak, and is followed by a palm-bearer, who turns around. Is he participating in a marriage ritual? Monument in the shape of a house. Beginning of the fifth century. Chiusi, Museo Nazionale.

a frontal head wearing the distinctive hat is associated, on the reverse, with typically sacerdotal objects: the axe, the knife, the libation vessel. These are the instruments of the sacrificial priest,[8] not of the haruspex. Do the images of men wearing this type of hat, but occupied in pouring a libation, depict haruspices? The absence of the fibula and short cloak advises caution. Is the profile figure who holds a palm and walks behind an *aulos*-player on a house-shaped monument from Chiusi (fig. 7.3) a haruspex or a priest?[9] Is the man who leads a two-horse chariot, to the right of the door in the Golini II Tomb, also a haruspex? Does the hat placed on a *liber linteus* on a funerary group in Berlin (see fig. 3.1) indicate that the deceased was a haruspex or a priest?[10] Finally, the large acroterial statues of Murlo wear immense hats that are clearly related to these.[11] Do they depict figures who practiced haruspicy (see fig. 5.10)? It is impossible to answer these questions, at least within the framework of this book, so prudence seems the wisest course.

In any case, these characters were certainly important and were granted evident respect. At Tarquinia there have been found lists (the *fasti*) of the sixty haruspices[12] who, at the beginning of the Empire, comprised an order that was more honorific than functional. The personages whose names appear on these lists seem to be of equestrian rank. Cicero tells us (*Leg.* 2.9.21) that the holders of these offices were selected at birth, from within the important aristocratic families, so as "to prevent the religion from falling into the hands of people of low degree."

That is, however, what must have happened. It is likely that Cato's reticence toward

# Worshippers

the haruspices is due to the presence among them of people of low rank who did not come from the aristocratic world. Cicero describes them scornfully as "village haruspices."

### PRIESTS

We are much better informed about the priests. We know that their roles were of extreme importance; they are designated in the several ritual texts that have come down to us. Their names can be figured out rather easily, but their precise functions generally escape us.

The Zagreb *liber linteus* cites the word *cepen* more than fifteen times, always in stipulations of sacrifices and rites to be accomplished. We find this same word in inscriptions from Tarquinia, Musarna, and Heba. The Capua calendar cites it twice, but in its southern form, *cipen*.[13] The root is closely related to the Sabine word *cupencus*, meaning *sacerdos*, "priest." This resemblance suggests that *cepen*, too, means priest. But is this the general term, or does it designate a specific priesthood? While the expression *spurana cepen*[14] probably means "priest of the city," the more precise translations that have sometimes been proposed[15] seem unwise. The word *cepenar* or *cepnar* probably denotes "the priests" collectively, a sort of college.

Another word, *eisnev*, certainly designates another category of priests, but it is impossible to be more precise than that. This word is related to *aisna/eisna*, which very probably has the sense of "belonging to the gods," "destined for divine service."

The word *sacnicstra* occurs several times in the genitive form *sacnicstres*. Since the general meaning of *sacni* is "sacred" or "consecrated," it seems probable that *sacnicstra* is a collective term designating men devoted to a god: the clergy in general, or a college, an organized group of priests.

Finally, the word *tamera* or *tameru* may also denote a particular priest, perhaps the one in charge of managing the *tmia*,[16] the sacred buildings. Or was the *tamia* a college of priests?

On the other hand, *maru* could not have designated a sacerdotal function, as has been hypothesized: it seems rather to denote a magisterial office. The expression *maruchva cepen* probably only refers to the frequent association of priestly and magisterial functions. Likewise, *marunuch pachanati*,[17] which juxtaposes the word for magistracy with that for Bacchants (from the name *Pacha*, Bacchus), very likely designates the office of overseeing a religious college, not a religious function in a pure sense.

### L(a)ris Pulenas

The vocabulary, as so often, does not help us much. It would be more profitable to hear what a man who held one or more priesthoods and played a significant role in his city says about himself. A famous sarcophagus (see figs. 1.3, 1.4) serves as the burial place of L(a)ris Pulenas,[18] an important personage of Tarquinia. His epitaph, engraved on the stone *volumen* that he ostentatiously unrolls, comprises a long in-

# Worshippers

scription of nine lines.[19] In it he relates his ancestry back four generations and even mentions the surname of his ancestor Lars Pules the Greek! But he also lists his functions in the city of Tarquinia: he composed one or more books (*zich*) on haruspicy (*nethsrac*) or on sacrificial technique. This is probably the significance of the sacrificial knives, which are duly depicted in the scene of the voyage to the Afterworld carved on the sarcophagus chest. It is equally certain that he played an important role in the cults of Catha, Pacha, and Culs(ans). The word *hermu* and the form *hermeri* also appear. They could have a connection with the name Hermes[20] or with statues. One must compare his duties with the role played at Tuscania by one of his colleagues, Larth Statlanes, who was *maru pachathuras cathsc*. L(a)ris Pulenas may have held a very important office, which has been compared to that of the Roman *rex sacrorum*.[21] His religious duties seem to have mostly involved composing books and administering the cult of the solar divinity associated with Dionysus, as well as that of Culsans, the Etruscan Janus. This sarcophagus dates from the second half of the third century, and elsewhere at this time the importance of Etruscan worship of Dionysus is well documented (Livy, 39.9).

## Images of Priests

On a sarcophagus from the Tomb of the Triclinium at Tarquinia, now in the British Museum,[22] a woman reclines, wearing garlands, beautiful earrings, and a necklace of *bullae* and holding a thyrsus and kantharos. Her cloak is held on her left shoulder by a very unusual knot, which is so complicated that it seems, like the fibula of the haruspices, to obey a ritual clothing stipulation. A fawn lies beside her. Is she a priestess, as has been hypothesized? Nothing proves that she was. This woman was clearly a devotee of Fufluns/Pacha/Dionysus, and she illustrates the importance of this cult in the third century, but her sacerdotal nature is not assured. Other depictions of the same sort, in which fawns also appear,[23] evoke the same rites and the same atmosphere.

On the authority of a late bilingual inscription, it has become habitual to translate the word *tanasar* as "actor" or simply to use the Latin term *histrio*. The Etruscan word is inscribed[24] beside two characters in the Tomb of the Augurs who solemnly salute the false door on the back wall (see fig. 4.5). No one dares attribute a priestly function to them ever since it has been suggested that the word denotes actors. But if the bilingual inscription had not given that translation, no one would ever have dreamed of proposing such an interpretation. It is possible, in fact, to see their gesture of salute as a rite performed by funerary priests. But then one would have to conclude that the late equivalence of terms results from a homonym, or that the inscription is not a true bilingual.

The little bronze votive found in the deposit of the periurban sanctuary of Gabii[25] probably depicts a priest rather than an augur. The *lituus* that he holds in his right hand has been twisted, and we must mentally straighten it out and roll it up again. (This is the curled staff that is the insignia and the tool of the Roman augurs.) The figure has all a priest's characteristics, comparable to those on the Perugia base, with

## Worshippers

which it is contemporary (see fig. 3.4). It is all the more interesting because it is a votive object through which the priest offers his permanent presence to the god.[26]

In the rather large number of representations of priests performing their duties, the identifications are indisputable (fig. 7.4). We shall look first at the family priests who gather on either side of a flaming altar on the early fifth-century cylindrical base in Perugia mentioned just above.[27] The sculptor has presented the scene, by convention, as a double procession converging at the central altar. The two most important characters are situated just to the right and left. The one on the left is a bearded old man. He makes a gesture—usually viewed as a funerary or chthonian prayer—with his raised right hand, the palm turned toward the ground or the fire. He is followed by a young girl and a whole mixed troupe of men and women. This seems to be a family group, in which two men holding double-curved sticks[28] are noticeable. The figures on the other side are all male, but two of them hold a *lituus*. On this relief we may consider the *lituus* a sacerdotal emblem. Immediately to the right of the altar, a figure who is playing a major role in the scene holds a *lituus* in his left hand and makes a gesture of prayer with his right. A second man, who is five figures behind, approaches the altar and simply holds his curled staff. It is difficult to interpret the scene without an inscription but the major figure with the *lituus* does seem to be the priest, and the bearded man standing at the left of the altar, the head of the family. A stele from Fiesole (fig. 7.5),[29] earlier by a good half-century, depicts one of these priests, distinguished by that staff which at Rome will later be considered augural.

7.4. Chianciano, limestone (*pietra fetida*) base. Procession of men carrying the insignia of rank or office. The second from the left bears a *lituus*. Beginning of the fifth century. Rome, Museo Barracco.

## Worshippers

7.5. Stele depicting a priest: note the *lituus*. From the region of Fiesole. End of the sixth century. Berlin, Staatliche Museen.

Other representations show us the sacrificants: a Chiusine relief in the Louvre is excessively restored (see fig. 3.6); a mirror from Palestrina (see fig. 3.7) is probably the best illustration; and a bronze repoussé plaque and an amphora of the Orvieto group help complete the scene.[30] In these sacrificial rites the priest is distinguished from the other participants only by his action: in almost every case, he performs a preliminary libation on the altar. A mirror of mediocre quality in Berlin shows Hercle and Menrva preparing to sacrifice a goat.[31] The goddess holds a libation vessel in her right hand, and by this act assumes the role of priest.

A frequent auxiliary in these sacrifices is the musician, the *aulos*-player. He stands at the foot of the altar and plays without interruption during the whole ceremony. Never do we see him put down his instrument. He was so necessary for this rite that ex-votos representing *aulos*-players were offered in some sanctuaries. One of these, a terracotta relief formed from partial over-molds, shows the priest standing at the right of the altar. He holds a phiale in his right hand, almost directly above a goat, which is half blocked from view. Depicted frontally to the left of the altar, the musician provides accompaniment (fig. 7.6).[32] These musicians played an essential role in Roman sacrifices, which could not take place without their presence. A strike of

## Worshippers

7.6. Musician playing his *aulos* in a sacrifice depicted on a small terracotta votive. From Caere. Second century. Boston, Museum of Fine Arts.

*aulos*-players in the fourth century brought Roman religious life to a complete stop and became a veritable state crisis (Livy, 9.30.5). We must picture specialists in this sacrificial music performing in the sanctuaries and religious ceremonies. One of these religious auxiliaries accompanies Fufluns on a fragment of a small bronze tripod from Vulci that was found in the excavations on the Athenian acropolis.

In these scenes of religious life, the worshippers appear to be few. In contrast to the abundant family on the circular Perugia base, attendance in sacrifice scenes was often limited to one person. On the mirror from Praeneste, it is a child. On the bronze plaque from Bomarzo (fig. 7.7), Sileni appear to be the sacrificants. This scene may show the beneficiary of the sacrifice. To the left of the altar, seated on a folding *diphros* (stool), a majestic bearded character, holding a long scepter in his left hand, appears to

7.7. Sacrifice performed by Sileni in the presence of a god. Repoussé bronze, perhaps a furniture appliqué. From Bomarzo. End of the sixth century. Rome, Museo Naz. di Villa Giulia

## Worshippers

receive a sacrifice performed by a standing man wearing a narrow-brimmed hat. Is the sacrificant Turms? Is the god honored by this rite Tinia? This depiction of a sacrifice is, to our knowledge, the only one in which the honored god plays a role.

### PRAYERS

In front of altars or statues, figures stand in an attitude of prayer, as we see on one of the Campana plaques.[33] The "orant" gestures, well known for funeral prayer, can be observed in a considerable number of depictions: for example, on the decorations impressed by cylinders onto small bucchero vases from the middle Tiber region. Prayer can be identified by a series of gestures, and in particular by the position of the hands, held with palms open toward the statue of the god.

Nor is the content of these prayers completely unknown to us. The *liber linteus* is not in fact limited to serving as a calendar.[34] From a careful comparison with the text of the Gubbio tablets, we can distinguish the stipulations concerning dates and rites to be performed and repetitive formulae whose structure is invariable. Within this uniformity we find variations in detail. Furthermore, five of these prayers, from a ritual of Nethuns, run in almost the same manner.

One of these five prayers begins with the word *nunthenths*, which can be translated as: "let us invoke" or "while invoking." The other prayers begin with *tin*, "say," "pronounce," or "recite." This is thus a prescription. Then comes the address of this prayer:

*Flere nethunsl un mlach nunthen*
Divinity of Nethuns, you who are good, I invoke you.

A place name follows, probably designating the location where the sacrificial act must be accomplished. This topographic detail is followed by a specification of the offering that must be made: for example, wine (*vinum*), and boiled meat (*faśei*) of pure victims (*zusleve zarve*).

Several words then specify who should make the offering: "the civic community" (*spurestres*), or a religious college (*sacnistres*). A line then mentions the date of the month in which the ceremony must occur, then those who expect a blessing from the god in return for this offering. These can be members of a religious confraternity or even the city as a whole (*methlumeri-c enas*).

This formula is found five times in this same text for the cult of other deities, with variations in the modifiable elements: the place, the nature of the offerings, the dedicants, and the beneficiaries. The general structure is rigorously similar to that of the prayers translated from the Gubbio tablets.

Several terms in this tentative translation are still unclear, but we can safely draw a few conclusions. We know the structure of the Greek liturgical prayer as it was practiced around the fourth century. It differs from the Etruscan in several respects. The Greek prayer begins by recalling earlier offerings and the blessings that resulted from them. Only then come the invocation of the god, the description of the offering that is about to be made, and the request that matches it. The general impression is that of a trade, a systematic application of the principle *do ut des* ("I give that you might give"). The same principle appears in the *liber linteus* prayer, but its expression is less abrupt, and the request is not formulated in the same way. Here the worshipper takes care to specify who should benefit from this offering, but not what the expected benefit is. While the destined recipient is stipulated, the nature of the god's response is left open.

VOTIVE OFFERINGS

The food offerings, animal sacrifices, and libations of wine or milk have naturally left no trace, but the objects substituted for these perishables tell us much. In addition, large numbers of nonsacrificial offerings have come down to us. Votive deposits document individual worship at all levels.[35]

It might seem inaccurate to call by the same name the sumptuous and ostentatious objects offered in the temples by the *Principes Etruriae* and the cheap mass-produced terracottas bought by workers for a plebeian sanctuary. The goals are the same, however: to embellish the sanctuary, and to present an offering that will permanently represent the worshipper in the eyes of the god.

We shall consider here only a few ex-votos dedicated in sanctuaries by princes or members of the high aristocracy. A princely offering previously mentioned (see chapter 5), is the terracotta group depicting Hercle and Menrva which was offered about 510–500 in the Portonaccio Sanctuary at Veii. This impressive group, whose particularly strong modeling was clearly executed by a talented sculptor, can only be a gift from a person of high rank who desired to show the goddess Menrva his piety in exchange for the kind of protection that she gave Hercle. The theme would perfectly suit the climate of the late sixth century, when tyrant-kings loved to compare their actions to those of the hero. If the similar group from the sanctuary of Sant'Omobono (see fig. 6.19) does not turn out to be the acroterion that the majority of scholars think it is, but instead another votive group of the same theme (which seems equally possible),[36] it would further confirm the ideological role of these ex-votos. Dating from the very end of the sixth century, the Veii terracotta group must have been a present from the unknown "king" who then ruled the city, and who is known to have been connected with the last of the Tarquins and certainly with Porsenna.

An offering of exceptional quality, a large bronze group dating from the 470s, was dedicated at Chianciano in a now-lost sanctuary that must have been connected with the site's curative waters.[37] It was a statue of a god mounted on a chariot, of which only a few elements are preserved. These sumptuous dedications evoke, indubitably but too allusively, the rich donors of these temples. They are the same donors who offered large metal vases and monumental lamps. The famous Cortona lamp is certainly not the largest of these, because a fragment of another, gigantic, example has turned up at Chianciano.

Worshippers

7.8. The Chimaera of Arezzo, part of a large votive group representing Bellerophon vanquishing the monster. End of fifth to beginning of fourth century. Florence, Museo Archeologico Nazionale, Soprintendenza Archeologica per la Toscana Firenze.

Another outstanding monument has come down to us in a fragmentary state: the famous Chimaera of Arezzo (fig. 7.8).[38] Even incomplete, it is clearly a masterpiece of Etruscan bronze manufacture. The monster, fatally wounded by Bellerophon (*Melerpanta*) as he rode Pegasus, is the only remnant of a monument that must have been impressive. The myth of the Sicyonian hero was very popular in the years 400–350, as evidenced by the numerous mirrors that reproduce this theme, and by the Faliscan vases and the sarcophagi that take up this motif a little later. The inscription *tinścvil* on the monster's right paw signifies that this was an offering to Tinia.

One naturally wonders why the horse and the horseman have disappeared, why the left paw, which probably bore the name of the dedicant, was broken, and, finally, why the monument was destroyed. One hypothesis, at best only a tenuous construction of likelihoods and possibilities, suggests that the group was dedicated in the first half of the fourth century by an aristocratic family, one of those *gentes* that appropriated heroic Greek myths for political ends. We know only a small number of these great families of Arezzo—their links with the Roman aristocracy were forged later—but we know that a serious political and social conflict broke out in 303, a kind

## Worshippers

of civil war that pitted the local nobility against the *demos*, the population of slaves and freedmen. It took pressure from Rome for "the parties to be reconciled" (Livy, 10.3.259). One is tempted to attribute the destruction of this ex-voto to a sort of *damnatio memoriae* of the aristocratic family that dedicated it. Some scholars have identified these as the Cilnii of Arezzo, ancestors of Maecenas.[39]

This whole chain of hypotheses is plausible but unverifiable; we shall not linger on it. It is the overall pattern that is interesting: the fact that some families exercised a veritable domination over the important sanctuaries and, in ostensibly serving the god, used the site as a monument to their own greatness. This phenomenon was a constant. The concentration of the priesthoods within these familial lines only reinforced it. We are reminded of the prescription on the Tabula Capuana that stipulated offerings to be made in the month of June by the Pacusna community (*Pacusnasie*), which draws its name from the cult of Pacha/Fufluns, and by another community named *Velthur*, which seems to have had an aristocratic territorial structure.[40]

It is likely that the most prestigious of the extant large bronzes are aristocratic ex-votos. In this category of offerings may be included a statue of a javelin-thrower, produced in a strongly Hellenized workshop to commemorate the athletic victory of some aristocrat of Etruscan Campania.[41]

### At Fanum Voltumnae

According to the historiographic sources (Pliny the Elder, *HN* 34.34), Roman conquerors in 264 pillaged two thousand statues from Volsinii, probably from the sanctuary of Voltumna. Almost all of them would have been votive offerings in bronze or precious metal, and probably nothing remains of them now. On the other hand we know who might have brought valuable offerings to a prestigious sanctuary. Cities, village communities, and grateful wealthy individuals probably left their gods tokens of their piety. Many acts of worship must have ended in the offering of objects and statues. The large statue known as the Mars of Todi (fig. 7.9)[42] was probably made by one of the early fourth-century Volsinian workshops associated with the sanctuary. The statue was found ritually buried near Todi. Its dedication is in Umbrian, but engraved in the Etruscan alphabet by someone familiar with that script: "Ahal Trutidius offered this as a gift." This offering must be a good example of the sort of statues that were stolen by the conquerors when the sanctuary was destroyed.

### Private Votive Deposits

The small sanctuaries received gifts too, some prestigious, others infinitely modest. Among the poorest and crudest of these offerings are the expressive figurines in sheet bronze[43] or even lead.[44] Their schematic quality often does not allow us to date them, but many were made later than the fourth century. They are found in the same sanctuaries with small, almost shapeless bronzes cast in the lost-wax process, and, not uncommonly, with statuettes of quite respectable quality.[45]

## Worshippers

7.9. Laran, the so-called Mars of Todi: large votive statue of an offerent. Beginning of fourth century. Vatican, Museo Gregoriano Etrusco.

The site of Brolio in the Val di Chiana[46] is an example of those places of worship where, from the seventh to the sixth century, travelers from all social levels mingled at the passage of a sort of frontier between Etruscan territory and Umbria, which was not yet under Etruscan control. Here have been found ceramic offerings, toilet items, fibulae, images of soldiers, and female figurines that give evidence for a cult practiced here by women of relative affluence. One finds images of stags, fawns, and hares, the offerings of hunters, as well as sumptuous gifts like cauldrons and a bronze *perirrhanterion* (vessel for lustral water) on anthropomorphic supports.[47] One might almost call this a sort of divine toll booth. This was the last sanctuary on the eastern routes where one could thank a purely Etruscan deity. It is not surprising that after neighboring Umbria came into the Etruscan orbit, the offerings disappear abruptly and the votive deposit ceases to receive gifts. Its role was linked to its border position, which ended around the beginning of the fifth century. Votive terracottas of the last centuries of Etruscan worship are totally absent from this site.

The site of Falterona is equally fascinating (see chapter 5). It initially had the same functions as a passage sanctuary and frontier point between Etruscan land and the

## Worshippers

valley of the Po, but its period of activity was considerably longer. In fact, coins of the Roman Republic have been found there. Numerous anatomical ex-votos, representations of body parts, document the late evolution of the sanctuary, which became a place of healing connected with the waters of the small lake of Falterona. All strata of society frequented this cult place, too, as the extremely variable quality of the offerings shows. The sanctuary of passage became a neighborhood cult.

*Expression of Religion*

The statuettes most frequently dedicated before the fourth century are depictions of offerers. This genre seems to originate with figural art itself, in the multitudes of bronze figurines derived from Ionian *kouroi;* but the Etruscan young men wear the *perizoma,* a sort of loincloth, or are ithyphallic. Corresponding to these male figurines are small female statuettes, their heads covered by a fold of the thick cloak that envelops them. These Archaic figurines are then closely followed by versions of *korai*. The young women often wear the Ionian costume, but also the *tutulus,* the characteristic Etruscan conical headgear. These small figures served as models for all the awkward, poor, and shapeless images that abound in the numerous deposits all the way to the periphery of Etruria, especially toward the Adriatic. These earlier, rather stiff images are followed by depictions of the worshipper in prayer, the left hand open, the right ready to pour a libation (fig. 7.10). There has been a transition from the representation of mere presence to that of the religious act itself.

Less numerous are depictions of gods. Some deposits lack them completely. One must avoid identifying every armed figure brandishing a lance as an image of Laran; these images may be simple representations of warriors, which should be counted among the depictions of dedicants. The relative rarity of images of gods results in part from the fact that such figures were more complex and thus more costly. To depict their attributes and movement necessitated more careful work and often a more skilled workshop. Nonetheless, this rarity is surprising. One wonders, at least as concerns the most ancient periods in some rural or outlying sanctuaries where the deities honored were well defined, whether their attributes and iconography were yet fixed in a recognizable way. It is significant, too, that the gods are rarely named in the dedicatory inscriptions on the most ancient objects.

A considerable percentage of the Archaic and Classical period votives are objects of daily use, often on a miniature scale. These include local or imported ceramics, articles for the costume or toilet, fibulae, and other jewelry. Some of these objects carry a particular meaning: weapons, magisterial chairs, and, especially, insignia of power. When found in votive deposits, they illustrate the connection between the political and the religious. A deposit at Tarquinia produced a curved trumpet, called a *lituus,* folded in three.[48] This typically Etruscan trumpet accompanied those who held power, no doubt political rather than military.

## Worshippers

7.10. Votive bronze offerent statue from Monte Acuto Ragazza: the figure holds a phiale for libations. Beginning of the fifth century. Bologna, Museo Civico Archeologico.

Building models were also dedicated to the gods: sometimes only a small *naiskos* (see fig. 6.29), sometimes an open-pediment temple with a portico resembling those on the structures in the large *temene*.[49] They remind us of fifteenth-century French or Flemish portraits of pious donors holding the model of the sanctuary that they have vowed to build.

Behind these votive objects hides a spirituality that is difficult to grasp. It seems to stress the physical presence of the worshipper, the gestures of salutation and adoration, the attitude of prayer, the importance of libations and offerings. These objects—substitution offerings, statues of worshippers, and, only secondarily, images of the gods themselves—allow us to sketch a picture of the religious practices of the Archaic and Classical periods. The relations established with the god do not seem directed toward a specific end—a request for health or power, for example. The relationship with the divine world is a sustained and ritualized one.

### Late-period Votive Deposits

Images of gods become more frequent around the middle of the fourth century in *favissae*, ritual burials in sanctuaries. They are much easier to identify because they imitate Greek gods in their poses, physical traits, and attributes. Tinia adopts the

## Worshippers

majesty of models in the Severe Style, then in the style of Pheidias. With the lightning bolt in his hand, he cannot fail to be recognized. Menrva, Laran, Hercle, Aplu, and Fufluns, too, follow Greek models. A statuette (see fig. 8.1) of Aplu/Apollo, from northern Etruria, bears the following dedicatory inscription:[50]

> mi : flereś : spulare : aritimi : fasti : rufriś t(u)rce : clen : cecha.
> *Fasti*, wife of *Riufri*, consecrated me to *Spulare Aritimi* in thanks for her son.

Appearing here at the same time are the dedicant, who is a woman, the recipient god (either one of the functions of Aplu/Apollo worshipped under his epithet *Erethimios*, or else a god named Aritimi), and the beneficiary of the divine aid, the dedicant's son. In other words, this is virtually the structure of the prayer that we attempted to reconstruct above. These are all indications of an increasingly personal relationship with the gods.

Finally, let us mention those less costly offerings found in almost all sanctuaries: the little backless terracotta figurines poured into singled-sided molds, the images made from used molds, the statuettes modified before firing to suit the exact desires of the worshippers. From the Vignaccia deposit at Caere[51] have come a number of female figurines, some depicting a pair of women seated with a child between them. Are these the two goddesses of Eleusis flanking Triptolemus? Also found were figures of Athena, Aphrodite, and goddesses nursing or carrying babies (*kourotrophes*): in essence, the whole world of femininity and maternity only loosely connected to myth.

Elsewhere, babies wrapped in swaddling clothes can be counted by the dozens. These document a cult to a maternity goddess who was probably also protectress of the newborn child (*infans*). When the baby is no longer in swaddling clothes, he is depicted nude, seated on the ground, playing. He has become *puer*, and another god takes charge of him. A famous bronze statue[52] from an urban sanctuary in Tarquinia depicts a young boy less than two years old. He wears the *bulla* and lifts his face toward an adult above him. The dedication, unfortunately fragmentary, states, according to the formula that we know well, that the child's father had dedicated this votive offering (*cver*) to the god Selvans on behalf of his son. Another statue of a child, similar in theme, was found near Lake Trasimene (fig. 7.11). It had been offered to Tec (*flereś tec sanśl cver*),[53] probably the goddess Tecvm (Menrva?). Still others, such as an example from Cortona,[54] could have been offered to Thufltha (which may be merely the *epiklesis* of a feminine divinity known by another name) on behalf of the child whom it depicts. These are votive offerings made by rich people, aristocrats, or perhaps even by groups of worshippers. Identical statues, but in terracotta and of little cost, are found in the same sanctuaries. In these, the children do not always wear the *bulla*, which means that they were not born citizens.[55] Thus the same sanctuaries receive the same kinds of offerings for the same reasons, but from very different strata of society.

We cannot know what grave danger the child endured that the parents should have

# Worshippers

7.11. Ex-voto from the shore of Lake Trasimene, in the area called Sanguineto. Around 150 B.C. Rome, Vatican, Museo Gregoriano Etrusco.

thanked the god with such an offering. But we do know the sufferings from which many worshippers hoped to be freed (fig. 7.12). In second-century votive deposits, small terracotta representations of the uterus (often a sheep's uterus, but sometimes a human one, which implies the practice of dissection),[56] of the female or male sexual organs, or of breasts give evidence for sterility or impotence, difficulties with nursing, or other disorders. Sanctuaries did not specialize in a single type of malady. In the same votive deposits occur feet, arms, and sometimes curious groupings of internal organs, which include the intestines, lungs, trachea, and heart. One can almost diagnose the malady from which the visitor suffered: a varicose ulcer, an underactive thyroid, a deformation caused by rheumatism. It is unlikely that these last three afflictions, though identifiable, could have been cured. These ex-votos are offerings of request rather than of thanks. They document religious practice and can perhaps shed light on Late Etruscan worship.

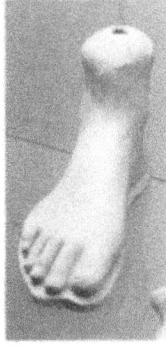

7.12. Anatomical ex-voto: a right foot. Beginning of the second century. Tarquinia, Museo Nazionale.

141

## Worshippers

A considerable number of vaguely personalized "busts" or heads raises some questions about late-period ex-voto worship. Do these individualized heads have the same function as the anatomical ex-votos—that is, do they suggest suffering in the head, the face, the brain? Or is their individualization a way for the worshipper to place his likeness permanently before the god? In the religious belief that they imply, are these heads the late equivalent of the Archaic *korai* and *kouroi?*

At the same time that the sanctuary of Aesculaepius/Asclepius was founded in Rome on the Tiber Island, and healing sanctuaries, *Aesclepia*, multiplied in Greece itself, the most widely documented religious practice in Etruria, too, was the request for a cure. Here is an everyday, popular religiosity that touched all social levels and affected the cults of many gods, who were invoked under their local names or functional epithets, often curative. This movement was not limited to Etruscan or Etruscanized Italy. It spread over the whole peninsula and generated a confused series of religious practices that seemed to lack a coherent ideology. This phenomenon is a symptom of the slow dissolution of Etruscan religion.

CHAPTER 8

# Gods

ETRUSCAN GODS, GREEK RELATIONS

In our brief look at Etruscan popular worship, we have come across dedicatory inscriptions or inscribed offerings that mention names of gods, but we have sometimes hesitated to identify them. The buildings discussed in earlier chapters have not always preserved the names of the gods to whom they were dedicated. The divine names inscribed on mirrors are often perplexing, since the deities seem vague, and several appear to share the same name. In the latest ex-votos it is scarcely possible to identify from the inscription the deity who received the offering; the most ancient, in fact, are not inscribed at all. The Etruscan gods sometimes appear to be an undefined and somewhat indistinguishable mob. Many names have no corresponding image, and many almost identical images accompany different names that occur only once. The whole motley crew seems to lack points of comparison. Our ignorance has often led us, in our need for intellectual comfort, to focus on the ones who spark a glimmer of recognition.

In fact, some Etruscan gods resemble Greek gods and some prefigure Roman ones. Their names, images, attributes, functions, even their histories, adventures, and natures are often largely comparable.[1] Some gods, though bearing an Etruscan name, exist only as characters in Greek myths and in scenes engraved on bronze mirrors that borrow imported designs to illustrate fragments of Greek epics or tragedies. The cult places of these gods occur only in the *emporia* or *asyla* inhabited by Greek merchants, and it is useless to try to identify the sector of the universe where the haruspices would have observed their presence. If there existed an "Etruscan pantheon"—an expression that needs nuance and may be contested altogether—we must ask whether much of it was not merely a regional variation of the Greek pantheon. We shall first discuss the gods whose cults are attested in Etruria but whose usual names do not occur on the Piacenza liver. Some may only appear to be missing: they may actually be found there under another name that would reveal their Etruscan origins.

# Gods

### *An Imported Greek God? Aplu/Śuri (Apollo)*

The Etruscan god Aplu or Apulu is the Greek Apollo. He has Apollo's appearance and mythology, as well as his curative and mantic functions. Initially he was the god of the bow, slayer of Pytho and Tityus, and thus the bringer of death; but he was also the purifying god who eliminated the serpent. His first known images are found on Pontic or La Tolfa vases,[2] on one of the painted plaques from Caere,[3] and on several bronze reliefs. But the large acroterion of Veii (see fig. 6.23) offers the finest Archaic depiction of the god. He later became the cithara god, the master of musical competitions, and the leader of the Muses (fig. 8.1), and from this point on his images generally follow Greek Classical models. He appears often on engraved mirrors, frequently with Menrva. Depictions of laurel abound in the tomb paintings of Tarquinia or on the corners of monuments from Chiusi. Their frequency suggests that sacred groves must have existed in association with funerary areas. Their Apollonian symbolism is not certain,[4] however, and these plants may simply have served to combat the natural impurity of necropoleis. The many bronze statuettes that represent him,

8.1. Aplu/Apollo. The "Ferrara Bronze," from the Po plain. Inscription: *mi : fleres : spulare : aritimi : fasti: ruifris : t(u)rce : clen : Cea,* "Fasti, Riufri's wife, gave me to the goddess Spulare Aritimi (or to the god *Pylaoros Erethymios,* Apollo, keeper of the door) in grateful thanks for her son." First quarter of the fourth century. Paris, Bib. Nat., Cabinet des Médailles.

## Gods

especially from the middle of the fifth century, probably indicate that he did have a cult, although this has often been disputed.

Curiously, his name is not an Etruscan transposition of the Greek *Apollon* (if it were, the *n* would remain and he would be called *Aplun*), but derives from the Latin *Apollo*. Thus Apollo was probably not imported into the Etruscan world directly from Greece through the ports, *emporia*, or *asyla* of the Tyrrhenian coast, but indirectly, by way of Rome or, more likely, the Latin territory. The presence of the Greek Apollo was strong in the Archaic settlements of the lower Tiber and the Latin coastal plain, and likely at the site of Rome itself. But Greek worshippers of the god did frequent the Etruscan coast; at Gravisca, one of Tarquinia's ports, the rich Aeginetan merchant, Sostratos, dedicated a marble anchor to Apollo around 530. Many other emigrés in Etruria must have worshipped the god of Delphi and Delos.[5]

The cult of Apollo was practiced by Greeks of the *emporia*, with the result that the Etruscan cities of the coast, in certain very grave situations when their haruspices were mute, sought the opinion of the Delphic god. Herodotus (1.167ff.) relates the atrocities that were committed at Caere on the day after the Battle of the Sardinian Sea, which was later named the Battle of Alalia (c. 540):

> Carthaginians and Etruscans drew lots for the possession of the prisoners from the ships which were sunk. Of the Etruscans, the Caeretans got by far the largest number, and they took them all ashore and stoned them to death.

But a deadly epidemic struck the men and beasts that passed by the place of the massacre:

> Wishing to expiate the crime of the murder, the men of Caere sent to Delphi, and were told by the priestess to begin the custom, which they still observe today, of honoring the dead men with a grand funeral ceremony and the holding of athletic and equestrian contests.

One can see in this episode the two faces that Apollo showed the inhabitants of Caere: on one hand, the purifier and healer (Apollo Medicus); on the other, a god whom they could interrogate through a procedure that differed completely from Etruscan divination. It may have been on this occasion that the Caeretans, whom the Greeks called the Agylleans, built a *thesauros* in the sanctuary of Delphi. At the other extremity of Etruscanized territory, at the mouth of the Po, the inhabitants of Adria and Spina, both deeply Hellenized, also rendered a cult to Apollo. Fragments of vases dedicated to him there provide the proof. Moreover, the Spinetans are also thought to have erected a treasury at Delphi. Spina was a mixed city in which the Greek component was probably as large as the Etruscan. But we cannot know whether the stele "of the Tyrrhenians" at Delphi, which supported a votive tripod, was offered by a private worshiper or by an Etruscan city, or even by the inhabitants of Lemnos, who were also called Tyrrhenians.

## Gods

8.2. Aplu/Apollo, head of the "Lorenzini Kouros." This cult statue, possibly of Greek manufacture, may illustrate the very Hellenized character of Apollo's cult in Etruria. End of the sixth century. Volterra, Museo Guarnacci.

Of all the Greek gods who were adopted in Etruria, Apollo is the only one who seems not to be a substitute for some earlier deity, at least not fully, nor to inherit any specific function from the Etruscan divine world.[6] We must not be surprised that he does not appear under his usual name on the Piacenza liver.

Recent excavations at Pyrgi, however, in a sanctuary that Aelianus attributes to Apollo (*V. H.* 1.2), have produced dedications to Śuri, a name sometimes associated with Aplu on lots. While Apollo's solar dimension does not seem to be found in Aplu, it is apparently present in some related deities. Thus at Pyrgi, Śuri, who could locally have functioned as Aplu, is associated with Cautha, who is quite obviously a solar deity. Other deities of purely Etruscan origin are also defined by this solar dimension. Aplu thus was not an intrusive figure, but a god both foreign and necessary, new and indispensable, especially in a mixed Greco-Etruscan environment (fig. 8.2). For this reason, he was certainly widely worshipped. We must probably interpret similarly the dedication to "Apollo of Ferrara,"[7] in which the god is designated by the epithet *Erethimios* ("the exciter," "the provoker").

# Gods

## *Artumes, Artames, Aritimi (Artemis)*

Unlike Aplu, the name of the god's sister did not pass into Etruscan through an Italic language. Artumes and Artames came directly from the Dorian dialect; Aritimi from the Ionian. She is depicted at her brother's side when he is the bow-wielding god. She is again beside him on a fifth-century mirror[8] where she is depicted playing the lyre. She seems to have received offerings in sanctuaries that were not hers, with the result that for a while it was believed that the Portonaccio Temple at Veii had been dedicated to her instead of Menrva. In fact, she was tightly linked to the cult of Aplu and was detached from it only at a late period when she became, like most female deities, *kourotrophos* and protectress of the child. Although she appeared in Etruria at the same time as Aplu, she seems to have appropriated to herself, as did all the other goddesses of Etruria, attributes that belonged *en bloc* to a more ancient divinity. But she never became mistress of the wild animals or even goddess of the hunt, as she had been in Greece. She appears in that role only in late-period representations of the myth of Actaeon.

## *Menerva, Menrva, Tecum? (Athena)*

The goddess's Etruscan name, especially in its ancient form *Menarva*, is so close to the Latin Minerva that one might think it came from there. But it is known that the Roman Minerva was of Sabine origin (Varro, *Ling.* 5.158), and the same name occurs in Faliscan and Oscan, where the terms seem to derive from Etruscan. It is thus probable that the name, if not the cult, spread from Etruria throughout Italy.

But the goddess, important as she was, is not inscribed on the Piacenza liver—at least not under that name. This is a surprising absence, since Menrva wielded a lightning bolt[9] and was supposed to have a street and a temple dedicated to her in every city of any size. We are thus tempted to look on the liver model for sectors right next to those of Tinia (nos. 1–3) and Uni/Mae (no. 4) that could house the goddess whom tradition, at least in the triple-cella temples of the late period, associates with them. But then, if we found it on the liver, would we not conclude that this triad simply derived from the three cellae of the Capitoline temple at Rome? Without disregarding this objection, let us look at those sectors on the liver. The sector after Uni's (no. 5) bears the inscription *tec/um*.[10] Could this be one of Menrva's names—one linked to her cosmic function?

There is no doubt that this goddess had a considerable importance: to her were consecrated the Portonaccio Temple and the one at Santa Marinella in the territory of Caere, and she plays a major role on the pediment of the temple at Pyrgi. Votive statuettes of her (fig. 8.3) are found in abundance in many deposits: at Arezzo, Perugia, Cerveteri,[11] and in the Etruscanized sites of the Po region and Campania. These indicate worship of the goddess, if not a temple dedication.

Many characteristics of Menrva seem to come directly from Athena. She often wears the aegis and always the helmet. She is often depicted as *promachos*, brandishing

## Gods

8.3. Menrva/Athena Promachos: small bronze of unknown provenance. Middle of the fifth century. Paris, Musée du Louvre.

her lance, the *hoplon* (round shield) on her arm, or, according to a more static and perhaps more ancient design, standing with her lance held vertically. Sometimes she has wings, an allusion to her speed; this detail seems to come from Ionian models. Mirrors, in particular, depict her being born fully armed from the head of Tinia, with the help of Thanr, Ethausva, Thalna, and of course Sethlans.[12] In Etruria, too, the goddess aids her usual heroes, primarily Hercle. We have discussed above (chapter 6) the political use of these myths. All this makes her appear to be directly imported from Greece, or, more precisely, from Attic areas. But she has nothing to do with crafts, as if Athena Ergane (the Worker) were too alien to Etruscan aristocratic society.

When one digs a little deeper, however, Menrva shows a surprising originality. Some of her altars at Veii and Santa Marinella are *bothroi*, which communicate with the world below. On Etruscan soil the goddess certainly had a chthonic component. Lots found in these two sanctuaries indicate that she had a divinatory function. Late-period anatomical ex-votos suggest that she acquired a role as healer. Exercising a function she had had in part in Athens,[13] Menrva also appears holding infants, as a nurse or adoptive mother for a whole series of male babies. She takes charge of these mysterious children, who are called Maris, and of Epiur,[14] probably Hercle's son, whose mother she was mistakenly believed to be. Finally, an unusual mirror in Florence[15] shows two Menrvas face to face, both with the aegis, lance, and shield. They

Gods

are united by an owl that rests on the arm of one of them. This strange duplication must be merely decorative: the taste for symmetry has banished logic. It is possible, however, that Menrva/Athena was not the only female deity to bear arms and the aegis. There may even have been a sort of divine college of armed goddesses (see chapter 9).

Lightning-wielding, chthonian, mantic, curative, kourotrophic, Menrva seems rather different from the Greek Athena, from whom she very early on borrows attributes, physical appearance, and some myths. If *Tecum* should turn out to be one of her epithets, the absence of the name Menrva from the Piacenza liver would merely show that this complex indigenous deity, who existed before any representational form, had only a superficially Hellenized face.

*Turan (Aphrodite)*
During the Archaic period, Turan/Aphrodite was worshipped in practically all of Etruria. At Gravisca, vases and statuettes were dedicated to her, equally in Greek and Etruscan. At Orvieto, she may be the goddess depicted in a statue of Greek marble in the funerary sanctuary of the Cannicella necropolis (fig. 8.4). She appears again in numerous vase-painting scenes, principally the Judgment of Paris, as well as on

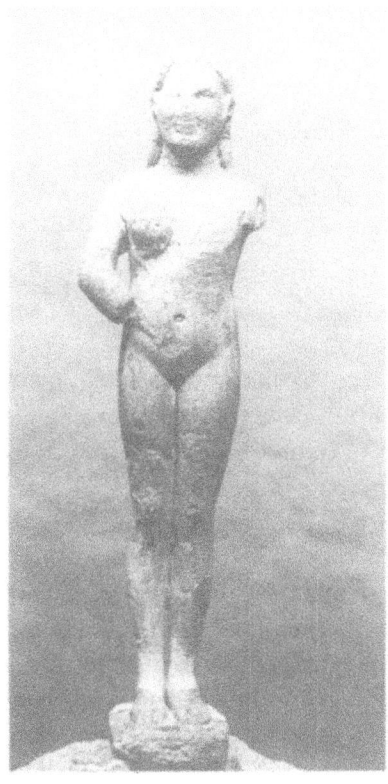

8.4. Funerary Aphrodite/Turan: a statue from the chthonian sanctuary of La Cannicella, Orvieto: Greek marble, Asian Greek manufacture, perhaps reworked in Etruria. Sixth century. Orvieto, Museo Claudio Faina.

Gods

8.5. Mirror with Turan, Atunis, and secondary deities of Turan's circle: on the upper right, Alpan, usually female, is here a young boy. Unknown provenance. End of the fourth century. Saint Petersburg, Hermitage Museum.

objects of feminine use, particularly mirrors. On one famous mirror she is shown with two pairs of wings and winged sandals, flanked by two nude boys, perhaps *erotes,* one of whom carries the palm of the suppliant.[16] Mirrors often show Turan with Adonis, called *Atunis* (fig. 8.5). Burial rites for this child were performed in the Gravisca sanctuary. She appears with Laran/Mars, of course, and is accompanied by children named Maris, who could be the many offspring of this divine couple. Frequently young women carrying toilet objects or crowns accompany the goddess: they are called Zipna, Munthc, Mean, Alpan. Sometimes her attendant is a winged young man named *Acvistr,* who holds a ribbon. Turan is also present at the toilet of Malavisch, who is shown seated as she is being decked out in her jewelry.[17] Figures called Lasa (whom we have incorrectly pluralized as "Lasas"—see chapter 9), generally female genies who sometimes bear secondary names or qualifying epithets, often gravitate around her.[18] All these characters from Turan's circle are otherwise

## Gods

completely unknown to us. They do not seem to have any Greek equivalents or to be included in any myths.

Turan was so important that she gave her name to a month (*Traneus*, probably from *turane*, "July"). Her name is surely Etruscan. It has long been thought to come from the same Mediterranean root as *tyrannos*, and would thus mean "mistress." More likely, it is formed from the verb *tur*, "to give"; she would thus be "she who gives."[19] The nature of her cults is difficult to define. The chthonic role that she is believed to have played at Orvieto may not have been a usual one for her; and the sanctuaries where prostitution was perhaps practiced (for example, Pyrgi), do not seem rightfully to belong to her. She may once have been depicted armed, like Laran or the Spartan Aphrodite Enoplios, and may have received a cult for that function. Given the importance of this deity, however, we are astonished that she does not appear on the Piacenza liver and did not have a single sector attributed to her in that microcosm of the world.

Turan is not easy to define. Etruscan in name, she borrowed an assortment of Greek characteristics from myths of Aphrodite, especially after the fourth century; but she never completely fused with the Greek goddess and remains surrounded by her own Etruscan followers. She often appears with the traits of other female deities, Menrva or even Uni. The erotic is not her only sphere. She is also a mother; she bears arms; she has a place in the funerary world. Like most Etruscan female deities, she seems to show the traits of an earlier great goddess from whom she inherited cult forms, but not the celestial domain.

### Vea

Vea may be an Etruscan Demeter. She had cults in the *temenos* of Gravisca and in the Cannicella sanctuary at Orvieto, where some scholars think she is depicted in the nude female statue that we believe represents Turan (see fig. 8.4). Her altar at Gravisca is cylindrical, like that at Eleusis. It may be she who appears on some late votive terracottas found both at Gravisca and La Vignaccia (Caere), in which two women are depicted enthroned with a standing child between them.[20] It appears that she also had a cult in the Po region of Etruria. Her name may derive from that of Veii, or vice versa; everyone agrees about the resemblance. Several inscriptions mention her, but there is no known allusion to her myths. Under these conditions, it is difficult to know whether or not she was of Greek origin.

### Turms (Hermes)

Turms does not appear on the Piacenza liver either. In spite of his perfectly Etruscan name, he was almost completely borrowed from the Greek world. His many representations—from the Veii *columen* to mirrors with mythological subjects, from Judgment of Paris scenes to "sacred conversations" with Tinia, Uni, and Menrva—only reproduce images of Zeus's messenger under an Etruscan name.

# Gods

8.6. Bronze handle from Spina with doubled Turms: one serving Tinia, the other, Aita. Ferrara, Museo Archeologico.

But there is a second face to Turms, or a second Turms: another messenger whom an inscription calls *Turmś Aitaś*, the Turms of Aita. He is the messenger of the god of the dead. This character is a close relative of Charu(n), whose mallet he sometimes carries—as on a bronze from Spina[21] or on various late sarcophagi—but whose physical traits (see chapter 4) he does not share. Here he is not a god in the full sense, merely a psychopomp genie (fig. 8.6). It is interesting to observe the cooptation of this figure from the Etruscan Afterworld by a Hellenized deity.

Neither Turms seems to have had a cult. We know of no ex-voto intended for him and no city that made him its patron god. It was mistakenly believed that Populonia had struck an image of Turms on its coins, but that turned out to be Sethlans. Actually, the Turms most often depicted or named, who appears on so many mirrors, is only a walk-on character in Greek myths, a secondary actor needed for a borrowed iconography. He has a cultural existence, but not a religious one. The funerary nature of his character seems to suggest that the role of a messenger god, an agent of the major deities, did not exist in Etruria.

## Sethlans (Hephaistos), Velchans

In spite of his Etruscan name, Sethlans was also an imported god. This probably explains his lack of a sector on the physical model of divine space, the Piacenza liver. If Servius (*Ad Aen.*) can be believed, Sethlans had the power to throw the lightning bolt. He may be merely the reduplication of Hephaistos; he has donned his appearance, adopted the attributes of god of the forge, and taken on his myths, primarily the birth of Menrva. He sometimes works, however, with a young character named *Tretu*, who is totally unknown in the Greek myths. Sethlans seems to be merely a

## Gods

functional god, connected with the work of the forge. The metal-working city of Populonia duly depicted him on its coins.

Oddly, a Velchans did occupy one of the houses of the Piacenza liver.[22] He has sometimes been compared to the Roman Vulcan, sometimes to the Cretan Zeus Velchanos, a god of vegetation. If the former comparison is correct, we would have here a doubling of Sethlans, and the placement of his name in a sector (no. 34) touching those of the subterranean world would be appropriate. The month of March bears his name in its Latinized form, *Velcitanus*. This shows his importance but would plead in favor of an identification with Zeus Velchanos.

Sethlans and Velchans seem to differ in their level of integration with their Greek parallels. Their unusual natures offer some evidence that they were originally Etruscan. A sector named and codified for Velchans on the Piacenza liver is certainly one of the most important criteria for his autochthony. Other strong indications are the ex-votos and offerings to him, as well as the mention in one of the ritual texts of a ceremony to both gods. The attribution to Velchans of functions considerably different from those of the Greek model argues that he was a local divinity, only superficially Hellenized. On the other hand, the abundance of images of Sethlans on mirrors, as well as their heterodox variations, would indicate that his importance was more cultural than religious.

### Calu, Aita (Hades), Phersipnai (Persephone)

The name Aita, obviously derived from the Greek *Aides* (Hades), appeared in Etruria only in the fourth century, first in the Tomb of the Ogre II at Tarquinia, then in the Golini Tomb at Orvieto (see chapter 4). His image appears at the same time as his name, both in these tombs and on the sarcophagus of Torre San Severo (fig. 8.7). He is shown as a bearded man resembling Tinia, but distinguished from him by a scepter with a coiling serpent and by the skin of a dog or wolf that he wears on his head. He is thus a relatively late figure who owes much to Greek depictions of Hades and even more to an adaptation of the Hellenized Tinia. He is inseparable from his wife, Phersipnai; she, too, comes directly from a Greek model, Persephone. At the same time, Nethuns is depicted with the same features as Aita, but with his head covered with the skin of a dolphin or a *ketos*. It is as if the same model served for all three deities, differentiated only by an attribute defining each one's element. This dependence on Greek imagery and names leads us to wonder about Aita's origin and the reason for his appearance.

There is in fact a god of the dead who seems to be earlier than Aita: this is Calu. Line 15 of the early fifth-century Capua Tablet prescribes an offering to Calu of "perfect victims" (*zusleva*). On the Magliano lead tablet, in the first line on side B, two deities appear: *mlach thanra Calusc*, "offering to Thanr and to Calu" (or "that which is good for Thanr and Calu"). A small bronze dog bears a dedication to Calu;[23] and we have

Gods

8.7. Aita and Phersipnei attending the sacrifice of Trojan prisoners for Patroclus. Sarcophagus of Torre San Severo, near Orvieto. Mid-fourth century. Orvieto, Museo Claudio Faina.

already (chapter 4) discussed the figure, dressed in the skin of a canid, who comes up from the world below to seize a man. But the most puzzling inscription, mentioned above in connection with Tinia, is engraved on the bottom of a cup from Orvieto: *tinia Calusna*. Whom does it mean? Calu here could be called "Tinia of the dead," as Charu(n) was transformed at Spina into *Turms Aitas*. Or perhaps the world of the dead was ruled by one of Tinia's forms, his chthonic component. Thus Calu and Tinia could be considered to have originated together. Or did Calu, after Aita had arrived as ruler of the Afterworld, continue on in a sort of subordinate role, limited to the moment of death and cut off from the world of the afterlife: a role scarcely superior to that of Charu(n)? It is certain that Calu had a cult but no myths, while Aita received no sacrifices, but figured in a collection of stories transposed from Greek myth.

*Castur and Pultuce, Tinias Cliniiar (the Dioscuri)*
A marvelous cup by Oltos was dedicated to the purely Greek deities, the Dioscuri, at Tarquinia toward the end of the sixth century. An inscription was elegantly engraved under its foot: *itun turuce venel atelinas tinas cliniiar*, "Venel Atelinas offered this to the sons of Tinia."[24] The expression occurs here for the first time, and it is merely the literal translation of *Dioskouroi*, "sons of Zeus"). The divine twins are considered collectively here. It is only around 480 at Vulci that their own names appear. This is

# Gods

an example of an importation, pure and simple, which not only translates the name and the lineage of Zeus (and ignores that of Tyndareos), but also directly transfers their appearance and their worship. As a result, the Dioscuri figure significantly in the iconography of mirrors, and their repetitive, symmetrical poses become a cliché of less inventive late-period workshops. Their cult, so important at Lavinium and Rome, was probably brought to coastal Etruria at the same time that it settled in Latium. However, Etruscan epigraphy and iconography both document twin male divinities, the *Thuluter*,[25] who have totally unknown functions but an appearance very close to that of the Dioscuri.

Artumes, the Dioscuri, and Sethlans appear simply to be direct imports. Aplu, imported indirectly by way of Latin territory, probably took over the characteristics of solar divinities like Cautha. The mantic functions of Śuri, Turan, and Menrva seem to result from a dividing up of an earlier deity's functions. Turms is an imported god, one of whose functions coincides with that of a preexisting Etruscan deity. Aita, who partially succeeds the Archaic Calu, again shows that Hellenization did not completely erase the earlier religious strata.

### A DIVINE ORDER?

According to Hesiod, the Greeks imagined a divine world structured according to the generations and hierarchies of the gods. Noticing that the same generations and hierarchies appear in Etruria, one might conclude that the Etruscans had a concept of a divine order—structured, perceptible, if not comprehensible—and that their great gods were organized into a coherent pyramid, essentially a "pantheon." We shall see that the reality was rather different. The divine order of the Etruscan world was instead organized according to spheres of activity, a structure that Martianus Capella echoes (see chapter 2). The series of sectors on the Piacenza liver will serve as an itinerary for us to visit other gods. Their organization will then seem not hierarchic, but functional.

### *Velthumna, Velthumena, Voltumna, Tinia (Zeus)*

Voltumna was, as Varro says (*Ling.* 5.46), *deus Etruriae princeps,* the chief and most important of the Etruscan gods. He was worshiped in Volsinian territory in the famous sanctuary where, from the fifth century on, the delegations of the Twelve Peoples met. This famous Fanum Voltumnae, which played a major role in the official Etruscan religion, has been mistakenly interpreted as the seat of a federation, whereas it was merely a sanctuary common to the *nomen etruscum*. In Rome at the time of Propertius and Ovid, however, this god was merely a minor deity called Vortumnus, of changeable form, but with the appearance of a young man.[26] Gardeners and peasants came to worship him in his sanctuary on the Vicus Tuscus by bringing beans! His most ancient name was probably Velthumena, but it does not occur in the Etruscan written sources.

## Gods

8.8. Tinia/Zeus, from a model by Pheidias. Architectural terracotta from the San Leonardo temple at Orvieto. Beginning of fourth century. Orvieto, Museo Claudio Faina.

It is evident from elsewhere, however, that the great god of Etruria was Tinia, who wielded three kinds of lightning, who appears in five positions on the Piacenza liver, and who Seneca (*QNat.* 2.45.1–3) says ruled over the universe. He is the father of the Dioscuri, whom the Etruscans call the sons of Tinia (*Tinas Cliniiar*); he is the master of Turms, who does his bidding; he has more than one chthonian domain (like Zeus Chthonios), and he was thus called Tinia Calusna, a name that links him to Aita/Calu. He did not take on the physical traits of Zeus until after the spread of the Pheidian type from Olympia; a magnificent terracotta copy of that type (fig. 8.8) is from the San Leonardo temple at Orvieto. Earlier, both in sculpture and painting and then on mirrors and vases, he is shown beardless with the features of a young man. In this figure it is easy to recognize Voltumna, who initially seemed much different.

Tinia thus is not merely the Etruscan form of Zeus or the prototype of Jupiter. He has nothing in common with them except his dominant position in the divine world and some mythological episodes that the mirror-engravers tirelessly repeat: the birth of Athena/Menrva, the birth of Dionysus/Fufluns, and "divine conversations." Young, sometimes chthonian, probably linked to vegetation, as was Vertumnus, his ultimate and restrictive Roman embodiment, Tinia had an existence completely different from that of his Greek and Roman equivalents. The Magliano lead tablet and

## Gods

section V of the *liber linteus* prescribe rites in his honor. The former clearly designates him in a chthonic context; the latter provides invocations in which he is associated with Thesan (Eos or Aurora). Thus are expressed the two poles of his domain. He was worshipped at Orvieto, probably in two different sanctuaries,[27] as well as at Tarquinia, at Arezzo, where the Chimaera group had been dedicated to him, at Bolsena, and in northern Etruria generally. It seems entirely likely, in fact, that every city was obliged to have a street and a temple named for him.

It is interesting that this name doubling is so common in Etruria. In this case, however, it seems that the name Voltumna should only be used for the deity of the Fanum Voltumnae who, after the Roman sack of Volsinii in 264, was transferred to a temple on the Aventine, and thus became Vortumnus. But most striking is the complex and multiple nature of this chief god. Did his apparent Hellenization limit his functions, which were initially much broader?

### From Uni to Juno

Uni occupies an essential place on the Pianceza liver, in the sector (no. 4) that follows that of Tinia. She was believed to have thrown the thunderbolt and is thus a major deity, long integrated into the circle of the great Etruscan gods. The name Uni, however, comes from the Latin Juno, as may her cult. In fact, she had a number of temples in Latium, where she was most often addressed as *sospita* ("savior, liberator") and represented armed, her head covered with a goat skin. A beautiful Archaic bronze shows her in the act of fighting; on a Pontic amphora representing the fight against Hercle, she wears her goat skin.[28]

The problem is more complex outside Etrusco-Latin areas, where one would look for possible equivalences between Uni and Greek deities. In Pyrgi's Temple B, which was consecrated to her, the Carthaginians called the goddess *strt*—that is, Astarte, who was a sky deity like Uni. The texts mention sanctuaries dedicated to her; a temple to Uni is cited in the Capua ritual, and another in the *liber linteus*.[29] She had temples at Caere and Perugia, and another at Veii, where she was "called out" by Camillus in 392. Her role at Cortona was very important. She was its patron deity, to judge from a dedication: *mi unial curtun*, "I belong to Uni of Cortona."[30] She maintains special relations with Hercle. Sometimes she fights him; sometimes the two deities are shown reconciled on engraved mirrors; and sometimes Uni nurses the hero, who through that act becomes her son (cf. *infra*, under "*Hercle*").

Depictions of her from the middle of the fourth century on show a transformation. Uni is now often half-nude like Turan, and at Gravisca Uni and Turan may even have shared the same cella. Leucothea (Ino), called the Mater Matuta at Rome, shared many traits with her, as did Eileithyia, protectress of births. Some ex-votos designate Uni as protectress of all small children. For the Punics of the free port of Caere, Astarte was her corresponding celestial deity. Uni shared many characteristics with Turan/Aphrodite; she functioned as the patron deity of many cities and was a warrior like Menrva/Athena. Her many connections suggest that there was a profound

# Gods

commonality among the major goddesses, the heiresses of a mother who had embodied all of these female functions.

### *Tecvm (Menrva?)*

Without knowing for certain the nature of Tecvm, we have connected her with Menrva above. Her place on the Piacenza liver seems to authorize this comparison. It is difficult to connect Tecvm with Tece, the name that appears on the Arringatore dedication,[31] but the seated bronze child in the Vatican (see fig. 7.11), dedicated to *Tec*, seems to refer to her.

### *Lusl, Lusa*

If one follows the peripheral strip of the Piacenza liver, from the domain of Uni across that of Tecvm, one comes to a deity named Lusl. In spite of her probable importance, she is otherwise unknown, even if her name is restored to Lusa, mentioned in the *liber linteus*. Perhaps this was a cult name or the epithet of a known deity who is currently absent (there are several) from this document.

### *Nethuns*

The next domain belongs to Nethuns. This god also appears in two other sectors of the Piacenza liver, one of them in association (as *synnaos*) with Tinia (*tinsth/neth*). His name probably comes from Umbrian. He may originally have been a god of the border with Umbria and ruled over sweet waters, brooks, and sources. He is sometimes depicted making water spring from the earth. Only rather late is he identified with Poseidon. He takes on the latter's attributes and myths and is depicted with a goddess who looks like Amphitrite. Toward the middle of the fourth century, his borrowed Greek appearance becomes definitively fixed and he assumes maritime functions, which he did not have initially. A little later still, he appears with a dolphin skin on his head. At the same time, a deity with the features of a young man, his head covered with the skin of a *ketos*, is depicted on the coins of Vetulonia. We think that these are the two faces of the late-period Nethuns. They recall the two faces of Tinia/Voltumna and, to a lesser degree, the double personality of Calu/Aita. This teaches us less about the nature of this specific god than about the process of formation of the Etruscan divine world from various sources. Here, an Umbrian god, Greek outer forms, and a youthful marine deity combine to produce a major god, to whom the *liber linteus* prescribes many rites and offerings. An image of Nethuns on several coins,[32] all probably originating in coastal Etruria, probably at Vetulonia, suggests that this god served as patron deity there.

### *Cautha, Cath, Usil, Cathesan (the sun) and Thesan (the dawn)*

While Aplu, whose Greek model is a solar deity, does not appear on the Piacenza liver, Cath occupies the sector immediately beside that of Nethuns. In fact, if Apollo had been imported into Etruria with all of his functions, he could have dethroned the

## Gods

solidly attested solar deity named Cautha or Cavtha. Under this name, the deity was feminine and may correspond to "Celeritas, the daughter of the Sun," in Martianus Capella's beautiful phrase. She also possesses a second sector on the Piacenza liver (no. 23), near the pyramidal lobe. This is proof of her importance. She was worshipped in many sanctuaries: at Cortona and Populonia, at Magliano and Tarquinia, and on the shores of Lake Trasimene, where the dedications indicate that she enjoyed much favor. The sacred zone of Pyrgi/south seems to have been devoted at one time to Cautha,[33] as well as to Śuri and Aplu (mentioned on lots). Curiously, at Tarquinia, the college of priests that served her also served Pacha (that is, Bacchus).[34] The name Cautha, however, designates only one aspect of this deity: the one under which she was most widely worshipped, the one by which she is named in the ritual texts.

Images on mirrors that depict the solar deity, however, especially those that show him crowned with rays, emerging from the sea, running in the blinding light of day, are accompanied by the name Usil. This god is undeniably masculine (fig. 8.9). Perhaps it is also he who runs, crowned with light, on the antefixes of the small building at Pyrgi. He appears on the Piacenza liver, but on the back, where he denotes the

8.9. Nethuns, Usil, and Thesan on a mirror from Tuscania. Fourth century. Rome, Museo Naz. di Villa Giulia.

luminous part of the sky (the sun or the daylight). Usil ultimately takes on the features of solar Apollo, and he drives a four-horse chariot.

On a mirror from Orbetello,[35] we encounter the inscription *ca Thesan*: "this is Thesan (the dawn)," and she is clearly adopting the myths of Ino. She appears in scenes of the death of Memnon (*Memrun*). Thesan is well known to be the deity of origins: the birth of the day, but also all births. She is none other than the Mater Matuta, to whom so many sanctuaries were dedicated and whose worship extended from Satricum to Pyrgi.

This disconcerting *mélange* nonetheless illustrates the real relations within the Etruscan divine world. Multiple names appear and attach to the same function. These deities—sometimes youthful, sometimes older, sometimes masculine, sometimes feminine, sometimes autochthonous, sometimes marked by foreign influences or totally imported—are only rarely organized according to family genealogies. While gods of different origins had related duties or attributes and could be substituted for one another, they were not completely equivalent. For this reason Etruscan gods remained resistant to the *interpretatio graeca* or *latina*, whose simplifications and assimilations could not account for their complexity. In this particular case, it is as if there were a kind of divine solar essence that could have different names or appearances according to the situation. Under one name it received a cult; under another, myths.

*Fufluns (Dionysus), Pacha (Bacchus)*
The name Fufluns is engraved on the Piacenza liver in the sector for chthonic or nature divinities. In a fifth-century inscription,[36] he is named *Fufluns Pachies*—that is, Bacchus. He is depicted on a tripod from Vulci that was dedicated on the acropolis of Athens, and a very old Greek tradition (*Homeric Hymn to Dionysus* 7), connects him with the Tyrrhenian pirates. From that time Fufluns, who was initially associated with spring vegetation, became the god of the vine and wine. This would have been an important function in Etruria, which became the Mediterranean's wine producer *par excellence*.

It is only in the Hellenistic period that a clear distinction is drawn between the deity name, Fufluns, and the cult name, Pacha. The cult spread throughout the Etruscan world. Its importance is attested by the violent repression of the "Bacchanalia" in 186 (Livy 39.6ff.), by the destruction of a sanctuary of Dionysus/Pacha at Bolsena,[37] and by the many late-period ex-votos depicting the god.[38] His worship was well anchored, and it had in Etruria, as it did in Apulia, both a mystic dimension and a "national" connotation. At this same time, Pacha began to play an important role in the turning of the seasons, thus presaging the function he ultimately served in Roman religion. One of the most widely reproduced scenes depicts his birth. Another, more refined and delicate, shows the god, in the grace of adolescence, exchanging a kiss with his mother, Semele. Artists vie with each other to depict this theme on mirrors,[39] as if it were the one most preferred by Etruscan aristocratic women.

## Gods

The name Fufluns was certainly connected with the city of Fufluna (Populonia), but did the god serve as its patron deity? That question has no answer yet.

### Selva, Selvans (Sylvanus?)

The name Selvans follows that of Fufluns on the border of the Piacenza liver, but he also occupies a second section (no. 31) in the left part of the interior space below the pyramidal lobe. These two positions touch those of the mysterious Letham, whom we shall discuss next. Selvans received many offerings, particularly bronzes with dedicatory inscriptions. His name is very often specified or modified by a surname or a simple epithet. He is defined[40] as *canzate, enizpetla,* or *sanchuneta.*[41] The last modifier connects him with the Latin god of oaths, Sancus. His major function, however, was to stand guard over limits and borders, the frontier between cultivated and uncultivated places. This function is symbolized by the skin of a feline, which covers the god's head on an interesting statuette from Cortona (fig. 8.10). At Tarquinia, his name is found associated with that of Śuri on a stele that reads: *(ś)uris selvansl.*[42] The texts of the *gromatici,* a Late anthology of surveying treatises, attribute to Silvanus,

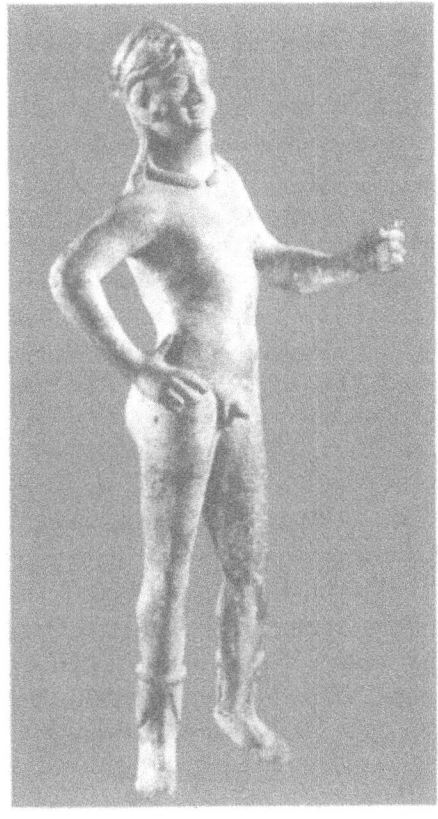

8.10. Votive statuette depicting Selvans, god of the wild border. First half of third century. Cortona, Museo dell'Accademia Etrusca.

161

his Roman heir, the placement of the first boundary cippi. Selvans was probably believed to guard and guarantee the boundaries of the numerous cities in which he was worshipped, such as Bolsena, Sarteano, and Cortona.

*Letham, Lethns, Letha, Lethms, Leta*
Named five times on the Piacenza liver, prescribed more than six ceremonies by the Capua ritual, this deity is certainly one of the most important, to judge from these objective criteria. The name appears only once on a mirror, whose theme is a "divine conversation" or, more likely, a "birth of Menrva," and this document is mutilated in such a way that one cannot even tell whether Letham is a god or a goddess. The ritual prescriptions of the Capua text do not offer any more information. It has been proposed, without proof, that this was a warrior deity or a Vesta-Hestia parallel. But we must admit our ignorance. This god's diverse positions on the Piacenza liver would associate him or her with the chthonian realm or with fertility. Such slender (and hypothetical) information on such a major deity is an incitement to further study.

*Tluscv*
Three sections of the Piacenza liver, as many as Tinia holds, are assigned to Tluscv or Tlusc. We do not know anything about this deity, whose name appears only on this one document. It is probable that this name is an unknown, perhaps merely haruspical, surname for an important deity associated with the earth. On the other hand, the god mentioned in the next section on the liver is well known.

*Cel, Cels (Ge, Gaia)*
Cel is the earth. On a mirror from Populonia, in fact, a giant is called "son of the earth": *Cels clan*.[43] This name, in this position, clearly establishes a chthonian environment for the neighboring deities, and consequently for Tluscv. No representation of Cel is preserved. This is perfectly logical, since the Etruscan deities were at first aniconic and only adopted anthropomorphic form under Greek influence. And since Gaia did not have an image in Greece itself, she could not have offered one to Cel.

*Culsans, Culsu, Vanth*
Culsans is the god of the door, *cvl*, and, like Janus, has two faces, one facing forward, the other backward.[44] He occupies the next section on the liver's border, which bears the name of *cvl alp*. A beautiful votive image of this god (fig. 8.11), discovered near one of the gates of Cortona, bears an inscription engraved on its thigh: *v. cvinti. arnt / ias. culśanśl. / alpan. turce*, "Vel Quintus for Arntia gave this gift to Culsans." In his long epitaph, L(a)ris Pulenas mentions the duties he performed for Culsans (see chapter 7). This suggests that the god had a regular cult; his statue probably portrayed him holding a key.

## Gods

8.11. Statuette of Culsans, god of doorways. Found at Cortona. First half of third century. Cortona, Museo dell'Accademia Etrusca.

A sort of female extension of Culsans appears on the Clusian sarcophagus of Hasti Afunei.[45] A young woman with all the characteristics of Vanth—the boots, the short skirt, the naked breast—slips through the half-open door to the Afterworld, a torch on her right shoulder and, in her left hand, what appears to be a key (really a pair of pincers to pull out the bolts of the gate: *karkinos*). Painted above her is her name, or perhaps a functional epithet: *Culsu*. Immediately to the right, however, another woman, identically dressed, leans on the enormous key for a city gate. The name painted above this second figure is *Vanth*, which ordinarily designates the bearer of a torch (*phane*, "torch"?) and the genie who guides the dead and lights the roads to the Afterworld (see chapter 4). Culsu here may be an epithet to define only Vanth, or both of the female figures holding keys.

Is it Alpan who hides in the second part of the Piacenza liver's inscription *Cvl.alp?* This seems impossible. Alpan appears among other young females in Turan's train, Achuvisr, Sipanu and Thanr, Zipan, Thalna, Mean. She belongs to Lasa's world and does not seem to fit in beside Vetisl and Cilensl.

## Gods

*Vetisl, Veive (Veiovis?)*
It is difficult to link the names Vetisl, Veive, and Veiovis with any certainty. Vetisl's presence in this unfavorable, infernal, and particularly somber zone of the Etruscan horizon would suggest that he is the Etruscan prototype of the Latin Veiovis.[46] The latter seems exclusively chthonian, ruling over marshes and sitting at the gates to the world of the dead. Linguistically, the name Veiovis can easily be associated with Vetisl, whose function is connected with *asyla* (international zones within port cities) and the welcome of foreigners.

*Cilensl, Cilen, Tin Cilen*
The last section in the peripheral band bears the name of a deity who appears two other times on the liver: once in the next section, where he is associated with Tin, and again between Satres and Letham in the radial sections of the left side. We do not know anything about this deity, who was certainly important, but the location of the sections assigned to him suggests that he was probably connected with the dead. The name Tin Cilen (no. 1) thus may have more or less the same meaning as a similar name pairing in the Orvieto sanctuary: Tinia Calusna, probably comparable to Zeus Chthonios. If so, Cilen could be one of the specific names of the god of the infernal world and might be compared to Aita Calu.

It is noteworthy that the number of gods' names whose significance is unknown corresponds more or less to the number of known deities whose names surprisingly do not appear on the bronze liver. Might we infer that the unrecognizable names on this object designate those deities as one would question them or look to them for signs—that is, under a function that was addressed by some other name? We have observed that some gods had both a cult name and a different mythic name. Might we suppose that they also had a third name that was haruspical?

*Laran and Maris*
Some identifiable deities occupy the inner sectors of the Piacenza liver. Maris has erroneously been identified as the Latin Mars, but actually Laran is the equivalent of the god of war.

The name Laran is Etruscan, but it appears late, in the first half of the fourth century. It is not on the Piacenza liver. This time it is not the name that betrays a strong Greek influence, but the iconography: no certain image of Laran illustrates anything but a Greek myth. He is depicted fighting a giant (*Cels clan*, the son of the earth), but most often he appears with Turan in a sort of insipid imitation of Ares and Aphrodite. The most original aspect of these scenes is the presence of the couple's children: three young boys who are all named Maris, but who are clearly not Mars. The Maris names that appear on the Piacenza liver, near a sector attributed to Hercle, are qualified by epithets or surnames: *Maris husrnana*, *Maris halna*, and *Maris isminthians*. In several scenes depicting Maris figures, Menrva draws a child out of a krater. Another

## Gods

scene, on a bronze cista from Praeneste, shows a child emerging, helmeted and armed, from a flaming krater. This is a thoroughly Etruscan myth, completely unknown, but it does correspond to a name inscribed on the liver. It seems that the Maris, children of Laran and Turan and raised by Menrva, had an origin and existence that were more authentically Etruscan than did their father, Laran.

We have no inkling of Laran's worship except through the great bronze statue known as the Mars of Todi (see fig. 7.9),[47] probably made by a Volsinian workshop. In spite of its private dedication in Umbrian, it could have functioned as a cult statue. The private worship of Laran is attested by countless bronze votive statuettes representing an armed man brandishing a lance. They are evidence for the spread of his cult, not only through Etruria, but throughout the areas of Italy marked by Etruscan influence.[48]

### Hercle

In Etruria, Hercle was not a hero but a god. His is the only virtually Greek name on the topography of the Piacenza liver: the other Hellenic or Hellenized deities appear there under their Etruscan or Italic names. This Greek-hero-turned-Etruscan-god had long been at home in Etruria. Monuments from the end of the seventh century or the beginning of the sixth already depict his adventures. On one ivory pyxis from Chiusi[49] he leads the cattle of Geryon and on another he escapes from Polyphemus' cavern. On a pyxis from the Montefortini Tomb of Comeana he escapes under a stag,[50] and on a plaque from Tarquinia[51] he lies in ambush for centaurs. Very quickly his labors took on a symbolic meaning, which political leaders manipulated. The images of Hercle mastering the lion and the bull on the terracotta plaques from a "residence" at Acquarossa[52] probably served as a political reference. We have linked his sculptures from Rome and Veii to the periods when the tyrants exercised power. Scenes of his combats against monsters and beasts and of his battles with other deities—Aplu and Uni, under her aspect as Juno Sospita—had both a political and a religious meaning.

But we suspect that he also had specifically Etruscan myths. On one mirror, Hercle carries off a woman named Mlachuch,[53] who is otherwise unknown. On other mirrors and on intaglios,[54] Hercle, sometimes still a child, sails on a raft of amphorae or flasks in a scene that may depict a voyage to the Afterworld. In other scenes, the god introduces Epiur, perhaps his son, also unknown in Greece, to Tinia. Others show him reconciled with Uni. He becomes her adoptive son (as an inscription on a mirror indicates: *hercle unial clan*, "Hercle, son of Uni"), and then the goddess nurses him (fig. 8.12). Surprisingly frequent are the scenes in which he and Menrva appear to be husband and wife. These myths, totally unknown in Greece, suggest that Hercle is merely the name given to an earlier deity, who had his own functions and history but also possessed some of the characteristics of the Greek Heracles.

Several small bronzes from northern Etruria depict a "god of the bow" or "hunter

Gods

8.12. Mirror from Volterra: Uni nursing Hercle and thus becoming his mother. Around 300. Florence, Museo Archeologico Nazionale, Soprintendenza Archeologica per la Toscana Firenze.

god" clothed in an animal skin. He is sometimes inadequately identified as Hercle.[55] Should we consider him a kind of proto-Hercle? In any case, although his name and many of his Greek myths were adopted very early (in the seventh century), Hercle is not an imported god. His Hellenization is certainly deep, but it cannot mask the traces of a complex earlier existence.

*Satre*

One radiating section (no. 35) on the Piacenza liver belongs to Satre. That position, with its particularly somber coloration, would suit an Etruscan version of the Roman Saturn. It is not certain that this is the god mentioned in the *liber linteus* (IX.3) with the words *satrs. enas. thucu*. We must admit that our knowledge stops there. Satre is

# Gods

known only from a single inscription of his name, which is perhaps only a false equivalent of his alleged Roman counterpart.

## ETRUSCAN GODS AND GREEK MYTHS: THE LIMITS OF OUR KNOWLEDGE

This long list of gods is discouraging. Several of them are relatively well known; others are listed in the calendars, inscribed in the cosmic cartography of the Piacenza liver, and offered dedications and sacrifices, but otherwise totally unknown. There are deities whose functions overlap, deities endowed with multiple names, deities who seem to combine multiple natures under the same name. To readers familiar with Greek and Roman religion, this divine structure must seem incomprehensible. Let us just say that it is profoundly different. In learning the nature of the Etruscan divine world, in distinguishing its Greek borrowings from original deities, we shall deepen our knowledge of Etruscan civilization.

For many years and using very different methodologies, Etruscan scholars have sought the real meaning and the force of Greek myths in Etruria. It would be impossible to resolve these nagging issues within the framework of this book, or to offer a general solution that would be valid in every case and for all periods. At best we can suggest partial answers, which must be modified with each century.

Diametrically opposed scientific opinions, involving different methods, have succeeded one another in Etruscan studies. Several decades ago, seemingly incomplete or noncanonical illustrations of myths, and their perceived "decorative" character, were explained away as merely a "banalization" of Greek themes. The apparent distortions were believed to lack meaning or demonstrate a failure of understanding on the part of the craftsman. According to this approach, the mirror with two Menrva figures, mentioned above, would merely be repeating the goddess as a decorative pattern, without any religious significance. This seemingly prudent method[56] ultimately resulted in denying all meaning to Etruscan mythic art, at least of the Archaic period. Its radical stance soon became impossible to sustain, if it had ever been viable.

Taking the opposite side, recent scholarship claims that Greek epic and myths were often well known and well understood, even in the Archaic period. Some myths were illustrated in Etruria before they took artistic form in Greece.[57] When these opposing attitudes become explanatory systems, however, they do not allow us to explore the ramifications of the Greek myths' penetration into Etruria.

Analysis of some surprising variants (especially those odd stories about Hera/Uni and Heracles/Hercle) suggests that the mythic models did not originate in Greece proper, but in Western Greece,[58] a culture that "Atticizing" scholars often neglect. Close attention to relations between Etruria and Western Greece has yielded fruitful religious parallels.[59] Western Greek mythic variants may often lie at the heart of discordances between the most widespread Attic version of a myth and its Etruscan interpretation. But the importance of the Oriental Greek component is now recognized

## Gods

as well. We should also search for the origin of mythic images in Asian Greece or among Hellenized neighbors in that part of the Greek world.[60]

There is no doubt that the Etruscans, selectively and often with subtle understanding, borrowed iconography and mythic images from the Greek world and integrated them into their figural repertoire. The themes are often Dionysiac, and derived from Athenian vase paintings. But we may still ask why, to what degree, and to what depth the Etruscans absorbed these borrowings.

Scholars have hypothesized, on the basis of a study of the François Tomb at Vulci,[61] an ideological and political reading for these epic and mythic scenes. The great megalographic paintings in the tomb depict the slaughter of the Trojan prisoners at the tomb of Patroclus on one wall and, opposite and eloquently parallel to it, the killing of the Tarquins and their allies from Volsinii, Sovana and Falerii, along with the liberation of *Caile Vipinas* (Caelius Vibenna) by *Macstrna* (Servius Tullius). The Homeric epic, rendered parallel to the history of the Italian peninsula, here acquires the force of a paradigm, symbol, or precedent. These scenes take place in an anti-Roman political context. The image of the slaughter of the Trojan prisoners evokes the battles of Vulci against Rome: of the Etruscan heirs of Greek culture against the descendents of the Trojans. No one can doubt the ideological use of this theme in the François Tomb, but does it have the same political charge on the so-called Sarcophagus of the Priest or that of Torre San Severo, or, above all, on the cheap terracotta urns that they inspired?[62] In these latter cases, its meaning instead seems religious or eschatological. This one example illustrates the complexity of the problem. In certain specific instances, from the fourth century at the earliest, the political or ideological reading of a work of art seems essential, but it is more difficult to accept in the artistic production of the lower class.

Admittedly, images of the Dioscuri, Castur and Pultuce, which increase in frequency in the fourth century, symbolize aristocratic youth and played an ideological role in the political context of the period. The labors of Hercle on the Acquarossa terracottas were set up as an ideal by the local ruler. The Minotaur on the frieze of the Regia at Rome likewise refers in some way to the Roman regime through the myth of Theseus; and the Chiusi aristocrat who owned and perhaps commissioned the François Krater may have wished to use the Athenian hero as a kind of model. But did the heroic and mythic images function merely as emblems, reference points for political propaganda?[63] Was Hercle exclusively linked to the regimes of the tyrants? Does the Calydonian boar hunt merely indicate philatticism on the part of the Tarquinian aristocrats who commissioned the Tomba della Scrofa Nera?[64] Is it certain that the temple's pediments were intended to demonstrate the ruler's political choices? Did Pyrgi's *antepagmentum* show the Syracusan threat or the tyrant's excess (see chapter 6)? Should the pediment of the Fucoli temple at Chianciano be read as a celebration of a Roman-Etruscan alliance (see chapter 5)? In contrast, the theme of the Bolsena temple (Volsinii II) is probably religious and could in essence refer to elements of the *etrusca disciplina*.[65]

## Gods

The political interpretation of Greek myths adopted in Etruria, as fruitful as it can be, should not exclude religious interpretations, which sometimes, indeed often, are compatible with the political message.

The nature of myth is that it can be read, interpreted, and utilized at multiple levels, in the culture that created it as much as in those that borrowed it. The Greek myths interpreted in a religious sense in Etruria do not necessarily carry the same meaning that they did in Greece. Some of them were distorted for magical-religious purposes and became associated with rites. This is probably the case with the myth of Phineus, who, in the course of a funeral ceremony, found himself transported in a dance ritual of purification and revitalization.[66] It is perhaps the same use of Greek myth we see illustrated on a bronze tripod in Berlin depicting the myth of Perseus and Medusa,[67] and in various illustrations of the story, both mythical and epic, of the death of Troilus. Achilles lies in wait for him in the Tarquinian Tomb of the Bulls, and on a relief from Chiusi[68] and a funerary amphora in Reading,[69] he is carried off to be sacrificed. In the depictions of these myths and probably of many others, the story is charged with a funerary meaning. The same is true of the many scenes of the sacrifice of Iphigeneia, particularly on the Late sarcophagi and urns of Perugia. The most flagrant case is probably the duel between Eteocles and Polyneices. This story served very different functions on the pediment at Talamone (see fig. 6.30), where it probably had a political meaning, and on Chiusine peasants' urns, where the image of these men killing each other most likely substituted for funerary gladiatorial combats. On the other hand, the myth of Alcestis and Admetus became a kind of doubling of the story of Orpheus; but was its meaning exclusively funerary? It seems excessive to limit the adopted myths to a single interpretation. Their religious dimension remains their underlying function, even if the socio-political meaning is often clearly of great importance.

One of the most important dimensions of Greek myth is its description of the world, and of its birth and structure. Etruria, however, had its own theogonic stories, its own conceptions of the universe, which were explained not by mythic narrative, but by revealed teaching. Thus Greek myth did not operate in this domain for the Etruscans. It was reduced to its most immediate meaning. Atlas holding up the heavens and Prometheus devoured by Zeus's eagle do not illustrate the omnipotence of Zeus/Tinia in punishing duplicity. They merely signify the two extremities of the world: the West of the Pillars of Hercules and the Orient of the Caucasus.[70]

We have to be extremely cautious in explaining how and why Greek myths penetrated into Archaic Etruria. The myths may have originated in the West, in Greece itself, or in the Orient; their influence may have stemmed from literary or artistic prototypes; their level of adoption may have been superficial or deep; their use in one place may have been political, in another symbolic, in another religious or eschatological. In its contact with the proliferating world of Greek myth, Etruria did not receive stories in a passive or haphazard manner. It chose them selectively, according to its beliefs and its needs of the moment.

Gods

Only this is certain: Greek myth was not "adopted" in Etruria. Some stories were chosen from the immense Hellenic repertoire and reworked to function in a different culture. Myth was not used to define, describe, or conceptualize the Etruscan gods. It was a catalogue of exempla, used sometimes for one purpose, sometimes for another. Etruscan thought (as we rather ambitiously claim to know it) was not mythic. For the Etruscans myth was only allegorical. Greek myths do not describe the world of the Etruscan gods, who were defined not by stories and acts, but by states of being, abilities, and functions.

Those multiple and poorly defined gods, the borrowed and reworked myths, the complex stratigraphy of divine names, functions, and images, all reveal the uniqueness of Etruscan religion.

CHAPTER 9

# The Divine

Our rapid overview of Etruscan gods has yielded some surprises. Although we possess many iconographic documents and a fair number of inscriptions, some deities are still completely unknown to us. Some names—for example Letham and Lusa—do not correspond to any image, any function, any cult location or, *a fortiori*, any myth. Other deities, whose cults are attested in Etruria purely through literary references in Latin, cannot be identified with any gods whose names we have. This is the case with Nortia, whose sanctuary at Volsinii is mentioned by Livy (7.3–7): "at Volsinii also appear, affixed to the temple of the Etruscan goddess Nortia, nails that indicate the number of years."

Śuri, an apparently male divinity attested at Viterbo, Tarquinia, Vulci, and Pyrgi, is poorly known (see chapter 8). He is sometimes associated with Selvans (at Tarquinia, on the Civita Hill), sometimes with Cautha (in the small southern sanctuary at Pyrgi), sometimes with Thufltha (at Vulci), but his connection to the god Soranos is pure hypothesis. Nonetheless, his mantic function is almost certain, and he may be at least partially identified with Aplu or even with Dis Pater, whose nature is infernal. Study of Śuri has, most annoyingly, yielded ignorance, imprecision, and abusive comparisons; and the same can be said of many Etruscan gods.

It seems useless to comment at length on these insufficiencies, which are largely due to our lack of sources, but they may also be due to the way we view and often overinterpret those sources. An organized theogony and mythology, even if purely theoretical, have fixed our notions of Greek and even Roman polytheism. In comparison, the profound confusion that reigns in the Etruscan "pantheon" is disconcerting to us. The original and apparently incoherent aspects of this divine world can be regrouped, however, in such a way as to generate new explanations and a different orientation.[1]

# The Divine

### "COLLEGIAL," MULTIPLE, AND NAMELESS GODS

Etruria is the homeland of anonymous gods. These were grouped into "colleges" or entities, and their number is both unknown and unknowable.

The most important are without doubt the *di involuti*. Their power is enormous—Tinia himself must ask their authorization to use his most powerful thunderbolt, according to Caecina (Seneca, *QNat.* 2.41)—but they remain hidden, surrounded by a curtain of clouds. They have no names, no number, no sex, no form. No cult and no ritual are known to have been performed to them. Their lack of name is clearly the primary reason they are completely foreign to the mortal world. They constitute the most secret and most distant stratum of the divine.

The *di consentes* are a little less distant (Seneca, *QNat.* 2.21). They do not have names, form, or sex, either, nor do they have any cult or sanctuary. But they are essential as counselors to Tinia/Jupiter and thus were inherited by Roman religion. To make them acceptable and comprehensible, to integrate and Romanize them, Roman tradition determined their number, sex, and form (Varro in Arnobius, *Adv. nat.* 3.40). They became twelve—six gods and six goddesses—and were associated with the twelve great gods. The emperor Julian built a portico to them at the foot of the Capitoline. The Romanization of the *di consentes* demonstrates, by what it changed, the essence of the Etruscan divine sphere. That which Roman religion believed to be lacking, and thus supplied, is precisely that which Etruscan religion primitively defined as the divine.

The same thing happens to other groups of multiple or plural deities. Take first the Penates, who, even at Rome, remained aniconic for a long time. The Penates of the city of Rome eventually took the form of two seated youths. But this definition was arbitrary, unrelated to the original Etruscan number and form of these superior deities, who were by nature unknowable. An arbitrary theological decision must have differentiated the Penates into four classes—the sky, the earth, the waters, and human souls (Nigidius Figulus in Arnobius, *Adv. nat.* 3.40)—and thus their internal order began to be established. The Penates who govern human souls are related to the *di animales* and are thus very different from the other three categories. They must have resulted from a relatively late elaboration of the order (see chapter 4), and are typical of the Roman adaptation called the *interpretatio latina*. The primitive Penates, like the unnamed Etruscan divinities, were probably divine beings of an undefined number, without images and without names, but they had a cult and were thus less distant from mortal concerns. When Varro identifies the *di consentes* with the Penates, he is imposing one of the first of the simplifications that occurred during this time in Roman religion as it came in contact with a foreign and aniconic divine structure.

The Lares are no less surprising, although Roman iconography, in order to fit them for the familiar life of roads and crossroads, shaped them as youthful figures always

## The Divine

in movement. Some scholars believe that Maris, that multiple child, was the prototype of the Lares. We know of a Maris Turms, probably a son of the messenger god, who is himself multiple. At Rome, Mercury was regarded as the father of the Lares (Ovid, *Fast.* 2.583), so this connection may be justified. This fabric of uncertainties reveals only one constant: the Lares were initially juvenile and plural deities. Their name is securely of Etruscan origin, and some legends attribute to them the supernatural conception of Servius Tullius/Macstrna.

In Rome, the Manes were the souls of the dead. They seem to be closely related to the *di animales*[2] and, for that reason, to come from the Etruscan divine world. Not individualized and hence not named, aniconic, and only worshipped collectively, they form another of its undifferentiated groups.

The *Aiser* or *Eiser*, on the other hand, appear in the rituals of the *liber linteus* and the Magliano lead tablet, where their sacrifices and rites are very precisely indicated.[3] It is prescribed to invoke them (*nunthen*), and to offer them boiled meat (*fasei*) and gifts (*turce*). An inscription from Venetia associates some *Aiser* with Tinia.[4] Other inscriptions mention the *Aiseras Thuflthicla* or simply *Thufltas*. This plural adjective, in which one finds the root *Thu* ("one"), may mean "united." These gods, always designated by a plural, do not have any visible or material existence. They are, as far as we know, incorporeal, and we do not know whether they are male or female,[5] or how many they are. Their name is collective and seems to be a plural. The inscription naming Tinia suggests that these deities are connected to gods that have an individualized identity. Are they counselors, like the *di consentes*? In an effort to be prudent and conservative, many Etruscologists translate *Aiser* as simply "the gods," even when the sense of "a group of gods" seems intended. Actually, it seems best not to translate *Aiser* at all, since they appear to be a sort of divine college formed of entities that are not individuated.

One must bear in mind the text of Herodotus (2.52) in which he speaks of the ancient gods of the Pelasges, who were closely related to the Etruscans:

> In ancient times, as I know from what I was told at Dodona, the Pelasgians offered sacrifices of all kinds, and prayed to "the gods," but without any distinction of name or title—for they had not yet heard of any such thing. They called the gods by the Greek word *theoi*—"disposers"—because they had "disposed" and arranged everything in due order, and assigned each thing to its proper division. Long afterwards the names of the gods were brought into Greece from Egypt and the Pelasgians learnt them—with the exception of Dionysus, about whom they knew nothing until much later.[6]

The gist of this overview is that a major part of the Etruscan divine world consists of groups that have functions, but are poorly defined, and thus are not depicted or named. Many of these group deities have no existence, body, or name as individual beings.

# The Divine

PLURAL DEITIES: LASA, VANTH, CHARU(N)

There are deities or genies, of a specific sex, who are variable in number and exist under a shared name. Because they are embodied, we have much more explicit information about them than we do about the nameless collegial gods described above: their forms are depicted in art and sometimes designated by precise epithets. The most famous are those collectively called Lasa,[7] a name that appears on the Piacenza liver. They are young and female, pretty and always elegant, rarely shown nude, usually elaborately clothed, bedecked in jewels, necklaces, bracelets, earrings, and often crowns. They accompany Turan. Sometimes they have wings. Their preferred attributes are the alabastron, containing perfume, and the *discerniculum*, a very delicate ivory stick that binds their hair and is used to draw out the perfumed cream. They are often depicted on mirrors, where they appropriately symbolize beauty.

Relatively rarely, Lasa can be distinguished by a surname: the adjectives *achununa* or *sitmica*, or adjectives that may refer to specific clans or functions, such as *vecuvia* (from *Vecu*, a clan name of Chiusi), *thimrae* (perhaps from the Apollonian epiklesis *thymbraios*), and *racuneta* ("of *Racune*"). Do these names define their function? Or are these female genies somehow attached to a single family, as these morphological similarities suggest? We also find Zipna, Munthuc, Achavisur (who is sometimes a young boy), Mean (who is often present at childbirths), and Alpan (who holds crowns). On a magnificent mirror in Saint Petersburg (see fig. 8.5), one Lasa, who is holding a cithara, is unfortunately the only figure without a name. Lasa appears in a surprisingly different context on a mirror in London (fig. 9.1), where she has abandoned the circle of Turan for the company of two heroes, Ajax (*Aivas*) and Am-

9.1. Lasa carrying a scroll inscribed with the names of the heroes Amphiarios and Aivas. Provenance unclear. Mid-fourth century. The British Museum.

## The Divine

phiaraos (*Hamphiare*). She holds a *volumen* inscribed with their names and hers. Did this figure result from a confusion between Lasa and Vanth, who often announces death by unrolling the book of fate? In any case, Lasa is not an individual but a plural deity; she is depicted as a collection of genies who are occasionally individuated. Comparing her to Greek nymphs sheds no light on her nature, which is essentially collective, plural, and not collegial.

Vanth seems to be of the same nature. We find multiple figures of Vanth depicted together, all guiding the dead. Almost every Vanth identified by a label (there is only one exception) carries a torch and illuminates the way.[8] All of them, either individually or in a group, are Vanth. Their supernatural quality is sometimes proclaimed by wings, and their chthonian character by serpents. Vanth's functions, discussed above (chapter 4), are assumed collectively. At the beginning of the second century, images of the Furies or Erinyes from Greece or southern Italy began to interfere with those of Vanth, as on the Talamone pediment or in a splendid bronze of Etruscan Campania (fig. 9.2). At that time her specific character as announcer of fate and guide of the dead became somewhat blurred, but not to the point that she turned into a goddess of justice.[9] The name Vanth always remained in the singular, evidence that her nature always remained plural.

Charu(n) too is a plural god or genie (see figs. 4.1, 4.2). Depicted at least eighteen

9.2. Fury or Vanth, a winged female genie holding serpents. From Etruscan Campania, the banks of the Volturno. Around 420. The British Museum.

## The Divine

times in the Tomb of the Cardinal at Tarquinia and very often two or three times on late-period sarcophagi and paintings, he usually carries the mallet as well as his other attributes as guide, doorman, and ferryman to the Afterworld. His name is sometimes modified by eloquent surnames. In the Tomb of the Charontes at Tarquinia, he appears as *Charun Huths* ("the fourth"), *Charun achrum(c)e* ("of Acheron"),[10] or *Charun chunchulis*. The name of the deity or genie Tuchulcha (which resembles *chunchulis* morphologically) is probably only an epithet of Charu(n). This psychopomp god is not a singular, but a plural entity, like Vanth or Lasa.

These three cases illustrate functioning divinities whose human form and sex are evident. They are deities of only secondary importance, but Hellenization did not modify them enough to hide their original plurality.

### DEITIES OF UNCERTAIN SEX

We poorly understand the gender of some nouns, and this is a serious handicap in identifying the sex of some deities who are known only through inscriptions:[11] for example, Letham. While our epigraphic sources are fragile, however, our figural sources are not. Let us immediately reject the alleged bisexuality of the statue from the Cannicella Sanctuary at Orvieto: she is without any doubt a female deity (see fig. 8.4). Let us also reject the alleged female gender of one aspect of Voltumna. His femininity is no different from that of Dionysus. On the other hand, Achavisur, sometimes called Achuvest or Achvistr, who was worshipped at Narce, can sometimes take the form of a charming young woman, sometimes that of a young man—not an Eros, but handsome and clearly adult. Some Greek heroes, such as Diomedes, can also become young women. This sort of indifference to a deity's sex is less frequent than has been claimed, and it is not easy to draw a conclusion from it. It may simply be the survival of a primitive concept of the divine as not having human form or sex.

### SEVERAL DEITIES, A SINGLE FUNCTION

We have observed the phenomenon of several gods governing a single functional domain (see chapter 8). The solar divinities, individualized enough to have their own cults even though their "division of labor" is otherwise undefined, are a particularly eloquent example. These gods seem to have flowed together out of various cults and regions and regrouped themselves around the same function without losing their original name and appearance.

This phenomenon is even more evident among the great female deities: Turan, Menrva, Uni, and others. They all have different aspects, their names come from different origins, their myths are borrowed from different Greek gods, but they are all *kourotrophes*, warrior goddesses, protectresses of infants, mistresses of cities, and, later, healers. When the Greeks tried to equate them with their own goddesses, as Herodotus did for the Egyptian deities, the Etruscans demurred or proposed various translations. These deities seem to have taken over the various functions of a

# The Divine

female deity who originally discharged all these duties. They did not divide these duties up judiciously among themselves, but indiscriminately took them all. They have names and cults born in Italy, images and legends born in Greece, but they all assume the same role: that of "the goddess," the female function in its totality.

### ONE DEITY WITH SEVERAL NAMES

We have shown that Etruscan gods often had two names, one by which they were worshipped, and another by which they revealed their history and lived their myths. We have suggested that some even had a third name that was haruspical—that is, linked to divination. Some actually acquired even more when the Etruscan deity added the Greek name, and the local deity added the name by which all Etruria worshipped him. Tinia and Voltumna are in this last category, as are Calu and Aita, Fufluns and Pacha, and perhaps Catha and Usil.

In addition to several names, these gods also had several faces: Tinia is adult and Voltumna is juvenile; Calu has no human form, but Aita is the very image of Hades. These multiple names and images suggest that the gods derived from a divine entity that was both protean and aniconic, both of changeable form and formless.

### SEVERAL GODS WITH A SINGLE NAME

The ultimate oddity is that sometimes two gods function under the same name. *Turms* designates the messenger of Tinia, but the same name, attached to that of Aita (*Turmś Aitaś*) designates the envoy of the god of the dead. Tinia is certainly the sky god *par excellence*, but the name *Tinia Calusna* may designate his chthonic function as a "Tinia of the Underworld." Maris appears to be the son (or sons) of Turan and Laran, but there was also a *Maris Turms*, a *Maris Hercles*, and a *Maris Tiusta*. It has been hypothesized that Maris was a formless being reduced to a kind of symbol, a *genius*. Why then would Turan and Laran have three of them? Why would Maris have surnames almost as diverse as those of Lasa? Why would he be in the shadow of three other gods?

Several deities have the same name; several names designate the same deity; several gods clearly have the same function; the same function is performed by a whole series of physically differentiated gods with the same name—it seems that a germ of incoherence has slipped into what appeared to be a system and has rendered it absurd. We must look to the origins of Etruscan religion for a global explanation that takes into account all of these contradictions.

### THE PRIMITIVE DIVINE SPHERE: DIVINATION WITHOUT INTERLOCUTORS

The Etruscans' original concept of divinity was probably generalized, aniconic, and fairly confused. The surprising number of divine groups without names or images, the survival of collective entities such as the Lares and the Manes, the plurality of

## The Divine

Charu(n), Vanth, and Lasa, the duality of Thulute and the triple nature of Kiaiser (who is known only for that)[12]—all suggest that the Etruscans originally perceived their gods as vague and mysterious beings, as collective or plural divine powers. Was this a sort of primitive pantheon, a profusion of "spirits" associated with acts or objects?[13] We do not think so. But the nonindividualized nature of the divine beings may explain a number of strikingly original elements, the most important of which is divination.

When the Greek worshipper went to Delphi, he posed a question to the god: "Is it better and more profitable to cultivate the lands of Eleusis?" or "To which god should I sacrifice before leaving on a journey?" The Pythia responded, and the priests put her answer into meter. Invoked and interrogated, the god spoke. The oracles functioned to establish a relationship between a mortal and a god. The relationship consisted of a question and a response—in a sense, a conversation. Etruria did not know this method, so it had to turn to the god of Delphi when it needed a precise answer to a specific question (see chapter 8). Tages had merely transmitted a code for reading reality, a translation guide, an interpretive system that could be refined or made endlessly more complicated, but denied any direct contact with the gods (see chapter 1). The haruspex did not question the god. He observed reality: the liver of a victim, the horizon, lightning, the flight of birds. In real and ordinary things, he read the state of the world, the attitude of the divine sphere and of each god within it. This is divination by observation, not interrogation. The method is passive: initiative cannot come from a mortal; it must come from the gods. "Lightning occurs in order to express a meaning," said Seneca. The lightning-wielding gods sent signs; mortals did not ask for them. Man did not try to penetrate the divine world. The gods, by a kind of grace, allowed a Tages to emerge from a field in Tarquinia and reveal the rites. Who sent Tages, and whose message did he carry? Who asked him to come? A different mentality would have asked these questions. The undifferentiated nature of the original Etruscan divinities suits this form of divination, which is merely a supernatural reading of worldly appearances. There were no individual gods to interrogate.

Only a few fragments of Etruscan prayers are preserved, all from the *liber linteus*. They are associated with prescriptions for offerings and sacrifices, specifically to the *Aiser*, to Nethuns, Tinia, Uni, Letham, Thesan, or Culsu. Their content is not exactly known, but the organization of their repetitive elements reveals a consistency in the way the Etruscans approached the divine (see chapter 7). Like the dedicatory inscriptions on private ex-votos, these prayers never precisely mention the worshippers' requests. There is no listing of earlier blessings, so characteristic of Greek prayers, nor are there requests expressed in terms of *quid pro quo*, at least in the preserved examples. The distance between the worshipper and the god seems much greater in Etruscan than in Greek practice. Would this not be a result of the Etruscan gods' originally undifferentiated nature?

# The Divine

INDIVIDUATION, ANTHROPOMORPHISM, HELLENIZATION

Did the crystallization of the gods into individual entities arise from a local religious need or from a Greek "theological" model inspired by imported images and myths? The first anthropomorphic images of gods reached Etruria from the Near East in the second half of the eighth century, and increased with Orientalizing imports from Greece. From that time on, some Etruscan deities seem to have had an individualized existence. It is difficult to determine when the most significant gods took individual form, but the concept seems to have preceded the importation of their images. M. Pallottino has suggested that Tinia was the first to emerge as a discrete deity.[14] There is no proof of this, nor is there anything to suggest a date. On the other hand, several factors indicate that Tinia had a very ancient origin and must have been differentiated very early: his chthonic dimension, which is much more extensive than that of Zeus, the extreme importance of lightning in Etruscan religion, and his double aspect as both juvenile and adult. In fact, the more contradictory the characteristics of an Etruscan god, the more likely it is that his or her formation as an individual deity was ancient. These gods seem to have integrated scattered elements into their being, before there was a need to separate and categorize. That need, which resulted from contact with Archaic Greek thought, probably arose late, when the names of the gods were already defined.

It is not possible to offer a solid chronology, but we may posit several stages in the formation of Etruscan divinity.

Departing from a divine world where functions were performed collectively by groups of divinities with poorly defined attributes, a first movement toward individuation occurred toward the end of the Villanovan period, when several deities of clearly defined sex made their appearance. The first of these was probably Tinia (but was his name also fixed?), who was the god primarily of lightning, but also of vegetation. Then came a deity with very broad female functions, as mother, nurse, lover, and perhaps also protectress of the dead. Finally, there emerged a solar deity who was probably still sexually undefined.

The second step was partial anthropomorphism. This stage of development seems to coincide with the arrival of the first Orientalizing images and the establishment of Greek cults on the coast. It also seems linked to the formation of cities.[15] Probably at this time as well the female deities became differentiated, and some sanctuaries were attributed to specific gods. The High Archaic goddess now took on her warrior aspect, no doubt borrowed from Athena, whose closest equivalent, Menrva, shared it with two other goddesses, Uni and Turan. The first non-Etruscan names intruded from Greek or the Italic languages. These diversified the pantheon while it was being formed. At this time, too, local heroes were slowly transformed into Greek-like gods. These included Hercle and Laran, influenced by Heracles and Ares. Parallel to this, some of Tinia's functions—as the superior power on sea or among the dead—which

The Divine

in Greece belonged to other gods, were partially detached and assigned to Nethuns or Calu, who was not yet equated with Aita. This was also the time when images of hybrid creatures from Asia began to appear in funerary iconography. These came to populate and characterize that intermediary space in the world of the dead where Virgil would later place them.

The emergence of individual gods must be linked to the formulation of the *etrusca disciplina*, and specifically the haruspical division of the world. The Etruscans' theological concept of the universe (or of its microcosm, a victim's liver) implies four major sectors, which at this time may not yet have been definitively subdivided into sixteen "dwellings." The rational ordering of this system must have taken place toward the end of the seventh century, as the formation of individual gods was being completed and they were beginning to take human form. The orientation of religious and funerary buildings of this period unmistakably reveals the traces of this concept of the universe, and marks the degree to which the individual gods have been defined.

The evolution of Etruscan concepts of the divine in the seventh century reveals two contrasting images. One is an undifferentiated stratum of primitive groups and entities that remains perceptible up to the last centuries of Tuscan culture; the other is an emerging "pantheon," organized not by genealogy, but by division into sectors according to divine function.

The final stage was Hellenization, which occurred in two very different phases. The first, in the Late Archaic period, involved the assembling of the great texts and the reworking of Greek myths to fit local use. This is the period when Artumes and the Dioscuri appeared, when epic stories were illustrated in Etruscan art, sometimes even earlier than in Greece itself. It is the time when variants of myths were adopted or created to meet specific local religious needs. The iconographic and literary repertoire from Greece and Magna Graecia was a strong force in defining Etruscan religion. At this time the gods' individual characters became definitively fixed. But the world of plural divinities continued its parallel existence, and permanently affected the appearance and sometimes the Hellenized names of the individualized gods.

The second phase of Hellenization was more cultural than religious (see chapter 8). In the mid-fourth century, Greek myths and legends, worship practices, and iconographic models spread at a such pace that Etruscan religion began to resemble all its neighbors superficially. Tinia took on Olympian Zeus's traits, which the coroplasts of Orvieto reproduced in the sanctuary of San Leonardo (see fig. 8.8). On engraved cistae and sarcophagi depicting the voyage to the Isles of the Blessed, the marine *thiasoi* are thoroughly Hellenized[16] yet nonetheless evoke very ancient and genuine native beliefs. In the large painted tombs, megalographies selectively borrowed from southern Italy illustrate gods very differently than their earliest images,[17] and scenes of the Afterworld sometimes adopt the colors of the Greek Hades.[18] Etruscan artists borrowed material from southern Italian, Pergamene, and Asian

## The Divine

Hellenistic iconography, and from it they developed mythical themes eschatological or political implications were often quite distant from those of their origins. The myths of Actaeon or Amphiarios illustrate a link to a religious substratum that had never been forgotten. The dogs that devour Actaeon recall Calu, who in more Hellenized contexts has yielded to Aita. The earth that opens beneath Amphiarios' chariot lets out a troop of anonymous subterranean deities who evoke the plural divine sphere. Masked as Furies or Greek-looking genies are envoys from a divine world that is anachronistic and yet alive. Dionysiac myths took on a political connotation in Etruria, but the Etruscan sanctuaries of the Naxian god continued to celebrate the rites of Fufluns.

Having embraced the cause of Marius and been forced into exile in Africa, the Etruscans of Volterra or Chiusi continued to perform the sacrificial customs of ancient Etruria, around chthonian altars identical to those of their distant homeland, but on the banks of a Tunisian wadi. In the first century B.C., another exile reached Egypt and lived and died on the Nile delta. As a mark of his identity he had brought with him a *liber linteus,* the only ritual book that has, via Zagreb, come down to us. Integrated into the life of the Hellenistic Mediterranean, the Etruscans of the second and first centuries B.C. adopted not only the forms of the dominant culture, but also the stories and images that conveyed it. They reused these to transcribe a religion that remained profoundly original.

The Etruscan divine world was a surprising mixture of archaisms and borrowings, of Greek relations and local heritage. It contrasted so strongly with the official Roman religion that the Etruscan gods worshipped in the city of Rome had only a distant connection with those worshipped in the cities of Etruria. Rome had "called forth" the goddess from Veii, but once she was at Rome she was no longer Uni but Juno; and Voltumna, in the Vicus Tuscus, was no longer the *deus Etruriae princeps,* but the god of the small farmer. What the Romans revered in Etruscan religion was not their gods, too contradictory in their view, but the *disciplina,* which nonetheless was indissolubly linked with the world of the gods.

# Conclusion

Etruria was conquered city by city. One by one, the Etruscan city-states were bound to Rome by treaties. The whole of Italy finally acceded to Roman citizenship, and the political existence of the Tyrrhenians ceased. The fate of the people was fixed. When the last of its ten allotted *saecula* had turned, the history of Etruria ended. The use of the language slowly died, too, and by the second century A.C., few could still read the sacred books. The emperor Claudius resurrected the college of the sixty haruspices with an obvious political goal. This act did, however, allow one of the major functions of Etruscan religion to survive, that function which, once the Etruscan gods had been assimilated into the official Roman religion and the festal calendars integrated into those of the state, remained unique and original: the *etrusca disciplina*.

This system was perceived as odd and unusual. We have seen that the gods of Etruria emerged only after complex reworkings and multiple contaminations. They lost their appeal at the same time as the other pagan gods, when a new personal spirituality, born from anguish in the face of death, nourished by unanswerable philosophical questions on the nature of man's being and becoming, reached the cultivated classes of the Roman world. But on three essential points Etruscan religion brought new elements to the old Roman paganism.

At the foot of the famous statue of Augustus of the Prima Porta is a small naked child—perhaps his *genius*. This bit of divinity, through whom the emperor received a cult, does not merely arise out of philosophical speculation. The idea that every person is accompanied by a small divine being to advise or protect him, a being who is a part of his nature yet belongs to the divine sphere, does not derive only from Stoic doctrines; it is also rooted in a long Etruscan tradition. The Lasa, who bears an individual proper name and is attached to a person, is at the core of this concept of an accompanying divine presence. Lasa is not really a *genius* or a *daimon*. In fact she arose even earlier, and helped prepare the ground for these later beliefs. In her form, Lasa, along with the *erotes*, later served as the models for angels, who owe much to these *genii*. The idea that each person has a bit of divinity at his or her side is evidence of a tired paganism tending toward a vague monotheism.

# Conclusion

But Etruscan divination, unique in the Classical Mediterranean, did not undergo the same type of degradation as the rest of the traditional religion. This divination had nothing to do with the gods of the pantheon, whom no one believed in any more and who served only as a pretext for civic rites. Based on a topographic organization of divine functions, it was born and gradually defined without mythology. The independence of haruspical divination from gods accounts for its survival in a world where paganism could be maintained only on a cultural or political level.[1]

Moreover, it had derived from a supernatural revelation, and late antiquity, this troubled age that welcomed the revelations of Hermes Trismegistos, could not scorn the message of Tages. As a prophet born from the soil of Italy, Tages appealed to the western Roman world. An African priest, Longinianus, confessed to Augustine the importance that he accorded to the pagan Tages, whom he regarded as comparable to Hermes Trismegistos and Orpheus, and much preferable to the prophets of Jerusalem.

The most important question posed by late antiquity concerned the nature of humanity and the possibility of life after death. Neither Roman nor even Greek religion offered answers. Hades and Orcus were literary themes, not objects of hope or fear. It is presumptuous to prejudge the content of the *libri acheruntici,* but it is certain that the Etruscan depictions, both troubling and reassuring, of a journey toward the Afterworld were very different from the much vaguer images that traditional paganism offered. The concept of a quasi-divine afterlife, as explained in the *libri acheruntici,* and the belief that the *di animales* could ritually attain immortality were reassuring and seductive. The Orphics and the sect of Mithras also proposed this, although they did not promise anything else. At least the hopes that the Etruscan rites offered had one advantage over those of their competitors: they were born in Italy and could not be accused of being foreign superstitions.

It is surprising that in 410 A.C. the Roman haruspices could have approached the pope with a proposal to unleash a barrage of lightning on Alaric's approaching Visigoths. The pontiff's refusal clearly marks the end of their importance. Etruscan religion had joined the camp of fallen gods and forgotten rites. The little bronze statuettes and the figures in painted tombs from that time on merely served the artists of the Christian world as models for their demons.

But even as late as the nineteenth century, despite the power of the Catholic Church, one could still hear in the remote hills of Tuscany the magical chant of the wine grower:[2]

Faflon, Faflon, Faflon!
A vuoi mi raccomando!
Che l'uva nella mia vigna
E multa scarsa
A vuoi mi raccomando,
Che mi fate avere
Buona vendemmia!

## Conclusion

Faflon, Faflon, Faflon!
A vuoi mi raccomando!
Che il vino nella mia cantina
Me lo fate venire fondante,
E molto buono,
Faflon, Faflon, Faflon!

[Faflon, Faflon, Faflon!
Oh, listen to my prayer.
I have a scanty vintage,
My vines this year are bare;
Oh, listen to my prayer!
And put, since thou canst do so,
A better vintage there!

Faflon, Faflon, Faflon!
Oh, listen to my prayer.
May all the wine in my cellar
Prove to be strong and rare
And good as any grown,
Faflon, Faflon, Faflon!]

The Etruscan Fufluns was surely unknown, but the wine god's hidden presence was still alive in the rural mind.

Notes
Thematic Bibliography
Glossary
Index
Illustration Credits

# Notes

## PREFACE

1. A. J. Pfiffig, *Religio Etrusca* (Graz 1975).
2. See the publication of the 1992 colloquium on the Etruscans and religion: *Les Étrusques, les plus religieux des hommes* (Paris 1997), hereafter *LPRH*.
3. D. Briquel, "La religion des anciens toscans," in *Religions de l'Antiquité* (Paris 1999) 7–78; D. Briquel, *Le regard des autres* (Besançon 1997); D. Briquel, *Les Étrusques, peuple de la différence* (Paris 1993); J.-P. Thuillier, *Les Étrusques, la fin d'un mystère* (Paris 1990); J.-R. Jannot, *A la rencontre des Étrusques* (Rennes 1987); I. Krauskopf, *Todesdämonen und Totengötter im vorhellenistischen Etrurien* (Florence 1987); L. Bonfante, ed., *Etruscan Life and Afterlife* (Detroit 1986); entries by I. Krauskopf, M. Cristofani, and A. Maggiani in M. Cristofani, ed., *Dizionario della civiltà etrusca* (Florence 1985); entries by A. Maggiani and E. Simon in M. Cristofani, ed., *Gli Etruschi, una nuova immagine* (Florence 1984).
4. G. Dumézil, *La religion romaine archaïque* (Paris 1966), appendix, 593–660.

## CHAPTER 1. THE *ETRUSCA DISCIPLINA*

1. The remaining fragments of these texts have been published by C. O. Thulin, *Die etruskische Disciplin*, 2 vols. (Göteborg 1905–9).
2. T. J. Cornell, "The Tyranny of Evidence," *JRA* Suppl. ser. 3 (Ann Arbor 1991) 26–32.
3. Cicero, *De div.* 2.23; Ovid, *Met.* 15.553; and the later writers: Censorinus, *DN* 4.13; Festus, *Gloss. Lat.* s.v. Tages.
4. Tradition transmitted by John Lydos.
5. Ordo LX haruspicum: M. Torelli, *Elogia Tarquiniensia* (Florence 1975).
6. M. Pallottino, "Deorum sedes," *Saggi di Antichità* (Rome 1979) 2: 679–709; M. Cristofani, "Sul rinvenimento dell'Arringatore," *Prospettiva* (1987) 464–68.
7. J. Heurgon, "The Date of the Vegoian Prophecy," *JRS* 41 (1959).
8. D. Briquel, *Le regard des autres* (Besançon 1997) 101; J. P. Small, *Cacus and Marsyas in Etrusco-Roman Legend* (Princeton 1982).
9. *CIE* 5430; J. Heurgon, "Influences grecques sur la religion latine," *REL* 35 (1957) 106–26.
10. Listed in Thulin, *Etruskische Disciplin*, 2 vols. (Göteborg 1905–9).
11. There is some dispute about which Caecina Cicero defended. B. Frier, *The Rise of the Roman Jurists* (Princeton 1985) 18, believes it was the father.
12. Cited in D. Briquel, *Chrétiens et haruspices* (Paris 1997).
13. Tarquinia, Tomba del Biclinio, *kline* D, cf. Byres, IV, pl. 8; Steingräber, *Catalogo ragionato della pittura etrusca* (Milan 1984) 294.
14. All three are illustrated in F. Roncalli, *Scrivere etrusco* (Milan 1985) 23.
15. From the Tomb of the Sarcophagi of Caere, Vatican, Mus. Greg. Etrusco, inv. no. 14949.
16. M. Cristofani, *Tabula Capuana* (Florence 1995) 69.
17. Other elements appear in Martianus Capella, Seneca (*QNat.*), and Cicero (*De div.* 2.42).

18. F. Prayon, "Deorum sedes," *ArchCl* 43 (1991) 1285–95; idem, "Sur l'orientation des édifices cultuels," *LPRH*, 357–73.

19. Heurgon, "The Date of Vegoia's Prophecy," *JRS* 49 (1959) 41–45.

20. H. Lachmann, *Gromatici veteres*, 1.359; J. Heurgon, *Daily Life of the Etruscans* (London 1964) 231.

21. From the corpus of the *gromatici*, Lachmann, *Gromatici veteres*, 1.350.

22. On a cippus from Pozzarello (Bolsena) *TLE* 900.

23. Berlin, Antiquarium, c. 310. See Bonfante and Bonfante, *The Etruscan Language*, second ed. (Manchester 2002) source 38.

24. Catalogue, *La Chimera e il suo mito* (Arezzo 1990).

25. F. Coarelli, "Le pitture della Tomba François, une proposta di lettura," *DialArch* 3 (1983) 43–69.

26. Briquel, *Le regard des autres*, 102ff.

27. Nigidius Figulus, *Brontoscopic Calendar*, in Arnobius, *Adv. nat.* 3.40. This has recently been translated by J. M. Turfa, in N. de Grummond and E. Simon, eds., *The Religion of the Etruscans* (forthcoming from University of Texas Press), appendix A.

## CHAPTER 2. RITES OF DIVINATION

1. A. Maggiani, "Le iscrizioni di Asciano e il problema del cosidetto 'M cortonese'," *StEtr* 50 (1982) 53–88; L. B. Van der Meer, *The Bronze Liver of Piacenza* (Amsterdam 1987).

2. Catalogue, *Les Étrusques et l'Europe* (Paris 1992) 146, no. 196.

3. Cf. chapter 1, p. 12. Martianus Capella, *De nuptiis Mercurii et Philologiae* (ed. A. Dick, Leipzig 1925), the first part of an encyclopedia of the liberal arts; he devotes many pages to the theological description of the sky.

4. A. J. Pfiffig, *Religio Etrusca* (Graz 1975) 118–19.

5. G. Colonna, "A proposito degli dei del fegato di Piacenza," *StEtr* 59 (1993) 123ff.

6. Cicero, *De div.* 2.42; determination of the *templum:* Pliny the Elder, *HN* 2.143–44. Seneca, *QNat.* 2.

7. That is, having two rows of complete teeth, or having two teeth longer than the others: s.v. Lewis and Short, *A Latin Dictionary*. Alternatively, the term may refer to the fact that lightning is forked.

8. Examples: "April 3. If it thunders, it signifies profit out of a grain supply brought from abroad." "June 2. If haply it should thunder, women in labor will have an easy delivery, there will be a loss of domestic animals by death, there will be an abundance of fish." "October 21. If it thunders, there will be a coughing sickness and oppression of the heart." Translations by J. M. Turfa, in N. de Grummond and E. Simon, eds., *The Religion of the Etruscans* (forthcoming from University of Texas Press), appendix A.

9. D. and R. Rebuffat, *Latomus* 37 (1978) 88ff.

10. Diminutive of Arnth ("little Arnth").

11. C. Thulin, *Die etruskische Disciplin* (Göteborg 1905–9), vol. 2, 89.

12. Dated to the second century B.C. A. Maggiani, "La divination oraculaire en Étrurie," *Caesarodunum* Suppl. 56 (1986) 26–41.

13. Ibid. 17.

14. M. Pallottino, "Uno specchio di Tuscania e la legenda etrusca di Tarchon," *RendLinc*, ser. 6, vol. 6, fasc. 3–4 (1930) 49–87.

15. Cf. H. Brunn and G. Körte, *I rilievi delle urne etrusche* (Berlin 1870–1916), vol. 2, pl. CXIX.

16. G. Colonna, "Apollon, les Étrusques et Lipara," *MEFRA* 94 (1984) 557ff.

CHAPTER 3. SACRIFICIAL AND FUNERARY RITES

1. These books are discussed previously in chapter 2, under "Omens."

2. H. Rix, *Etruskische Texte* (Tübingen 1991) 1–8 (hereafter *ET*). For the latest bibliography about the Zagreb *liber linteus:* F. Roncalli, ed., *Scrivere etrusco,* catalogue of the exposition (Milan 1985) 88.

3. H. Rix, "Les prières du Liber Linteus de Zagreb," *LPRH,* 391–98.

4. M. Cristofani, *Tabula Capuana* (Florence 1995) 69; A. J. Pfiffig, *Religio Etrusca* (Graz 1975): s.v. *litatio;* Roncalli, *Scrivere etrusco,* 51: s.v. libation.

5. Vatican, Mus. Greg. Etrusco, inv. no. 14949. F. Roncalli, "Osservazioni sui 'libri lintei' etruschi," *RendPontAcc* (1980) 51–52.

6. Berlin, St. Mus. SK 1261; *infra*, chapter 7, p. 126.

7. H. Blanck and G. Proietti, *La Tomba dei Rilievi di Cerveteri* (Rome 1986) 19, fig. 7.

8. Cristofani, *Tabula Capuana*.

9. Perugia, Mus. Arch. no. 634. J.-R. Jannot, *Les reliefs archaïques de Chiusi* (Rome 1984) D.I.14, figs. 519–24.

10. Paris, Louvre, CP 6626. F. Roncalli, *Le lastre dipinte di Cerveteri* (Florence 1965) pl. III.N.3.

11. Paris, Louvre, MA 3611. Jannot, *Reliefs*, B.I.5a, fig. 105.

12. Coin of Cortona, third century. On the obverse, a frontal head of a haruspex. D. Tripp, "Coinage" in L. Bonfante, ed., *Etruscan Life and Afterlife* (Detroit 1986) 214, fig. VI-19.

13. F. Sokolowski, *Lois sacrées des cités grecques* (Paris 1969) 36ff.

14. Tuscania, Mus. Arch. Bonfante, *Etruscan Life and Afterlife*, 263, fig. VIII-42.

15. On Veiovis, see *infra*, chapter 8.

16. As it is depicted on the Revil Cista, London, British Mus.: Bordenache Battaglia, *Le Ciste Prenestine* (Rome 1979) 112ff. It takes place in front of a tomb on the sarcophagus of Torre San Severo (Orvieto): R. Herbig, *Die jüngetruskischen Steinsarkophagen* (Berlin 1952) N. 73, pl. 36. It occurs near a funeral column on the stamnos from Sovana: catalogue, *Artigianato artistico* (Milan 1985) 208ff.

17. Mirror: Florence, Mus. Arch. Naz. Here fig. 3.7. Relief: Vatican, Mus. Greg. Etrusco, inv. no. 12268. Amphora: Dresden, Skulpturensammlung, ZV 1635; catalogue, *Die Welt der Etrusker* (Berlin 1988) 151–52, B 5.33.

18. Berlin, St. Mus. 1226: Jannot, *Reliefs*, C.III.8, figs. 332–34. Palermo, Mus. Arch., unnumbered: Jannot, *Reliefs*, C.III.9. Urn from Chiusi, Mus. Naz. 2277: Jannot, *Reliefs*, C.I.37.

19. Brit. Mus. Cat. vases B 64: N. Spivey, *The Micali Painter and His Followers* (Oxford 1987) no. 102, pl. 18.

20. L. B. Van der Meer, *Italian Iron Age Artefacts* (London 1986) 439; Spivey, *The Micali Painter,* 19. J.-P. Thuillier, *Les jeux athlétiques dans la civilisation étrusque* (Rome 1985) 148–49.

21. F. Prayon, "Sur l'orientation des édifices cultuels," *LPRH,* 357–73.

22. Principally Varro, *Ling.* 5.143; Festus, s.v. *Rituales*.

23. Aquileia, Mus. Arch. Naz. inv. 1171.
24. Rome, Mus. Villa Giulia, inv. 24562: M. Cristofani, *I bronzi degli Etruschi* (Novara 1985) 140.
25. I. Edlund-Berry, "Ritual Destruction of Cities and Sanctuaries," in R. D. De Puma and J. P. Small, eds., *Murlo and the Etruscans* (Madison 1994).
26. F.-H. Massa-Pairault and J.-M. Pailler, *Bolsena* 5.1 (Rome 1979).
27. D. Kurtz and J. Boardman, *Greek Burial Customs* (London 1982).
28. S. Stopponi, *La Tomba della Scrofa Nera* (Rome 1983).
29. J.-R. Jannot, "A propos de la tombe du lit funèbre," *Studia Tarquiniensia* (Rome 1988) 53–68, pls. 8–12.
30. Sarcophagus of Ramtha Visnai, Boston, Mus. of Fine Arts, inv. no. 1975–799.
31. Thuillier, *Les jeux athlétiques*.
32. J.-R. Jannot, "Phersu, Phersuna, Personna," in *Spectacles sportifs et scéniques* (Rome 1991) 281–320.
33. J.-P. Thuillier, "Une base di Chiusi avec représentation de jeux funéraires," *RA* 2 (1997) 243–60.
34. Rome, Mus. Villa Giulia. Around the middle of the third century. M. Falconi Amorelli, *Vulci, Scavi Bendinelli* (Rome 1983) 13.
35. J.-R. Jannot, "Sur les fausses portes étrusques," *Latomus* 43.2 (1984) 273–83.
36. E. Colonna di Paolo, *Necropoli rupestre del Viterbese* (Novara 1978).
37. F. de Polignac, *La naissance de la cité grecque* (Paris 1984) passim.
38. P. Zamarchi Grassi, "La sezione topografica: Il Melone II del Sodo," in *Il Museo dell'Accademia Etrusca di Cortona* (Cortona 1996) 95–112; idem, "Un edificio per il culto funerario: Nuovi dati sul tumulo II del Sodo a Cortona," *RdA* 22 (1998) 19–26; idem, *La Cortona dei Principes* (Cortona 1992) 128; *Cortona Etrusca: Esempi di architettura funeraria* (Cortona 1999).
39. G. Paolucci, "La diffusione dei tumuli nell'area chiusina e l'errata provenienza della seconda pisside della Pania," in P. Gastaldi, ed., *Studi su Chiusi arcaica*, *AION* 5 (1998) 22.

CHAPTER 4. THE AFTERWORLD

1. D. Briquel, "Regards étrusques sur l'Au-delà," in *La mort, les morts et l'Au-delà* (Caen 1987) 263ff.
2. G. Colonna, "Note di lessico etrusco," *StEtr* 48 (1980) 161–79.
3. M. Cristofani, "Ricerche sulle pitture della Tomba François di Vulci," *DialArch* 1 (1967) 186.
4. Volsinies, *TLE*, 330.
5. G. Colonna, "Farthan, huze, hinthial," *StEtr* 48 (1980) 143ff.
6. E. Gerhard and G. Körte, *Etruskische Spiegel* 2 (Berlin 1870) no. 213.
7. A. J. Pfiffig, *Religio Etrusca* (Graz 1975) 163; Colonna, "Farthan, huze, hinthial," 174ff.
8. H. Hencken, *Tarquinia, Villanovans, and Early Etruscans* (Cambridge, Mass., 1968).
9. Ibid., 34, fig. 6; G. Bartoloni, F. Buranelli, V. d'Atri, and S. de Santis, *Le urne a capanna rinvenute in Italia* (Rome 1987) fig. 106c; J.-R. Jannot, "Rites villanoviens et rites étrusques, quelques continuités," *StEtr* (2002) 4–12.
10. F. Prayon, *Frühetruskische Grab- und Hausarchitektur* (Heidelberg 1975); idem, "Architecture" in L. Bonfante, ed., *Etruscan Life and Afterlife* (Detroit 1986) 174ff.
11. Prayon, *Grab- und Hausarchitektur*, pl. 82, 2.

## Notes to pages 56–65

12. A. Naso, *Architetture dipinte* (Rome 1996).
13. Ibid. 417; J.-R. Jannot, "Sur les fausses portes étrusques," *Latomus* 43.2 (1984) 273–83; B. D'Agostino, "L'immagine, la pittura e la tomba," *Prospettiva* 32 (1983) 2–12.
14. J.-R. Jannot, "Sur la représentation étrusque des morts," in *La mort, les morts et l'Au-delà* (Caen 1987) 279 ff.
15. R. D. Gempeler, *Die Etruskische Kanopen* (Einsiedeln 1975).
16. L. Bonfante, *Etruscan Dress* (Baltimore 1975) 159ff.
17. As O. Brendel mistakenly thought: *Etruscan Art* (Harmondsworth 1978) 103ff.
18. Florence, Mus. Naz., Chianciano group; M. Cristofani, *Statue-cinerario chiusine* (Rome 1975) 34ff.; A. Rallo, ed., *Le donne in Etruria* (Rome 1989), pl. LXXX.
19. M. F. Briguet, *Le sarcophage des époux (Louvre)* (Florence 1989); M. Cristofani, "Reconstruction d'un mobilier funéraire archaïque de Cerveteri," *MonPiot* 63 (1980) 1–30. (Villa Giulia).
20. London, British Mus. 786; M. D. Gentili, *I sarcofagi etruschi in terracotta di età recente* (Rome 1994) 68. Most recently, S. Haynes, *Etruscan Civilization: A Cultural History* (Los Angeles 2000) figs. 266 a–c.
21. Florence, Mus. Arch. Naz. 70976; Gentili, *I sarcofagi etruschi*, 66, A.66.
22. Villa Giulia, around 550; A. Hus, *Recherches sur la statuaire* (Rome 1961). On seahorses: M. Boosen, *Etruskische Meermischwesen* (Rome 1986) 135ff.
23. Cups from Orvieto, Mus. Faina: M. Martelli, *La ceramica degli Etruschi: La pittura vascolare* (Novara 1987) nos. 107–8. "Pontic" amphora: B. Ginge, *Ceramiche etrusche a figure nere* (Rome 1987) 20, N.2.
24. F. Roncalli, "Iconographie funéraire et topographie de l'Au-delà en Etrurie," *LPRH*, 37ff.
25. End of the second century; Florence, Mus. Arch. Naz. 5514.
26. Second century; Chiusi, Mus. Naz. 860.
27. Tarquinia, Mus. Naz.; J.-R. Jannot, "Charu, Tuchulcha et les autres," *RM* 100 (1993) pl. VII, 3.
28. Tarquinia, Tomb of the Blue Demons. Cf. M. Cataldi Dini, "La Tomba dei Demoni Azzuri," in M. A. Rizzo, ed., *Pittura etrusca al Museo di Villa Giulia* (Rome 1989) 150–53.
29. Copenhagen, Ny Carlsberg Glyptotek; Jannot, " Charu, Tuchulcha et les autres," pl. XI, 2.
30. A drawing by Michelangelo, Casa Buonarotti, Florence, copies an Aita similar to that in the Tomb of Orcus.
31. F. Weege, *Etruskische Malerei* (Halle 1921) 31ff.; H. Blanck, in *Les Étrusques et l'Europe* (Paris 1992) 240ff.
32. Catalogue, *Artigianato artistico* (Milan 1985) 208ff.
33. *Cvl*, "door"; *Culsans*, "Janus"; cf. *infra*, chapter 8, 162. E. Simon, "Culsu, Culsans, und Ianus," in *2d Convegno Internazionale Etrusco*, 1271–81.
34. The *n* appears in only four inscriptions, all very late. The original name is *Charu*, and the final *n*, indicating a partial identification with the ferryman of the Styx, appears only under Greek influence.
35. In a newly discovered fourth-century painted tomb in Sarteano, a female demon, probably an innovative version of Charu(n), drives a swiftly-running quadriga, while a three-headed snake seems to guard the land of the dead. A symposium, set in the Afterworld as is that of the Golini Tomb in Orvieto, mingles the dead with the netherworld's rulers. A. Minetti, "New Tomb Discovered at Sarteano," *Etruscan News* 4 (Winter 2004) 5; and idem, *StEtr* (in press).
36. Jannot, "Charu, Tuchulcha et les autres."

37. Excellent copies: M. Moltesen and C. Weber-Lehmann, *Etruskische Grabmalerei* (Mainz 1992).

38. A new reading by G. Colonna and A. Morandi, "La gens titolare della tomba tarquinese dell'Orco," *StEtr* 61 (1995 [1996]) 95–102, which supersedes the interpretation of M. Torelli, *Elogia Tarquiniensia* (Florence 1975) 45ff.

39. F.-H. Massa-Pairault, "Religion étrusque et culture grecque," *LPRH*, 325ff.

40. M. Cataldi Dini, "La Tomba dei Demoni Azzuri," in *Tarquinia, Ricerche, scavi e prospettive* (Milan 1987) 37–42; idem, in Rizzo, *Pittura etrusca al Museo di Villa Giulia*, 150ff.

41. Arnobius, following Nigidius Figulus (3.40), confesses that he does not understand this himself!

42. Festus, 108; Briquel, "Regards étrusques sur l'Au-delà," 272.

43. P. Defosse, "Génie funéraire ravisseur (Calu) sur quelques urnes étrusques," *AntCl* 41 (1972) 487ff.; Perugia, Mus. Arch. Contra: E. Simon, "Sentiment religieux et vision de la mort," *LPRH* (Paris 1997) 449–58.

44. Volterra, Mus. Guarnacci 350.

45. E. Brunn and G. Körte, *I rilievi delle urne etrusche* (Berlin 1870) III.

46. *StEtr* 37 (1969) 334ff.; J.-R. Jannot, "Charu(n) et Vanth, divinités plurielles," *LPRH*, 139–66. G. Colonna on the same matter: "Divinités peu connues du panthéon étrusque," *LPRH*, 170–85.

47. *CVA*, Paris, Louvre, III, 1b, t. 1, 5–8. J.-R. Jannot, "Charun et Charôn," *CRAI* (1991) 443–64, and "Charu, Tuchulcha et les autres"; disputing these conclusions: Colonna, "Divinités peu connues du panthéon étrusque," 171, fig. 5.

CHAPTER 5. SANCTUARIES

1. *Selvans sanchuneta cvera* (*TLE* 900).
2. M. Torelli, "Veio," in *Mélanges T. Dohrn* (Rome 1982) 471ff.
3. Festus, 318 L: *loca dis sacrata sine tecto*.
4. Aulus Gellius, 7.12: *locus parvus, deo sacrato, cum ara*.
5. I. Edlund, *The Gods and the Place* (Stockholm 1987).
6. A. Andrén, *Archaeological Terracottas from Etrusco-Italic Temples* (Lund 1939); Catalogue, *Santuari d'Etruria* (Milan 1985) 67ff.
7. Torelli, "Veio," 471.
8. The *evocatio* is mentioned here for the first time.
9. But an electrical resistivity survey has revealed another, not yet published; this temple seems, from an inscription, to have been dedicated to Tinia.
10. P. Romanelli, "Tarquinia," *NSc* (1948) 238–68.
11. M. Bonghi Jovino, "La phase archaïque de l'Ara della Regina," *LPRH*, 69–97.
12. Torelli, "Veio."
13. A. J. Pfiffig, *Religio Etrusca* (Graz 1995) 75.
14. *CIL* 4920 and *CIE* 4919.
15. On these divine appellations consisting of a god's name followed by a function name, see C. De Simone, *LPRH*, 185ff., who distinguishes them from double (binary) names.
16. A. Maggiani and E. Simon, "Il pensiero scientifico e religioso," in M. Cristofani, ed., *Gli Etruschi, una nuova immagine* (Florence 1984) 143; *infra*, chapter 8.

17. Inscription from Cortona: Rix, *ET*, 8.1; G. Colonna, *Santuari d'Etruria* (Milan 1985) 172.

18. M. Cristofani, "La Venere della Cannicella," Convegno Orvieto 1984, *AnnFaina* 3 (1987) 27–39.

19. As its discoverer, R. Mancini, believed.

20. Most of the Cerveteri tumuli, the famous "meloni" of Sodo, and obviously the funeral buildings of Blera, San Giovenale, San Giuliano, etc.

21. L. Banti, *Il mondo degli Etruschi* (Rome 1969) 227ff. Cf. most recently, E. Pacciani and F. Sonego, "La tomba dell'iscrizione," *AION* 5 (Naples 1998) 103ff.

22. G. Colonna, "Strutture treatriforme in Etruria," in *Spectacles sportifs et scéniques* (Rome 1993) 331.

23. J.-R. Jannot, "Deux édifices clusiens," *MEFRA* 86 (1974) 723–44.

24. To be performed by one or two family members: M. Cristofani, *Tabula Capuana* (Florence 1995) 22.

25. De Simone, *LPRH*, 185ff.

26. M. Cristofani, *I bronzi degli Etruschi* (Novara 1985) 127, 128; F. Buranelli, *Bronzi a figura umana* (Vatican City 1999) 110ff.

27. Catalogue, *Santuari d'Etruria* (Milan 1985)174; A. Maggiani, in *La chimera e il suo mito* (Arezzo 1990) 51ff.

28. On the sanctuary of Sillene: G. Paolucci, *Il territorio di Chianciano Terme: Dalla preistoria al medioevo* (Rome 1988) 58. Another is found on the site appropriately named Acquasanta, another at Casa del Savio, in a comparable location. All these sanctuaries are situated on a thermal spring. Cf. F. Prayon, "Wasserkulte in Etrurien," in *Die Welt der Etrusker* (Berlin 1988) 77–79.

29. Another lunar crescent comparable to the one from Sillene probably comes from Acquasanta. It is dedicated to "Tiur of Cathuna"—i.e., more or less linked to Catha. Cf. *infra*, chapter 8.

30. M. Cristofani, *Città e campagna nell'Etruria settentrionale* (Arezzo 1976) 128.

31. A. Rastrelli, "L'edificio sacro di Fucoli," in *La civiltà di Chiusi e del suo territorio* (Florence 1993) 463–76.

32. F.-H. Massa-Pairault, *La cité des Étrusques* (Paris 1996) 228.

33. Rastrelli, "L'edificio sacro di Fucoli," 272.

34. Massa-Pairault, *La cité des Étrusques*, 228.

35. G. Colonna, ed., *Il santuario di Portonaccio a Veio, 1: Gli scavi di Massimo Pallottino nella zona dell'altare (1939–1940)* (Rome 2002).

36. Stepped enclosure surrounding a circular altar; S. Steingräber, "Le culte des morts et les monuments de pierre étrusques," *LPRH*, 97–117.

37. Edlund, *The Gods and the Place*, 59; M. Cristofani, *Gli Etruschi in Maremma* (Milan 1981) 91–92; G. Jones, "Capena and ager Capenas," *BSR* 31 (1963) 100ff.

38. Dante, *Purgatorio* I.14.17: *un fiumicel che nasce in Falterona*, "a little river that rises in Falterona."

39. A. Fortuna and F. Giovannoni, *Il Lago degli Idoli* (Florence 1975).

40. P. Zazoff, *Etruskische Skarabäen* (Mainz 1968) pl. 33.

41. S. Steingräber, *Pittura etrusca* (Milan, Tokyo 1984) 51.

42. A. Romualdi, *Catalogo del deposito di Brolio* (Rome 1981).

43. G. Colonna, "Divinazione e culto di Rath/Apollo," *StEtr* 62.2 (2001) 151–73.

44. G. Colonna, "Divinités peu connues du panthéon étrusque," *LPRH*, 178.

45. Colloquium, *Die Göttin von Pyrgi* (Tübingen 1979).

46. A. Morandi, *Nuovi lineamenti di Lingua Etrusca* (Rome 1991) 125ff.; Morandi's date, in our opinion, is too low.

47. Only the Phoenician Punic text can be translated: "To the Lady Astarte this is the holy place which has made and given Tiberie Vel(ia)nas ruler over Kisry—in the month of the sacrifice of the Sun as a gift in the temple and because Astarte has supported him by her hand[?] in the third year of his reign in the month of Karar on the day of the burying of the god—and [may] the years of the statue of the goddess in her temple be as many as these stars" (translation quoted by J. M. Turfa in L. Bonfante, ed., *Etruscan Life and Afterlife* [Detroit 1986]).

48. Lucilius writes of the *scorta pyrgensia* ("the debauchery of Pyrgi"), and Servius, *Ad Aen.* 10.184, alludes to the same tradition: but is this sufficient evidence and a correct interpretation?

49. M. Torelli, "Il santuario greco di Gravisca," *PP* 32 (1977) 398–458.

50. M. Torelli, "Les Adonies de Gravisca, archéologie d'une fête," *LPRH*, 233–93. The evidence is very slender: a stone case and a small coral piece. There are no inscriptions or allusions in the ancient authors.

51. M. Torelli, "Per la definizione del commercio greco-orientale, il caso di Gravisca," *PP* 37 (1982) 304–25.

52. E. H. Richardson, "An Archeological Introduction to the Etruscan Language," in Bonfante, *Etruscan Life and Afterlife*, 218, fig. VII-3.

53. Torelli, "Les Adonies de Gravisca," 233ff. Even in Greece, this type of sanctuary is exceptional.

54. Pfiffig, *Religio Etrusca*, 69–70.

55. *CIL* XI.5265: the so-called *Spello rescript*.

56. *TLE* 87, 99, 137, 233.

57. The interpretation of the excavators S. Stopponi and C. Bizzarri, "Excavations at the Campo della Fiera (Orvieto)," *Etruscan News* 2 (2003) 3–4.

58. G. Colonna, *Siena, le origini* (exhibition catalogue, Siena 1985) 194ff.

59. K. M. Phillips, *Gli Etruschi, nuove ricerche e scoperte* (Viterbo 1972). Most recently, R. D. De Puma and J. P. Small, eds., *Murlo and the Etruscans* (Madison 1994), esp. I. Edlund-Berry, "Ritual Destruction of Cities and Sanctuaries," op cit., 16ff.

CHAPTER 6. THE BUILDINGS

1. J.-P. Thullier, "Autels d'Étrurie," in *L'espace sacrificiel* (Lyon 1991) 243–48.

2. J. Hemelrijk, *Caeretan Hydriae* (Mainz 1984) 120, pl. 68, and also an amphora in the Louvre, E 703, by the Silenus Painter; an amphora in Reading by the Tityos Painter, Univ. Mas. 47.6.1.

3. On this point: L. T. Shoe, "Etruscan and Roman Republican Mouldings," *MAAR* 28 (1965).

4. F. Roncalli, *Le lastre dipinte di Cerveteri* (Florence 1965) pls. III, VI.

5. For example, on an urn from Volterra: E. Fiumi, "Volterra," *N Sc* (1972) 87, no. 9, fig. 44.

6. F. Parise Badoni, *Ceramica campana a figure nere* (Florence 1968) passim.

7. M. Cristofani, *Hellenismus in Mittelitalien* (Göttingen 1976) 170.

8. F. Giuliani and P. Sommella, "Lavinium," *PP* 32 (1977) 356ff.

9. A. Boëthius, *Etruscan and Early Roman Architecture* (Harmondsworth 1970); A. Boëthius,

"Vitruvio e il tempio tuscanico," *StEtr* 24 (1955) 137–42; H. Knell, "Der etruskische Tempel nach Vitruvius," *RM* 90 (1983) 91–101; S. Haynes, *Etruscan Civilisation* (Los Angeles 2000) 204–21, discusses several major temple sites.

10. P. Gros, *L'architecture romaine* (Paris 1996) 123.
11. R. A. Staccioli, *Modelli di edifici etrusco italici* (Florence 1968).
12. G. Bartoloni et al., *Le urne a capanna rinvenute in Italia* (Rome 1987); and see chapter 4 *supra*.
13. H. Hencken, *Tarquinia, Villanovans, and Early Etruscans* (Cambridge, Mass., 1968); J.-R. Jannot, "Rites villanoviens et rites étrusques, quelques continuités," *StEtr* (2002) 4–12.
14. F. Prayon, *Frühetruskische Grab- und Hausarchitektur* (Heidelberg 1975).
15. R. A. Staccioli, *Modelli di edifici etrusco-italici* (Florence 1968) no. 35.
16. Cf. Prayon, *Frühetruskische Grab- und Hausarchitektur*, categories C1 and C2.
17. Zone F: M. Strandberg Olofsson, *Acquarossa* 5 (Stockholm 1984).
18. Prayon, *Frühetruskische Grab- und Hausarchitektur*, types C and following.
19. Shoe, "Etruscan and Roman Republican Mouldings."
20. Decorations in tufa or limestone: J.-R. Jannot, "Deux représentations d'édifices clusiens," *MEFRA* 86 (1974) 723–44.
21. N. T. de Grummond, "Rediscovery," in L. Bonfante, ed., *Etruscan Life and Afterlife* (Detroit 1986) 28.
22. Norchia, necropolis of Acqua Alta; Sovana, Ildebranda Tomb: J. P. Oleson, *The Sources of Innovation in Later Etruscan Tomb Design* (Rome 1982).
23. G. Colonna, "Tarquitius Priscus e il Tempio di Giove Capitolino," *PP* 36 (1981) 41–59.
24. A. Somella Mura, "L'area sacra di Sant'Omobono," *PP* 32 (1977) 172–73.
25. F. Brown, "Cosa 2: The Temples of the Arx," *MAAR* 26 (Rome 1960).
26. A. Frova, "Luni," *StEtr* 44 (1976) 468–72.
27. Catalogue, *Satricum, una città latina* (Florence 1982).
28. R. Knoop, *Antefixa Satricana* (Assen-Wolferboro 1987) 212.
29. R. Bartoccini, *Il tempio grande di Vulci* (Louvain 1963).
30. P. S. Lulof, *Late Archaic Terracotta Statues from Satricum* (Amsterdam 1991).
31. Translation quoted by J. M. Turfa in Bonfante, *Etruscan Life and Afterlife*, see chapter 5, note 47 *supra*.
32. The dance of the cranes: F.-H. Massa-Pairault, *Iconologia e politica* (Milan 1992) 67ff. For another very convincing interpretation: I. Krauskopf, "Influences grecques et orientales sur la représentation des dieux étrusques," *LPRH*, 25–36.
33. A. J. Pfiffig, *Religio Etrusca*, 75.
34. A. Somella Mura, *L'area sacra del Foro Boario* (Rome 1981) 119–20.
35. But F. Coarelli, *Il Foro Boario* (Rome 1988) 301–28, identifies her as Hera-Aphrodite, as does F.-H. Massa-Pairault.
36. G. Colonna, "Il Maestro dell'Ercole e della Minerva," *OpRom* 16.1: *Lectiones Boëthianae* 6 (1987) 7–41.
37. Haynes, *Etruscan Civilisation*, 205–10. Most recently, G. Colonna, ed., *Il santuario di Portonaccio a Veio, 1: Gli scavi di Massimo Pallottino nella zona dell'altare (1939–1940)* (Rome 2002).
38. N. A. Winter, "Architectural Terracottas Decorated with Human Heads," *RM* 85 (1978) 4.

39. Massa-Pairault, *Iconologia e politica*, 63ff.

40. I. Edlund-Berry, *The Seated and Standing Statue Akroteria from Poggio Civitate (Murlo)* (Rome 1992).

41. G. Stefani, "Veio," *NSc* (1953) 67.

42. Massa-Pairault, *Iconologia e politica*, 101.

43. Menrva: ibid., 103. Cinerary statues from Chiusi: Berlin, St. Mus. E 34; Bonn, Akad. Mus. Univ. B 148; Copenhagen, Ny Carlsberg, H 214; M. Cristofani, *Statue-cinerario chiusine di età classica* (Rome 1975).

44. F.-H. Massa-Pairault sees here the drawing of lots for the combatant who must face Hector: *La cité des Étrusques* (Paris 1996) 171ff. It is an extremely clever hypothesis, but we have no proof of its validity.

45. Massa-Pairault, *Iconologia e politica*, 105.

46. O. W. von Vacano and B. von Freitag, *Il frontone di Talamone* (Florence 1982); B. von Freitag-Löringhoff, *Das Giebelrelief von Telamon* (Mainz 1986).

47. Dated by von Vacano. F.-H. Massa-Pairault, *Iconologia*, places this creation much later, between the Gracchi and Sulla.

48. J. P. Small, *Studies Related to the Theban Cycle in Late Etruscan Urns* (Rome 1981).

49. Bologna, Mus. Arch.; M. Zuffa, "I frontoni e il fregio di Civitalba," in *Studi Calderini e Paribeni* (Milan 1956) 267ff.

50. A. Rastrelli, "L'edificio sacro di Fucoli," in *La civiltà di Chiusi e del suo territorio* (Florence 1993) 463ff. Cf. chapter 5 *supra*.

51. G. Colonna, "Ricerche sull'Etruria interna volsinese," *StEtr* 41 (1973) 505ff.

## CHAPTER 7. WORSHIPPERS

1. H. Rix, ed., *ET*, Um 1.7, T.II, 315.

2. M. Pallottino, "Uno specchio di Tuscania," *RendLinc*, ser. 6, vol. 6, fasc. 3–4 (1930) 51, fig. 41. The mirror is in Florence, Mus. Arch. Naz.

3. L. Bonfante, *Etruscan Dress* (Baltimore 1975) 202, no. 137.

4. Southern Etruria, Vatican, Mus. Greg. Etrusco, inv. no. 12040; M. Cristofani, *I bronzi degli Etruschi* (Novara 1985) 272, no. 60. A wider hat: Verona, Mus. Arch. inv. A4605.

5. P. G. Guzzo, *Le fibule in Etruria dal VI al I secolo* (Florence 1972) 157ff.

6. *ET*, Vs 3.7; T.II, 100.

7. *ET*, AS 4; T.II, 167.

8. M. Torelli, "Secespita, praefericulum," in *Etrusca et Italica* (Pisa 1997) 575–98.

9. J.-R. Jannot, *Les reliefs archaïques de Chiusi* (Rome 1984) C.I.30.

10. M. Cristofani, *Statue-cinerario chiusine* (Rome 1975) pls. 4, 2.

11. I. Edlund-Berry, *The Seated and Standing Statue Akroteria from Poggio Civitate (Murlo)* (Rome 1992).

12. M. Torelli, *Elogia Tarquiniensia* (Florence 1975) 103ff.

13. M. Cristofani, *Tabula Capuana* (Florence 1995), 90, line 8: *cipen apires racvanies*, etc; *cipen tar. tiria vaci(1)*, p. 58, line 28.

14. *ET*, AT, 1.171.T.II, 76.

15. S. P. Cortson, *Die etruskischen Standestitel* (Copenhagen 1925) 128.

16. It is certain that this is not a priesthood but a magistracy in charge of sacred buildings or offerings.
17. *ET,* Ta, 1.184.
18. *ET,* II, Ta 1.17, 47.
19. J. Heurgon, "Influences grecques sur la religion latine," *REL* 35 (1957) 106ff.
20. A meaning proposed by A. Morandi, *Nuovi lineamenti di lingua etrusca* (Rome 1991): "to lead."
21. M. Cristofani, *Civiltà degli Etruschi* (Milan 1985) 350.
22. British Mus. Sc. D, 22.
23. M. Cristofani, *L'arte degli Etruschi* (Turin 1978) fig. 165.
24. *ET,* II, Ta 7.9, 7.10, 63.
25. Rome, Mus. Villa Giulia, excavation inv. G 601.
26. Catalogue, *La grande Roma dei Tarquini* (Rome 1990) pl. XI.
27. Jannot, *Les reliefs archaïques de Chiusi,* 152, D.I.14.
28. Cf. a bronze plaque from Bomarzo, *infra,* note 30.
29. Berlin, St. Mus. inv. Sk. 1220; Catalogue, *Die Welt der Etrusker* (Berlin 1988) 211, B 9.5.
30. Cf. chapter 3, pp. 38–39; relief from Chiusi, Paris, Louvre, MA 3611; mirror in Florence, Mus. Arch. Naz.; amphora in Dresden, St. Kunstmus. ZV 1653; bronze plaque from Bomarzo, Vatican, Mus. Greg. Etrusco, inv. no. 12268.
31. St. Mus. Fr. 198. *LIMC,* s.v. *Hercle,* no. 264.
32. H. Nagy, *Votive Terracottas from the "Vignaccia," Cerveteri, in the Lowie Museum of Anthropology* (Rome 1988) 212–13; Boston, Mus. of Fine Arts, 89.364.
33. F. Roncalli, *Le lastre dipinte di Cerveteri* (Florence 1965) pl. VI.
34. H. Rix, "Les prières du Liber Linteus de Zagreb," *LPRH,* 391–99.
35. G. Colonna, "Le iscrizioni votive etrusche," *ScAnt* 3–4 (1989–90) 875ff.
36. Catalogue, *La grande Roma dei Tarquini,* 136.
37. The Sillene Spring: G. Paolucci, *Il territorio di Chianciano Terme* (Rome 1988) 58–59.
38. A. Cherici, in *La Chimera e il suo mito* (Arezzo 1994); M. Cristofani, *I bronzi degli Etruschi* (Novara 1985) 295.
39. Cf. S. Haynes, *Etruscan Bronzes* (London 1985) 302, no. 156, with previous bibliography.
40. Cristofani, *Tabula Capuana,* 101.
41. J.-R. Jannot, "Le lanceur de javelot du Musée du Louvre," *RA* (1987.2) 225–50.
42. Vatican, Mus. Greg. Etrusco, inv. no. 693.
43. G. Colonna, *Bronzi votivi umbro-sabellici a figura umana* (Florence 1970).
44. Catalogue, *L'art des peuples italiques* (Geneva 1993) 250ff.
45. E. H. Richardson, *Etruscan Votive Bronzes* (Mainz 1983).
46. A. Romualdi, *Catalogo del deposito di Brolio in Val di Chiana* (Rome 1981). Cf. chapter 5, p. 88.
47. Cristofani, *I bronzi degli Etruschi,* 248.
48. M. Bonghi Jovino, *Gli Etruschi di Tarquinia* (Milan 1986) 100, fig. 92, no. 197.
49. R. A. Staccioli, *Modelli di edifici etrusco italici* (Florence 1968) no. 16.
50. The figure is called the "Apollo of Ferrara"; Paris, B. N. Med. B. B. 101; A.-M. Adam, *Bronzes étrusques et italiques* (Paris 1984) 106, no. 244. Inscription: *ET,* OB, 3.2, 341.
51. Nagy, *Votive Terracottas from the "Vignaccia."*

52. Vatican, Mus. Greg. Etrusco, inv. no. 12180.
53. *ET*, Co. 3.8, 303.
54. Leiden, Rijksmuseum, Co.4.
55. They bear an obvious resemblance to Phoenician votive statues: Catalogue, *Les Phéniciens* (Milan 1988) 284.
56. J. M. Turfa, "Anatomical Votives and Italian Medical Traditions," in R. De Puma and J. P. Small, eds., *Murlo and the Etruscans* (Madison 1994) 224–40.

CHAPTER 8. GODS

1. In *LIMC*, the Etruscan gods appear between Greek prototypes and Roman equivalents!
2. Cf. amphora in the Villa Giulia with the "Apotheosis of Heracles": M. Martelli, *La ceramica degli Etruschi* (Novara 1987) no. 116. Aplu here is an archer.
3. Campana plaque no. 2; Paris, Louvre S. 4035; F. Roncalli, *Le lastre dipinte di Cerveteri* (Florence 1965) pl. 2.
4. E. Simon, "Die Tomba dei Tori und der etruskische Apollonkult," *StEtr* 24 (1955–56) 143ff.
5. P. Amandry, "On the Offering of an Etruscan Tripod in Delphi," *BCH* (1987) 126.
6. Is he related to the god Soranos? I. Edlund-Berry, *The Gods and the Place* (Stockholm 1987) 46.
7. A.-M. Adam, *Bronzes étrusques et italiques de la Bibliotèque Nationale* (Paris 1984) 166–67.
8. Berlin; E. Gerhard, *Etruskische Spiegel*, 2.93.
9. Servius, *Ad Aen.* 11.259, and on a mirror: Gerhard and Körte, *Etruskische Spiegel*, 246.
10. The only other mention: *liber linteus*, col. XII, line 5.
11. H. Nagy, *Votive Terracottas from the "Vignaccia," Cerveteri, in the Lowie Museum of Anthropology* (Rome 1988) pl. XXXVI.
12. Mirror in Bologna Mus. Arch. 1073. H. Salskov Roberts, "The Creation of a Religious Iconography," in *Aspects of Hellenism in Italy, Acta Hyperboria* 5 (1993) 287–318.
13. N. Loraux, *Les enfants d'Athéna* (Paris 1981); lekythos: FR, Louvre, CA 681.
14. Epiur appears at least twice on the Piacenza liver, once near Hercle, and Mars is mentioned as receiving offers on the lead inscription from Magliano.
15. Gerhard, *Etruskische Spiegel*, vol. 5, pl. 7.1: Florence, Mus. Arch. The anonymous manuscript reviewer notes that there is also a box mirror with two Menrvas: Gerhard, *Etruskische Spiegel*, vol. 3, pl. 241; M. Torelli, *StEtr* 34 (1966) 330–31.
16. London, British Mus. no. 84.6–14–56; S. Haynes, *Etruscan Bronzes* (London 1985) 263.
17. Gerherd, *Etruskische Spiegel*, vol. 4 (1867), pl. 344. *LIMC vi.1 s.v.* Malavish 1–11 (R. Lambrechts). B. Van der Meer, *Interpretatio Etrusca* (Amsterdam 1995) 201–3, 19.1, and fig. 96.
18. A. Rallo, *Lasa: iconografia ed esegesi* (Florence 1974). One is surely a boy: *Lasa Sitmica* (Gerhard, *Etruskische Spiegel*, vol. 1, pl. 115). And on the famous mirror from St. Petersburg (see fig. 8.5) at least two Lasa-like *genii* are young boys.
19. A. J. Pfiffig, *Religio Etrusca* (Graz 1975) 261ff.: *turan*, "gift"; *turuce*, "has given."
20. Nagy, *Votive Terracottas from the "Vignaccia,"* 76–77.
21. E. Hostetter, *Bronzes from Spina*, vol. 1 (Mainz 1986), pls. 6–7, c, d.
22. No. 34, *Lvślvelch*. Perhaps *Lusa/Velchansl*.
23. Leiden, Rijksmuseum van Oudheden.

## Notes to pages 154–166

24. *TLE* 156.
25. Saulini antefix, Florence, Mus. Arch. Naz.; G. Colonna, "Divinités peu connues du panthéon étrusque," *LPRH*, 169; *ET*, Vs. 7.40, 108.
26. See Propertius, 4.2; Ovid, *Met.* 14.643ff. Vortumnus' changing form is the last Roman avatar of the Etruscan god, whose importance suggests a very wide sphere of power before Hellenization.
27. The attribution of the Belvedere Temple to Śuri seems tenuous; G. Colonna, "Divinités peu connues," *LPRH*, 178.
28. Bronze: Florence, Mus. Arch. Naz. no. 8; amphora: London, Br. Mus. B 57.
29. Capua: line 13; *liber linteus:* XII, 10.
30. *ET*, Co. 4.6, 303.
31. It reads: *fleres tece sansl tenine . . . et fleres tec sansl cver.* M. Cristofani, *I bronzi degli Etruschi* (Novara 1985).
32. T. Hackens, "La métrologie," in colloquium: *Contributi introduttivi allo studio monetazione etrusca* (Naples 1976) 221–72.
33. Cf. chapter 9, p. 177, and chapter 5, p. 89.
34. On the well-known inscription of Laris Pulenas: *cathas pachanac a/umna the hermu* (*TLE* 131), which probably means "having performed in a place (named al umna) the cult (?) of Catha and Pacha."
35. Florence, Mus. Arch. Naz.: Gerhard, *Etruskische Spiegel,* vol. 5, pl. 159.
36. Volsinii, *TLE* 336: *Fuflunsl pachies velclthi.*
37. F.-H. Massa-Pairault and J. Pailler, *Bolsena* 5.1 (Rome 1979).
38. A. Pautasso, *Il deposito votivo presso la porta nord a Vulci* (Rome 1994) D, 5.
39. A famous example is in Berlin, Pergamon Mus.; *CSE* DDR, I, D.5.
40. Likewise: *smuc inthiun aitula: MonPiot* 61 (1961) 54.
41. In an inscription from Bolsena: *Selvans sancuneta cvera. ET* II, Vs. 8, 100.
42. M. Cataldi, "Nuova testimonianza di culto sulla cività di Tarquinia," in Viterbo colloquium: *Tyrrhenoi philotechnoi* (1994) 61–69.
43. *TLE* 368.
44. E. Simon, "Culsu, Culsans, und Ianus," in *2d Convegno Internazionale Etrusco,* 1271–81.
45. Palermo, Mus. Arch. Naz., Cassuccini Collection.
46. Pfiffig, *Religio Etrusca,* 236ff.
47. Vatican, Mus. Greg. Etrusco, inv. no. 693.
48. G. Colonna, *Bronzi votivi umbro-sabellici a figura umana* (Florence 1970).
49. From Pania and Poggio alla Sala: M. Cristofani, "Paideia, arete e metis," *Prospettiva* 81–84 (1996) 2ff.
50. Catalogue, *Principi Etruschi* (Bologna 2000) nos. 242ff., 246.
51. Called *"a scala,"* stepped. S. Bruni, *I lastroni a scala* (Rome 1986).
52. Catalogue, *Case e palazzi d'Etruria* (Milan 1985) 58; M. Strandberg Olofsson, *Acquarossa 5* (Stockholm 1984).
53. London, British Mus. 1772–3-4.7.4; Haynes, *Etruscan Bronzes,* 272, no. 71.
54. P. Zazoff, *Etruskische Skarabäen* (Mainz 1968) 160, pl. 33.
55. Da Contarina, Este, Mus. Arch. 15844; Vatican, Mus. Greg. Etrusco, inv. no. 12055; Paris, Louvre; and Geneva, Fol Mus. F. Buranelli, *Bronzi a figura umana* (Vatican City 1999) 159, no. 15;

## Notes to pages 167–176

P. Zanovello, "L'Heracles di Contarina," *Aquileia Nostra* 58 (1987) 154–88. Cf. S. Haynes, *Passion for Antiquity* (1994) 156; E. H. Richardson, *Etruscan Votive Bronzes* (Mainz 1983) 361; and see J. S. Schwartz, *LIMC* 6.196ff. s.v. *Hercle*.

56. L. Banti, *Il mondo degli Etruschi* (Rome 1969); G. Camporeale, "Banalizzazione etrusche di miti greci," *StEtr* 28 (1960).

57. R. Hampe and E. Simon, *Griechische Sagen in der frühen etruskischen Kunst* (Mainz 1964).

58. P. Zancani Montuoro, "Un mito italiota in Etruria," *ASAtene* (1950) 85–98.

59. Edlund-Berry, *The Gods and the Place*.

60. J. Hemelrijk, *Caeretan Hydriae* (Mainz 1984) shows the connections of Etruscan craftsmen with Asia and Egypt.

61. M. Cristofani, "Ricerche sulle pitture della Tomba François di Vulci," *DialArch* 1 (1967) 186–219; F. Coarelli, "Le pitture della Tomba François, una proposta di lettura," *DialArch* 3.1/2 (1983) 43–64; F. Buranelli, *La Tomba François di Vulci* (Rome 1987).

62. H. Blanck, "Die Malereien des sogennanten Preister-Sarkophage in Tarquinia," in *Mélanges T. Dohrn* (Rome 1982) 11ff.

63. F.-H. Massa-Pairault, *Iconologia e politica* (Milan 1992).

64. S. Stopponi, *La Tomba della Scrofa Nera* (Rome 1983).

65. F.-H. Massa-Pairault, *La cité des Étrusques* (Paris 1996) 229.

66. J.-R. Jannot, "Les danseurs aux haches ou le ballet de Phinée," in *Mélanges Jacques Heurgon* (Rome 1976) 471–85.

67. P.J. Riis, *Vulcentia Vetustiora* (Copenhagen 1997) 57. Perhaps, too, in Perugia bronzes: ibid. 65.

68. Palermo, Mus. Naz. 8382; J.-R. Jannot, *Les reliefs archaïques de Chiusi* (Rome 1984) B, II, 1a.

69. L. Cerchiai, "Achille e Troilos in Etruria, alcuni ipotesi su due cippi chiusini," *DialArch* 8 (1990–92) 64ff.

70. W. Dobrowolski, "I Dioscuri sugli specchi etruschi," in *Tyrrhenoi Philotechnoi* (Rome 1994) 173ff.

CHAPTER 9. THE DIVINE

1. M. Pallottino, *Etruscologia* (Milan 1968) chap. 7.

2. A. J. Pfiffig, *Religio Etrusca* (Graz 1975) 179.

3. H. Rix, "Etruskische Aiseras," in *Festschrift F. Altheim* (Berlin 1969) 280–92. *Liber linteus*, II, 12; V, 7; XII, 2.

4. *TLE* 718 (Venetia. Feltre).

5. *Contra* Pfiffig, *Religio Etrusca*, 180.

6. Herodotus, *The Histories* (trans. A. de Sélincourt, rev. A. R. Burn, Harmondsworth 1985) 150.

7. A. Rallo, *Lasa, Iconografia ed esegesi* (Florence 1974).

8. C. Scheffer, "Harbingers of Death? The Female Demon in Late Etruscan Funerary Art," in *Munuscula Romana* (Stockholm 1991) 51–63. The exception: a vase of the Vanth Group, Orvieto, Mus. Faina, no. 2645.

9. F.-H. Massa-Pairault, *La cité des Étrusques* (Paris 1996) 202.

10. J.-R. Jannot, "Charu, Tuchulcha et les autres," *RM* 100 (1993) 59–82.

11. On this topic cf. M. Cristofani, "Sul processo di antropomorfizzazione del pantheon etrusco," in *Miscellanea etrusco-italica*, *QArchEtr* 22 (Rome 1993) 9–21.

12. "The triple god" or "the god three": G. Colonna, "Divinités peu connues du panthéon étrusque," *LPRH*, 175.

13. A. Maggiani, "Réflexions sur la religion étrusque primitive," *LPRH*, 431ff.

14. Pallottino, *Etruscologia*, 242.

15. F. de Polignac, *Naissance de la cité grecque* (Paris 1984).

16. G. Bordenache Battaglia, *Le ciste prenestine* (Rome 1979).

17. Catalogue, *Artigianato artistico* (Milan 1985) 208ff.

18. Tomb of Orcus II; S. Steingräber, *Pittura etrusca* (Milan, Tokyo 1984) 334.

CONCLUSION

1. D. Briquel, *Chrétiens et haruspices* (Paris 1997).

2. G. Camporeale, *Gli Etruschi, storia e civiltà* (Turin 2000) 209, cites the folklorist Charles Godfrey Leland, whose work is reprinted as *Etruscan-Roman Remains and the Old Religion* (London 2002) 69.

# Thematic Bibliography

### GENERAL STUDIES, HISTORY, AND ART

Aigner-Foresti, L. *Etrusker nördlich der Alpen* (Vienna 1992).
Akerström, A. "Etruscan Tomb Painting, an Art of Many Faces," *OpRom* 13 (1981) 7–34.
Alföldi, A. *Early Rome and the Latins* (Ann Arbor 1963).
Altheim, F. A. *History of Roman Religion* (New York 1938).
Banti, L. *Il mondo degli Etruschi* (Rome 1969).
Barker, G., and T. Rasmussen. *The Etruscans* (Oxford 1998).
Bartoloni, G., and M. Sprenger. *The Etruscans: Their History, Art, and Architecture* (New York 1983).
Bayet, J. *Croyances et rites dans la Rome antique* (Paris 1971).
Becatti, G., and F. Magi. *Le pitture della Tomba degli Auguri* (Rome 1956).
Blanck, H., and G. Proietti. *La Tomba dei Rilievi di Cerveteri* (Rome 1986).
Blanck, H., and C. Weber Lehmann. *Malerei der Etrusker* (Mainz 1987).
Bloch, R. *The Etruscans* (London 1958).
———. "Problèmes religieux étrusques," *Ktema* 10 (1985) 143–48.
Boëthius, A. *Etruscan Culture, Land and People* (Malmö 1962).
Boitani, F., M. Cataldi Dini, and M. Pasquinucci. *Etruscan Cities* (London 1975).
Bonfante, L. *Etruscan Dress* (Baltimore 1975).
———. *Out of Etruria* (Oxford 1981).
———. "The Women of Etruria," *Arethusa* 6 (1973) 91–101.
Bonfante, L., ed. *Etruscan Life and Afterlife* (Detroit 1986).
Bonghi Jovino, M., ed. *Gli Etruschi di Tarquinia* (Milan 1986).
Bordenache Battaglia, G. *Le ciste prenestine* (Rome 1979).
Brendel, O. *Etruscan Art* (Harmondsworth 1978).
Briquel, D. *Les Étrusques, peuple de la différence* (Paris 1993).
———. "Une explication du nom des Étrusques," *Gerion* 9 (1991) 289–98.
———. "Gens ante alias magis dedita religionibus: Les Étrusques et le sacré," *BAssBudé* (1989) 247–62.
———. "Les plus religieux des hommes," *Lalies* 11 (1992) 75–81.
———. *Le regard des autres* (Besançon 1997).
———. "La religion des anciens toscans," in Y. Lehmann, ed., *Religions de l'Antiquité* (Paris 1999) 7–77.
———. "La religiosité étrusque ou le regard de l'autre," *LPRH* (Paris 1997) 415–31.
Camporeale, G. *Gli Etruschi, storia e civiltà* (Turin 2000).
———, ed. *Gli Etruschi fuori d'Etruria* (Verona 2001).
———, ed. *The Etruscans Outside Etruria* (Malibu 2004).
Cataldi Dini, M. "La Tomba dei Demoni Azzurri," in M. A. Rizzo, ed., *Pittura etrusca al Museo di Villa Giulia* (Rome 1989) 151ff.
Catalogue, *L'art des peuples italiques* (Geneva 1993).
———. *Artigianato artistico* (Milan 1985).

# Thematic Bibliography

———. *Case e palazzi d'Etruria* (Milan 1985).
———. *Les Étrusques et l'Europe* (Paris 1992).
———. *La grande Roma dei Tarquini* (Rome 1990).
———. *Mostra dell'Etruria Padana* (Bologna 1960).
———. *Les Phéniciens* (Milan 1988).
———. *Poggio Civitate Murlo* (Florence 1970).
———. *Principi Etruschi* (Bologna 2000).
———. *Spina, una città tra Greci ed Etruschi* (Ferrara 1994).
———. *Die Welt der Etrusker* (Berlin 1988).
Cerchiai, L. "Achille e Troilos in Etruria, alcuni ipotesi su due cippi chiusini," *DialArch* 8 (1990–92).
Clemen, C. *Die Religion der Etrusker* (Bonn 1936).
———. "Die Etruskische Sekulärrechnung," *Studi e materiali di storia delle religioni* 4 (1928) 235–42.
Cristofani, M. *L'arte degli Etruschi* (Turin 1978).
———. *I bronzi degli Etruschi* (Novara 1985).
———. *Città e campagna nell'Etruria settentrionale* (Arezzo 1976).
———. *Civiltà degli Etruschi* (Milan 1985).
———. *The Etruscans: A New Investigation* (London 1979).
———. *Gli Etruschi in Maremma* (Milan 1981).
———. *Gli Etruschi, una nuova immagine* (Florence 1984).
Cristofani, M., ed. *Dizionario della civiltà etrusca* (Florence 1985).
d'Agostino, B. "Image and Society in Archaic Etruria," *JRS* 32 (1983) 1–10.
de Grummond, N. *A Guide to Etruscan Mirrors* (Tallahassee 1982).
Del Chiaro, M. *Etruscan Ghiaccio Forte* (Santa Barbara 1976).
Dennis, G. *Cities and Cemeteries of Etruria*, 2 vols. (London 1848; 3rd ed. London 1883; reprint Rome 1968).
de Puma, R., and J. P. Small, eds. *Murlo and the Etruscans: Art and Society in Ancient Etruria* (Madison 1994).
Dobrowolski, W. "I Dioscuri sugli specchi etruschi," in *Tyrrhenoi Philotechnoi* (Rome 1994).
Dohrn, T. *Die etruskische Kunst im Zeitalter der griechischen Klassik* (Mainz 1982).
Dumézil, G. *La religion romaine archaïque* (Paris 1974), appendix, 593–660.
Enking, R. *Etruskische Geistigkeit* (Berlin 1947).
Fiumi, E. "Volterra," *NSc* (1972) 52–136.
Gerhard. E. *Etruskische Spiegel*, vols. 1–4 (Berlin 1843–67), vol. 5, ed. G. Körte (Berlin 1884–97), reprint, 5 vols. in 4 (Rome 1960).
Grant, M. *The Etruscans* (London 1980).
Haynes, S. *Etruscan Bronzes* (London 1985).
———. *Etruscan Civilization: A Cultural History* (Los Angeles 2000).
———. *Etruscan Sculpture* (London 1971).
Hemelrijk, J. *Caeretan Hydriae* (Mainz 1984).
Hencken, H. *Tarquinia and Etruscan Origins* (London 1968).
———. *Tarquinia, Villanovans, and Early Etruscans* (Cambridge, Mass. 1968).
Herbig, R. *Götter und Dämonen der Etrusker* (Mainz 1965).

# Thematic Bibliography

———. "Zur Religion und Religiosität der Etrusker," *Historia* 6 (1957) 123ff.
Heurgon, J. *Daily Life of the Etruscans* (London 1964).
Hus, A. *The Etruscans* (London 1961).
———. *Les Étrusques et leur destin* (Paris 1980).
———. *Recherches sur la statuaire en pierre étrusque archaïque* (Rome 1961).
Jannot, J.-R. *A la rencontre des Étrusques* (Rennes 1987).
———. "Deux représentations d'édifices clusiens," *MEFRA* 86 (1974) 723–44.
———. *Les reliefs archaïques de Chiusi* (Rome 1984).
Jones, G. D. B. "Capena and ager Capenas," *BSR* 31 (1963) 100ff.
*LPRH: Les Étrusques, les plus religieux des hommes* (colloquium 1992, pub. Paris 1997).
Maggiani, A., and E. Simon. "Il pensiero scientifico e religioso," in M. Cristofani, ed., *Gli Etruschi, una nuova immagine* (Florence 1984) 139–68.
———. "Réflexions sur la religion étrusque primitive, de l'époque villanovienne à l'époque archaïque," *LPRH* (Paris 1997) 431–49.
Martelli, M. *La ceramica degli Etruschi* (Novara 1987).
Massa-Pairault, F.-H. *La cité des Étrusques* (Paris 1996).
———. *Iconologia e politica* (Milan 1992).
Pallottino, M. *Etruscan Painting* (Geneva 1952).
———. *The Etruscans* (Harmondsworth 1975).
———. *Etruscologia* (Milan 1968).
———. *A History of Earliest Italy* (London 1988).
———. *Saggi di antichità*, 3 vols. (Rome 1979).
———. "Tarquinia," *MonAnt* 36 (1937–38).
Paolucci, G. *Il territorio di Chianciano Terme: Dalla preistoria al medioevo* (Rome 1988).
Parise Badoni, F. *Ceramica campana a figure nere* (Florence 1968).
Pfiffig, A. J. *Gesammelte Schriften* (Vienna 1995).
———. *Religio Etrusca* (Graz 1975).
Phillips, K. M. "Bryn Mawr College Excavations in Tuscany," *AJA* 77 (1972) 319–26.
———. *Gli Etruschi: Nuove ricerche e scoperte* (Viterbo 1972).
———. *In the Hills of Tuscany: Recent Excavations at the Etruscan Site of Poggio Civitate (Murlo, Siena)* (Philadelphia 1993).
Prayon, F. *Gli Etruschi* (Bologna 1999).
Radke, G. "Beobachtungen zur Religion der Etrusker," *WürzJbb* 14 (1988).
Rallo, A., ed. *Le donne in Etruria* (Rome 1989).
Richardson, E. H. *Etruscan Votive Bronzes: Geometric, Orientalizing, Archaic* (Mainz 1983).
Sassatelli, G. "Culti e riti in Etruria padana," *ScAnt* 3–4 (1989–90) 599–617.
Scullard, H. H. *The Etruscan Cities and Rome* (London 1967).
Simon, E. *Schriften zur etruskischen und italischen Kunst und Religion* (Stuttgart 1996).
Sokolowski, F. *Lois sacrées des cités grecques* (Paris 1969).
Spivey, N. *Etruscan Art* (London 1997).
———. *The Micali Painter and His Followers* (Oxford 1987).
Sprengel, U., and G. Bartoloni. *The Etruscans: Their History, Art and Architecture* (New York 1983).
Steingräber, S. *Pittura etrusca* (Milan, Tokyo 1984).

## Thematic Bibliography

Steingräber, S., D. Ridgway, and F. Serra Ridgway, eds. *Etruscan Painting: Catalogue Raisonné of Etruscan Wall Paintings* (New York 1986).

Swaddling, J., ed. *Italian Iron Age Artefacts in the British Museum*. Papers of the Sixth British Museum Classical Colloquium, 1985 (London 1986).

Taylor, L. R. *Local Cults in Etruria* (Rome 1923).

Thuillier, J. P. *Les Étrusques, la fin d'un mystère* (Paris 1990).

———. *Les jeux athlétiques dans la civilisation étrusque* (Rome 1985).

Thulin, C. *Die etruskische Disciplin*, 2 vols. (Göteborg 1905–9).

Torelli, M. "La Religione," in *Rasenna* (Milan 1986) 159–237.

———. "Veio," in *Mélanges T. Dohrn* (Rome 1982) 471ff.

Weege, F. *Etruskische Malerei* (Halle 1921).

### DIVINATION, SACRED LITERATURE, AND THE *ETRUSCA DISCIPLINA*

Agostiniani, L. *Le "iscrizioni parlanti" dell'Italia antica* (Florence 1982).

Agostiniani, L., and F. Nicosia. *Tabula Cortonensis* (Rome 2000).

Bentz, M. *Etruskische Votivbronzen des Hellenismus* (Florence 1992).

Blecher, H. "De extispicio capita tria," in *Religiongeschichtliche Versuche und Vorarbeiter* (1905) 171ff.

Bloch, R. *La divination dans l'antiquité* (Paris 1984).

———. *Les prodiges dans l'antiquité classique* (Paris 1963).

Briquel, D. "Art augural et Etrusca disciplina," *Caesarodunum* Suppl. 56 (1986) 68–100.

———. "Divination étrusque et mantique grecque: La recherche d'une origine hellénique de l'Etrusca Disciplina," *Latomus* 49 (1990) 321–42.

Capdeville, G. "Le tre manubiae di Tinia," *StEtr* 58 (1992) 155–70.

Chiaramonte Trere, C. "Alcuni dati sulla prassi rituale etrusca," *ScAnt* 3–4 (1989–90) 695–704.

Colonna, G. "A proposito degli dei del fegato di Piacenza," *StEtr* 59 (1993) 123ff.

———. "Divinazione e culto di Rath/Apollo a Caere," *StEtr* 62.2 (2001) 151–73.

———. "Il fegato di Piacenza e la tarda etruscità padana," in *Studi Zuffa* (Rimini 1984).

Cornell, T. J. "The Tyranny of Evidence: A Discussion of Possible Literacy in Etruria and Latium in the Archaic Age," in *Literacy in the Roman World*, *JRA* Suppl. ser. 3 (Ann Arbor 1991) 7–33.

Cristofani, M. "Ancora sul cosidetto specchio di Tarchon," *Prospettiva* 51 (1987) 46–48.

———. *Tabula Capuana: Un calendario festivo di età arcaica* (Florence 1995).

Devoto, G. *Le tavole di Gubbio* (Florence 1948).

Dumézil, G. "Remarques sur les trois premières regiones caeli de M. Capella," in *Hommages à Max Niedermann* (Brussels 1956) 102–7.

Heurgon, J. "The Date of Vegoia's Prophecy," *JRS* 49 (1959) 41–45.

Kettner, G. *Cornelius Labeo* (Naumburg 1977).

MacBain, B. *Prodigy and Expiation: A Study in Religion and Politics in Republican Rome* (Brussels 1982).

Maggiani, A. *La divination dans le monde italique* 3 (Tours 1986).

———. "La divination oraculaire en Etrurie," *Caesarodunum* Suppl. 56 (1986) 6–41.

———. "Qualche osservazioni sul fegato di Piacenza," *StEtr* 50 (1982) 53–88.

# Thematic Bibliography

Massa-Pairault, F.-H. "Sacra Acheruntica." *L'Etrusca Disciplina* (Orvieto 1987).

Morandi, A. *Epigrafia etrusca* (Rome 1982).

———. *Nuovi lineamenti di lingua etrusca* (Rome 1991).

Pallottino, M. "Deorum sedes," in *Mélanges Calderini e Paribeni* (Milan 1956–57) and in *Saggi di Antichità* 2 (Rome 1979).

———. "Uno specchio di Tuscania e la legenda etrusca di Tarchon," *RendLinc,* ser. 6, vol. 6, fasc. 3–4 (1930) 49–87.

Pfiffig, A. J. *Studien zu den Agramer Mummienbinden* (Vienna 1963).

Prayon, F. "Deorum sedes," *ArchCl* 43 (1991) 1285–95.

Rix, H. "Les prières du Liber Linteus de Zagreb," *LPRH* (Paris 1997) 391–99.

———, ed. *Etruskische Texte: Editio Minor* (Tübingen 1991).

Roncalli, F. *Scrivere etrusco* (Milan 1985).

Sassatelli, G. *La città etrusca di Marzabotto* (Bologna 1989).

Thulin, C. "Die Götter des Martianus Capella und der Bronzerleber von Piacenza," in *Religionsgeschichtliche Vers. und Vorarb* 3.1 (1906).

Torelli, M. *Elogia Tarquiniensia* (Florence 1975).

———. "Secespita, praefericulum," in *Etrusca et Italica* (Pisa 1997) 575–98.

Van der Meer, L. B. *The Bronze Liver of Piacenza* (Amsterdam 1987).

———. "Lecur Placentinum and the Orientation of the Etruscan Haruspex," *BABesch* 54 (1979) 57–131.

## DEATH, THE DEAD, TOMBS, AND THE AFTERWORLD

Akerström, A. *Studien über die etruskischen Gräber* (Lund 1934).

Andersen, H. "The Etruscan Ancestral Cult: Its Origins and Development and the Importance of Anthropomorphization," *AnalRom* 21 (1993) 7–66.

Andrén, A. "Il santuario della necropoli di Cannicella," *StEtr* 35 (1967).

Bartoloni, G. "Riti funerari dell'aristocrazia in Etruria (Veio)," *Opus* 3 (1984) 13–29.

Bartoloni, G., F. Buranelli, V. d'Atri, and S. de Santis. *Le urne a capanna rinvenute in Italia* (Rome 1987).

Bérard, C. *Anodos* (Rome 1974).

Blanck, H. *La Tomba dei Rilievi di Cerveteri* (Rome 1986).

Bonfante, L. "Human Sacrifice on an Etruscan Urn in New York," *AJA* 88 (1984) 531–39.

Boosen, M. *Etruskische Meermischwesen: Untersuchungen zu Typologie und Bedeutung* (Rome 1986).

Briguet, M.-F. *Le sarcophage des époux de Cerveteri du Musée du Louvre* (Florence 1989).

Briquel, D. "Regards étrusques sur l'Au-delà," in *La mort, les morts et l'Au-delà* (Caen 1987) 263ff.

Bruni, S. *I lastroni a scala* (Rome 1986).

Brunn, H., and G. Körte. *I rilievi delle urne etrusche,* 2 vols. (Berlin 1870–1916).

Bruschetti, P., and P. Zamarchi Grassi. *Cortona Etrusca: Esempi di architettura funeraria* (Cortona 1999).

Buranelli, F., *La Tomba François di Vulci* (Rome 1987).

———. *L'urna Calabresi* (Rome 1985).

# Thematic Bibliography

Camporeale, G. "Scene etrusche di protesi," *RM* 66 (1959) 37–44.

Cataldi-Dini, M. "La Tomba dei Demoni Azzuri," in colloquium on *Tarquinia: ricerche, scavi e prospettive*, 1986 (Milan 1987) 37–42.

Colonna di Paolo, E. *Necropoli rupestre del Viterbese* (Novara 1978).

Cristofani, M. "Pittura funeraria e celebrazione della morte: la Tomba dell'Orco." Colloquium on *Tarquinia: ricerche, scavi e prospettive*, 1986 (Milan 1987) 191–202.

———. "Ricerche sulle pitture della Tomba François di Vulci," *DialArch* 1 (1967) 186–219.

———. *Statue-cinerario chiusine di età classica* (Rome 1975).

———. "La 'Venere' di Cannicella," in *Santuario e culto nella necropoli di Cannicella* (Orvieto 1986).

D'Agostino, B. "L'ideologia funeraria nell'età del ferro in Campania," in *La mort, les morts dans les sociétés anciennes* (Ischia 1977) 203–21.

———. "L'immagine, la pittura e la tomba," *Prospettiva* 32 (1983) 2–12.

———. "La Sirene, il tuffatore e la porta dell'Ades," *AION* 4 (1982) 43–50.

Defosse, P. "Génie funéraire ravisseur (Calu) sur quelques urnes étrusques," *AntCl* 41 (1972) 487ff.

de la Genière, J. "Rituali funebri e produzione di vasi a Tarquinia," in colloquium on *Tarquinia: ricerche, scavi e prospettive*, 1986 (Milan 1987) 203–8.

de Ruyt, F. *Charun, démon étrusque de la mort* (Rome 1934).

Ducati, P. "Le pietre funerarie felsinee," *MonAnt* 20 (1910).

Gempeler, R. D. *Die etruskische Kanopen: Herstellung, Typologie, Entwicklungsgeschichte* (Einsiedeln 1975).

Guzzo, P. G. *Le fibule in Etruria dal VI al I secolo* (Florence 1972).

Haynes, S. "Thoughts on the Winged Female Figure in the Funerary Sculpture of Chiusi," in G. Maetzke, ed., *La civiltà di Chiusi e del suo territorio*. Atti del 17 convegno di studi etruschi ed italici, Chianciano Terme, 1989 (Florence 1993) 297–309.

Herbig, R. *Die jüngeretruskischen Steinsarkophage* (Berlin 1952).

Höckmann, U. "Gallierdarstellungen in der etruskischen Grabkunst des 2. Jh," *JdI* 106 (1991) 1991ff.

Hostetter, E. *Bronzes from Spina*, 2 vols. (Mainz 1986–2000).

Hughes, D. *Human Sacrifice in Ancient Greece* (London 1991).

Jannot, J.-R. "Charun et Charôn," *CRAI* (1991) 443–64.

———. "Charu, Tuchulcha et les autres," *RM* 100 (1993) 59–81.

———. "The Etruscans and the Afterworld," *EtrSt* 7 (2000).

———. "Phersu, Phersuna, Persona," in *Spectacles sportifs et scéniques* (Rome 1991) 281–320.

———. "A propos de la tombe du lit funèbre," *Studia Tarquiniensia* (Rome 1988) 53–68.

———. "Sur les fausses portes étrusques," *Latomus* 43 (1984) 273–83.

———. "Sur la représentation étrusque des morts," in *La Mort, les Morts et l'Au-delà* (Caen 1987) 279ff.

Krauskopf, I. *Heroen, Götter und Dämonen auf Etruskischen Skarabeen* (Mannheim 1995).

———. *Todesdämonen und Tötengötter im vorhellenistischen Etrurien: Kontinuität und Wandel* (Florence 1987).

Kurtz, D., and J. Boardman. *Greek Burial Customs* (London 1982).

Mansuelli, G. *Guida alla città di Marzabotto* (Bologna 1982).

# Thematic Bibliography

Massa-Pairault, F.-H. "Problemi di lettura della pittura funeraria a Orvieto," in *Lettura e interpretazione della produzione pittorica del IV secolo a.c. all'ellenismo, Dialoghi di Archeologia* (1983.2) 19–42.

Moltesen, M., and C. Weber-Lehmann. *Etruskische Grabmalerei* (Mainz 1992).

Naso, A. *Architetture dipinte: Decorazioni parietali non figurate nelle tombe a camera dell'Etruria meridionale (VII–V sec. a. C.)* (Rome 1996).

Oleson, J. P. *The Sources of Innovation in Later Etruscan Tomb Design (ca. 350–100 B.C.)* (Rome 1982).

Pairault, F.-H. *Recherches sur quelques séries d'urnes de Volterra* (Rome 1972).

Paschinger, E. *Die etruskische Todesgöttin Vanth* (Vienna 1992).

Prayon, F. *Frühetruskische Grab- und Hausarchitektur. RM-EH* 22 (Heidelberg 1975).

Rebuffat Emmanuel, D. "Le jeu de Phersu à Tarquinia," *CRAI* (1983) 421–38.

Roncalli, F. "Iconographie funéraire et topographie de l'Au-delà en Étrurie," *LPRH* (Paris 1997) 37–55.

———. *Le lastre dipinte di Cerveteri* (Florence 1965).

Sassatelli, G. "Una nuova stele felsinea," in *Studi Zuffa* (Rimini 1984) 107–25.

Scheffer, C. "Harbingers of Death? The Female Demon in Late Etruscan Funerary Art," in *Munuscula Romana* (Stockholm 1991) 51–63.

Simon, E. "Sentiment religieux et vision de la mort," *LPRH* (Paris 1997) 449–58.

Steingräber, S. "Le culte des morts et les monuments de pierre étrusques," *LPRH* (Paris 1997) 97–117.

Steuernagel, D. *Menschenopfer und Mord am Altar* (Wiesbaden 1998).

Stopponi, S. *La Tomba della Scrofa Nera* (Rome 1983).

Thuillier, J. P. "Une base de Chiusi avec représentation de jeux funéraires," *RA* 2 (1997) 243–60.

van Stratten, H. "Gifts for the Gods," in H. S. Versnel, ed., *Faith, Hope and Worship* (Leiden 1981) 64–151.

Zamarchi Grassi, P., ed., *La Cortona dei principes* (Cortona 1992).

———. "Un edificio per il culto funerario: Nuovi dati sul tumulo II del Sodo a Cortona," *RdA* 22 (1998) 19–26.

### MONUMENTS, TEMPLES, ALTARS, AND ARCHITECTURAL PROGRAMS

Aebischer, P. "Notes et suggestions concernant le culte des eaux," *StEtr* 6 (1932) 123ff.

Akerström, A. "Untersuchungen über die figurlichen Terrakottenfriese aus Etrurien und Latium," *OpRom* 1 (1954) 191–231.

Ampolo, C. "Il gruppo acroteriale di S.Omobono," in colloquium: *La formazione della città nel Lazio, DialArch* (1980) 32–35.

Andrén, A. *Archeological Terracottas from Etrusco-Italic Temples* (Lund 1939).

———. "Origine e formazione dell'architectura templare," *RendPontAcc* 32 (1959–60).

———. "Osservazioni sulle terrecotte architettoniche Etrusco Italiche," *OpRom* 8 (1971) 1–16.

Bartoccini, R. *Il tempio grande di Vulci* (Louvain 1963).

Bartoloni, G. "Palazzo o tempio, Poggio Buco," *AION* 14 (1992) 9–33.

Beazley, J. D. *Etruscan Vase Painting* (Oxford 1947).

Bloch, R. "Urbanisme et religion," in colloqium: *Studi sulla città antica* (Bologna 1970) 11–17.

# Thematic Bibliography

Boëthius, A. *Etruscan and Early Roman Architecture* (Harmondsworth 1970).
———. "Vitruvio e il tempio tuscanico," *StEtr* 24 (1955) 137–42.
Boldi, A. "Il culto delle acque e le stipi votivi salutari nel territorio aretino," *Atti Petrarca* (1938) 306–13.
Bonamici, M. *Volterra, l'acropoli e il suo santuario: scavi 1987–1995* (Pisa 2003).
Bonghi Jovino, M. "L'Ara della Regina," in colloquium: *Tarquinia: Richerche, scavi, prospettive,* Milan, 1986 (Milan 1987).
———. "La phase archaïque de l'Ara della Regina," *LPRH* (Paris 1997) 69–97.
Brown, F. *Cosa: The Making of a Roman Town* (Ann Arbor 1980).
———. "Cosa II: The Temples of the Arx," *MAAR* 26 (1960).
Brown, W. L. *The Etruscan Lion* (Oxford 1960).
Bruschetti, P. *Il lampadario di Cortona* (Cortona 1979).
Castagnoli, F. "Sulla tipologia degli altari di Lavinio," *BullCom* 77 (1959–60) 145–72.
———. "Il culto di Minerva a Lavinium," *Quaderni, Acc.Lincei* 246 (1979).
Catalogue. *Santuari d'Etruria* (Milan 1985).
———. *Satricum, una città latina* (Florence 1982).
Coarelli, F. *Il Foro Boario* (Rome 1988).
Colonna, G. *Bronzi votivi umbro-sabellici a figura umana* (Florence 1970).
———. "Le iscrizioni votive etrusche," *ScAnt* 3–4 (1989–90) 875ff.
———. "Strutture treatriformi in Etruria," in *Spectacles sportifs et scéniques*, CEFR, fasc. 172 (Rome 1993) 321–47.
———. "Urbanistica e architectura," in *Rasenna* (Milan 1986) 369–530.
———, ed. *Il santuario di Portonaccio a Veio, 1: Gli scavi di Massimo Pallottino nella zona dell'altare (1939–1940)*, MemLinc, Miscellanea 6.3 (Rome 2002).
Comella, A.-M. "Apollo Soranos? Il programma figurativo del Tempio dello Scasato," *Ostraka* 2 (1993) 301–16.
———. *Il materiale votivo tardo di Gravisca* (Rome 1978).
Cristofani, M. *Città e campagna nell'Etruria settentrionale* (Arezzo 1976).
———. *Gli Etruschi in Maremma* (Milan 1981).
De Waele, J. "I templi della Mater Matuta a Satricum," *Meded* 43 (1981) 7–68.
Edlund-Berry, I. *The Gods and the Place* (Stockholm 1987).
———. "Ritual Destruction of Cities and Sanctuaries: The 'Un-founding' of the Archaic Monumental Building at Poggio Civitate (Murlo)," in R. D. De Puma and J. P. Small, eds., *Murlo and the Etruscans* (Madison 1994) 16–28.
———. *The Seated and Standing Statue Akroteria from Poggio Civitate (Murlo)* (Rome 1992).
Fortuna, A., and F. Giovannoni. *Il Lago degli Idoli: testimonianze etrusche in Falterona* (Florence 1975).
Giuliani, F., and P. Sommella. "Lavinium," *PP* 32 (1977) 356ff.
Gros, P. *L'architecture romaine* (Paris 1996).
Jannot, J.-R. "Deux édifices clusiens," *MEFRA* 86 (1974) 723–44.
Knell, H. "Der etruskische Tempel nach Vitruvius," *RM* 90 (1983) 91–101.
Knoop, R. *Antefixa Satricana* (Assen-Wolferboro 1987).
Lulof, P. S. *Late Archaic Terracotta Statues from Satricum* (Amsterdam 1991).
———, ed. *Deliciae Fictiles*, 2 vols. (Amsterdam 1997).

# Thematic Bibliography

Orsi, P. "Ubicazione e ricostruzione dell'ara italo-etrusca," *StEtr* 16 (1942).
Prayon, F. "Sur l'orientation des édifices cultuels," *LPRH* (Paris 1997) 357–73.
———. "Wasserkulte in Etrurien," in *Die Welt der Etrusker* (Berlin 1988) 77–79.
Rastrelli, A. "La decorazione fittile del edificio sacro in località I Fucoli presso Chianciano Terme," in *I Cicli figurativi di età republicana, Ostraka* 2 (1993).
———. "L'edificio sacro di Fucoli," in *La civiltà di Chiusi e del suo territorio*. Atti del 17 convegno di studi etruschi ed italici, Chianciano Terme, 1989 (Florence 1993) 463ff.
Romualdi, A. *Catalogo del deposito di Brolio in Val di Chiana* (Rome 1981).
Roncalli, F. "Le strutture del santuario," in *Santuario e culto della necropoli di Cannicella* (Orvieto 1986).
Shoe, L. T. "Etruscan and Roman Republican Mouldings," *MAAR* 28 (1965).
Somella Mura, A. *L'area sacra del Foro Boario* (Rome 1981) 119–20.
———. "L'area Sacra di Sant' Omobono," *PP* 32 (1977) 172–73.
———. "Il gruppo di Apollo e Athena," *PP* 36 (1981) 59–64.
Staccioli, R. A. *Modelli di edifici etrusco italici: i modelli votivi* (Florence 1968).
Torelli, M. "Il santuario di Hera a Gravisca," *PP* 26 (1971) 44–67.
Turfa, J. M. "Anatomical Votives and Italian Medical Traditions," in R. De Puma and J. P. Small, eds., *Murlo and the Etruscans: Art and Society in Ancient Etruria* (Madison 1994) 224–40.
von Freitag-Löringhoff, B. *Das Giebelrelief von Telamon* (Mainz 1986).
von Vacano, O. W., and B. von Freitag. *Il frontone di Talamone* (Florence 1982).
———. "Osservazioni riguardanti la storia edilizia del tempio di Talamonaccio," in *La coroplastica templare etrusca*. 16 Convegno di Studi Etruschi (Florence 1992) 57–68.
Winter, N. A. "Architectural Terracottas Decorated with Human Heads," *RM* 85 (1978).
Zuffa, M. "I frontoni e il fregio di Civitalba," in *Studi Calderini e Paribeni* (Milan 1956) 267ff.

ETRUSCAN GODS AND HELLENIZATION

Adam, A.-M. *Bronzes étrusques et italiques de la Bibliothèque Nationale* (Paris 1984).
Bayet, J. *Herclè* (Paris 1926).
Bérard, Cl. "L'héroisation et la formation de la cité," in colloquium: *Architecture et Société* (Rome 1983) 43–59.
Bomati, Y. "Phersu et le monde Dionysiaque," *Latomus* 45 (1986) 21ff.
Bruhl, A. *Liber Pater* (Paris 1953).
Bruni, S. "Un nuovo rilievo tarquinese con suicido di Aiace," *Athenaeum* 64 (1986) 486–92.
Burkert, W. "La tragedia Greca e il rito del sacrificio," in *Origini Selvagge* (Bari 1991).
Camporeale, G. "Banalizzazione etrusche di miti greci," *StEtr* 28 (1960) 21–35.
———. "La mitologia figurata nella cultura etrusca arcaica," in *Secondo congresso internazionale etrusco, Florence 1985* (Rome 1989) 905–24.
———. "Thalna e scene mitologiche connesse," *StEtr* 28 (1960) 233–62.
———. "Variations sur le thème d'Héraclès et le lion," *LPRH* (Paris 1997) 13ff.
Capdeville, G. "Substitution de victimes dans les sacrifices d'animaux," *MEFRA* 83 (1971) 283ff.
Catalogue. *Le Chimera e il suo mito* (Arezzo 1994).
Cerchiai, L. "Achille e Troilos in Etruria, alcuni ipotesi su due cippi chiusini," *DialArch* 8 (1990–92).

# Thematic Bibliography

Chiadini, G. "Selvans," *StEtr* (1996) 161–79.
Coarelli, F. "Le pitture della Tomba François, una proposta di lettura," *DialArch* 3 (1983) 43–69.
Colloquium, *I culti stranieri in Etruria*, Fondazione Faina (Orvieto 1988).
———. *Die Göttin von Pyrgi* (Tübingen 1979).
Colonna, G. "La dea etrusca Cel e i santuari del Trasimeno," *RivStorAnt* 6 (1976) 45–62.
———. "Il Maestro del'Eracle e della Minerva: Nuova luca sull'attività dell'officina Veiente," *OpRom* 16.1: *Lectiones Boethianae* 6 (1987) 7–41.
———. "Novità su i culti di Pyrgi," *RPAA* 57 (1984–85) 101–31.
———. "Riflessi del epos greco nell'arte degli Etruschi," *Convegno Taranto* (Toronto 1980) 303–20.
———. "Tarquitius Priscus e il Tempio di Giove Capitolino," *PP* 36 (1981) 41–59.
Cristofani, M. "Celeritas Solis Filia, Kotinos," in *Mélanges E. Simon* (Mainz 1992) 347–49.
———. *Hellenismus in Mittelitalien* (Göttingen 1976).
———. "Masculin/féminin dans la théonymie étrusque," *LPRH* (Paris 1997) 209–23.
———. *Statue-cinerario chiusine di età classica* (Rome 1975).
———. "Sul processo di antropomorfizzazione del panteon etrusco," in *Miscellanea etrusco-italica*, QArchEtr 22 (Rome 1993) 9–21.
———. "La testa Lorenzini," *StEtr* 47 (1979) 85–92.
———. *Urne Volterrane* (Florence 1977).
Cristofani, M., and M. Martelli. "Fufluns Pachies: sugli aspetti del culto di Bacco in Etruria," *StEtr* 46 (1978) 119–33.
de Simone, C. *Die griechischen Entlehnungen im Etruskischen*, 2 vols. (Wiesbaden 1968–70).
de Visser, M. W. *Die nicht menschgestaltigen Götter der Griechen* (Leiden 1903).
Fauth, W. "Lasa Turan Vanth," in *Festschrift G. Radke* (Münster 1986) 116–31.
Hampe, R., and E. Simon. *Griechische Sagen der frühen etruskischen Kunst* (Mainz 1964).
Heurgon, J. "Influences grecques sur la religion latine," *REL* 35 (1957) 106ff.
Jannot, J.-R. "Charu, Tuchulcha et les autres," *RM* 100 (1993) 59–82.
Krauskopf, I. "Culsans und Culsu," in *Festschrift G. Radke* (Münster 1986) 156–63.
———. "Influences grecques et orientales sur la représentation des dieux étrusques," *LPRH* (Paris 1997) 25–36.
———. "Notices about Gods," in *Dizionario della civiltà etrusca* (Florence 1985).
———. "Notices about Gods," in *LIMC* (Zürich–München 1981–92).
———. *Der thebanischen Sagenkreis und andere griechische Sagen in der etruskischen Kunst* (Mainz 1974).
———. *Todesdämonen und Totengötter im vorhellenistischen Etrurien: Kontinuität und Wandel* (Florence 1987).
Kretschmer, P. "Die etruskische Gott Sethlans," *Glotta* 32 (1954) 159.
Maggiani, A. In *La Chimera e il suo mito* (Arezzo 1990).
———. "L'uomo e il sacro nei rituali e nella religione etrusca," in *La civiltà del mediterraneo e il sacro* 3 (Milan 1992).
Maggiani, A., and E. Simon. "Il pensiero scientifico e religioso," in M. Cristofani, ed., *Gli Etruschi, una nuova immagine* (Florence 1984).
Massa-Pairault, F.-H. *La cité des Etrusques* (Paris 1996).

# Thematic Bibliography

———. *Iconologia e politica nell'Italia antia: Roma, Lazio, Etruria dal VII al I secolo a. C.* (Milan 1992).

———. "Lasa Vecu, Lasa Vecuvia," *DialArch* ser. 6, vol. 3 (1988) 200–235.

———. "Sacra Acheruntia, Libri Acheruntici: culture grecque et Etrusca disciplina," in colloquium: *L'Etrusca Disciplina*, Fondazione Faina (Orvieto 1987).

Massa-Pairault, F.-H., and J.-M. Pailler. *Bolsena* 5.1 (Rome 1979).

Nagy, H. *Votive Terracottas from the "Vignaccia," Cerveteri, in the Lowie Museum of Anthropology* (Rome 1988).

Olzscha, S. "Das Aiseraproblem," *StEtr* 39 (1971) 95–105.

Pailler, J. M. *Bacchanalia, la répression de 186 à Rome et en Italie* (Rome 1988).

———. "Fufluns e Catha," 2d Convegno Internazionale Etrusco (Rome 1989) 1271–81.

Pautasso, A. *Il deposito votivo presso la porta nord a Vulci* (Rome 1994).

Pellegrini, G. "Divinità paleovenete," *PP* 6 (1951) 87–94.

Pfiffig, A. J. *Ein Opfergelubde an etruskischen Minerva* (Vienna 1968).

Radke, G. *Die Götter Altitaliens* (Münster 1979).

Rallo, A. *Lasa: iconografia ed esegesi* (Florence 1974).

Rebuffat Emmanuel, D. *Le Miroir étrusque d'après la collection du Cabinet des Médailles* (Rome 1973).

Rix, H. "Die Eindringen griechischer Mythen in Etrurien," in *Die Aufnahme fremder Kultureinflüsse in Etrurien* (Mannheim 1980) 96–106.

———. "Etruskische Aiseras," in *Festschrift F. Altheim* (Berlin 1969) 280–92.

———. "Rapporti onomastici fra il pantheon etrusco e quello romano," in *Gli Etruschi e Roma* (Rome 1981) 104–26.

Salskov Roberts, H. "The Creation of a Religious Iconography," in *Aspects of Hellenism in Italy*, Acta Hyperborea 5 (1993) 287–318.

Santangelo, M. "Una terracotta di Faleries e lo Zeus di Fidia," *Bollettino di Archeologia* 33 (1948).

Simon, E. "Culsu, Culsans, und Ianus," in 2d Convegno Internazionale Etrusco (Rome 1989) 1271–81.

Small, J. P. *Cacus and Marsyas in Etrusco-Roman Legend* (Princeton 1982).

———. "Herclè," in *LIMC*.

———. *Studies Related to the Theban Cycle in Late Etruscan Urns* (Rome 1981).

Spivey, N. *The Micali Painter and His Followers* (Oxford 1987).

Torelli, M. *Lavinio e Roma* (Rome 1984).

———."Per la definizione del commercio greco-orientale, il caso di Gravisca," *PP* 37 (1982) 304–25.

———. "Il santuario greco di Gravisca," *PP* 32 (1977) 398–458.

Van der Meer, L. B. "Archetype, Transmitting Model, Prototype: Studies on Etruscan Urns from Volterra," *BABesch* 50 (1975) 75ff.

———. "Etruscan Urns from Volterra: Studies on Mythological Representations," *BABesch* 52–53 (1977–78) 57ff.

———. "The Evolution of the Etruscan Pantheon," *Cosmos* 5 (1989) 77–91.

———. "Greek and Local Elements," in *Italian Iron Age Artefacts* (London 1986) 439–46.

———. "Maris, Birth, Life and Death on Two Etruscan Mirrors," *BABesch* 63 (1988) 115–28.

# Thematic Bibliography

———. "Religion ombrienne et religion étrusque," *LPRH* (Paris 1997) 223–33.

Van Essen, C. Cl. *Did Orphic Influence on Etruscan Tomb Painting Exist?* (Amsterdam/Paris 1927).

Verzar, A. "Pyrgi e l'Afrodite di Cipro," *MEFRA* 92 (1980) 35–84.

Von Freitag Löringhoff, B. "Die Bronze Statuette BM 1149: Vanth oder Erinys?" in *Italian Iron Age Artefacts* (London 1982) 453–57.

Zamarchi Grassi, P. *Il Museo dell'Accademia Etrusca di Cortona* (Cortona 1996).

Zancani Montuoro, P. "Un mito italiota in Etruria," *ASAtene* (1950) 85–98.

Zazoff, P. *Etruskische Skarabäen* (Mainz 1968).

# Glossary

**acroterion:** sculptural decorative element in the round surmounting the corners of the pediment gable and the ridge beam of the roof.

*adyton (ἄδυτον):* room on the interior of a temple to which access is forbidden to the uninitiated. Most commonly it is a small space situated behind the *naos*.

*agon (ἀγών):* sports competition. Adj: agonistic.

**Aita:** Etruscan god of the Afterworld, equivalent to the Greek Hades and the Latin Pluto. Also see *Calu*.

**alabastron:** small perfume vessel originally made of alabaster. Its form is long and narrow with a rounded base.

**aniconic:** having no figural representation.

**antefix:** terracotta decorative element serving to mask the open end of a line of tiles at the edge of the roof.

*antepagmentum:* decorated terracotta plaque that masks and protects the end of a roof beam.

**anthemion:** stylized floral or vegetal decoration placed at the peak of an architectural element.

**Acquarossa:** archaeological site of the Archaic Period in the area of Viterbo.

*asylon (ἄσυλον):* an area, often within a port, which enjoyed a certain autonomy and welcomed foreigners (Asylie).

*Atunis:* (Greek Adonis) Lover of Aphrodite/Turan. Frequently depicted on mirrors; worshipped in a cult at Gravisca.

*auguraculum:* space for observing the flight of birds. See *templum*.

*aulos (αὐλός):* double oboe. Sometimes (mistakenly) called a double flute.

**auspication:** observation of bird omens (or *ornithoscopia*).

**biga:** two-wheeled chariot pulled by two horses.

**Blera:** archaeological site to the south of Viterbo. Known for its rock-cut necropoleis.

**Bolsena:** city near the lake of the same name; here Roman Volsinii was founded after the destruction of Velzna (Orvieto).

*bothros (βόθρος):* altar for chthonian sacrifices; it is pierced by a central channel connecting it to the ground below.

**boustrophedon:** writing that changes direction at the end of each line, as an ox traces a furrow.

*Caere:* (Cerveteri) powerful Etruscan maritime city to the north of Rome; among its famous ports were Pyrgi and Alsium.

*Calu:* chthonian deity or demon, depicted covered with the skin of a dog and emerging from a well on urns from Perugia and Volterra. This scene alone would not make him very important, but his may be the most ancient name for Aita/Hades.

*carpentum:* four-wheeled wagon covered with a semi-cylindrical awning.

*Castel d'Asso:* site in inland Etruria, west of Viterbo, between Tarquinia and the Lago di Bolsena. Known for its rock-cut necropoleis.

*Catha:* solar deity.

*cella:* the room within a temple that contained the cult statue. (Greek: *naos*).

# Glossary

**Chiusi:** Etruscan city in the Val di Chiana; Etr. *Clevsi,* Lat. *Camars* or *Clusium.* North of Orvieto, south of Arezzo.

**chthonian:** related to the underworld, infernal or funerary.

**cippus:** vertical stone used as a marker, sometimes for religious purposes (for borders, tombs, etc.).

**cista:** box, often of metal, to hold objects of value. The majority are cylindrical and adorned with handles. The metal, usually sheet-bronze, carried engraved decoration.

**cithara:** musical instrument with strings stretched over a wooden body; a lyre, harp, or lute.

**Clusian/Clusine:** of Chiusi.

**Cosa:** Roman colony founded in 273. Near Orbetello. American excavation.

**crotalum:** castanet.

*ekphora (ἐκφορά):* transport of the dead body to the place of burial.

*emporion (ἐμπόριον):* Greek commercial establishment in a non-Greek land; these enjoyed a sort of extraterritoriality and often developed a mixed culture.

**epiklesis:** adjective accompanying the name of a deity and serving to define his or her function or place of worship.

*etrusca disciplina:* collection of sacred texts revealed to the Etruscans by the gods and containing Etruscan knowledge and laws.

*evocatio:* the ritual of "calling out"; turning away and adopting a deity that is protecting an enemy.

**Falerii:** (Città Castellana) city of south Etruria, capital of the Faliscan territory; taken and destroyed by Rome in 241.

**Faliscan:** (Faliscan territory) region situated to the north of Rome and to the east of the Lago di Bracciano. (Falerii, Capena).

*favissa: fossa,* or a reservoir for a votive deposit.

*genos (γένος):* or *gens,* a family broadly defined to include blood relatives and the intimates and dependents of a household.

**gentilicius:** belonging to a *gens* or *genos,* that is, to a great noble family extended in the broadest sense.

**Gravisca:** (Porto Clementino) the port of Tarquinia and the sanctuaries established in the area of the port.

**Grotta Porcina:** site in inland Etruria between Tarquinia and the Lago di Vico.

**hepatoscopy:** observation of the livers of victims for the purpose of divination.

*heroon (ἡρῷον):* small sanctuary for the cult of a hero (demi-god), the founder of a city or of a great family.

**hierodulus:** slave or servant of a deity.

*hybris (ὕβρις):* wanton excess. The greatest fault, for the Greeks: it is to refuse to admit that a human is only a human.

*in antis:* between two *antae,* that is, between the extensions of two lateral walls.

*kettos:* sea dragon with the neck and shoulders of a horse and a body in the form of a snake.

*kline (κλίνη):* bed or banquette for sleeping, eating, or laying out a corpse.

*kore:* depiction of a young girl standing, clothed, and making an offering.

*kottabos (κότταβος):* a game of skill played during banquets, its goal was to hit with the contents of a wine cup a small metal cup balanced on a vertical shaft. By extension, this word

# Glossary

designates the metal shaft and its decorative support. This object was part of the expensive furnishings of upper class households.

*kouros:* depiction of a young man standing, nude, with his arms down against his body.

**lectisternium:** meal offered to the effigy of a divinity placed on a dining couch.

*limitatio:* the procedure of marking out boundaries, assured by the surveyors and guaranteed by the state.

*lituus:* 1. the curled staff of augurs and priests; 2. straight trumpet with a curled-back bell.

*lucumon:* generic word for the kings of Archaic Etruria.

**lyre:** musical instrument with strings of equal length stretched across the shell of a tortoise.

**mantic:** of or pertaining to divination, prediction of the future; oracular.

**megalography:** large wall painting, whose composition presents figures close to human scale.

**Murlo:** Archaic archaeological site south of Siena. Perhaps the religious and political center of a northern Etruscan league.

*naiskos (ναΐσκος):* small sacred building; small *naos*. (pl. *naiskoi*).

*naos (ναός):* the most sacred part of a sanctuary, the room where the god resides. Lat. *cella*. The term sometimes refers to the entire interior of a sacred building.

**Norchia:** site in inland Etruria northeast of Tarquinia. Known for its rock-cut necropoleis.

*oikos (οἶκος):* in the evolution of architecture, a house consisting of a single elongated room.

**opisthodomos:** a temple's rear porch, supported by columns and comparable to the porch of the façade.

*opus quadratum:* building construction using squared, dressed stones.

*ostenta:* Latin term for omens. *Ostenta saecularia* = omens announcing the end of a *saeculum*.

**uranian:** relating to the sky. A uranian cult honors a celestial deity. Opp.: chthonian.

**Pacha:** Bacchus, Dionysos-Bacchos.

*panspermia (πανσπερμία):* sacrificial offering of a broth made of all comestible grains.

**peripteral:** surrounded by "wings," i.e., by porticoes supported on rows of columns. Peripteral temple: temple surrounded by columns.

*perirrhanterion:* sacred vessel for lustral water, on three or more supports, which are often anthropomorphic.

**Phersipnai:** queen of the Etruscan Afterworld and wife of Aita (Greek Persephone, Latin Proserpina).

*pixis:* ornamental covered box, usually cylindrical in shape. Archaic Etruscan *pixides* are of ivory.

**podium:** monumental terrace, or the base of the Etrusco-italic temple.

**Porsenna:** tyrant/king of Chiusi at the end of the 6th century. He extended his power southward (Orvieto) and seized Rome.

**princeps** (pl. **principes**): aristocrat having the function of political chief, king, tyrant, or supreme magistrate of an Etruscan city.

*pronaos:* vestibule which is located before the *naos*/cella.

*propylon:* monumental gateway to an enclosed area.

*prothesis (πρόθεσις):* exposition of the body of a dead person.

**psychopomp:** guide of souls. Role often attributed to Hermes. The hippocamp and, to a lesser degree, the centaur are psychopomp creatures.

*puteal:* a well serving as a channel of communication between the world of the living and the underground world of the dead.

# Glossary

**quadriga:** two-wheeled chariot pulled by four horses.

**sacellum:** small sanctuary.

**Satricum:** site in southern Latium near the Pomptine plain. Temple of *Mater Matuta*.

**Selvans:** Etruscan god whose name is inscribed twice on the Piacenza Liver. God of boundaries and probably of oaths.

***sunnaoi*** (σύνναοι)**:** those who have a common *naos:* term applied to deities who share a cult place.

**symmachia:** military alliance among Greek cities, usually for the purpose of defense.

**Tarquitius Priscus:** author of the 1st c. B.C. Macrobius has preserved a part of his work on omens.

***temenos*** (τέμενος)**:** in Greece, an enclosure sacred to a god.

***templum:*** sacred space oriented and delimited in the sky by an augur and used for the observation of the flight of birds or celestial phenomena. See *auguraculum*.

***taeniae:*** ribbons or fillets used to decorate sacred places or objects or the victims of sacrifices. They adorn, protect, and mark the sacred character of places.

***thalamos*** (θάλαμος)**:** chamber. *Thalamos* house: house consisting of one long room with an entrance on one of its short sides.

***thesauros*** (θεσαυρός)**:** or treasury: small votive building offered in an important sanctuary by a city or a people.

***Thesmophoria*** (Θεσμοφόρια)**:** religious ceremonies in honor of Demeter. Important in Athens and also in the majority of Greek cities.

**triga:** two-wheeled chariot drawn by three horses.

***tutulus:*** hairstyle of Etruscan women; the hair is twisted into a narrow conical shape.

**tyrant:** monarch whose accession to power does not appear legitimate and whose regime is usually hostile to the aristocrats. The term is not pejorative.

**Vea:** Etruscan deity equivalent to Demeter; honored particularly at Gravisca and Volsinii. Perhaps the origin of the name of Veii.

**Veii:** Etruscan city 17 km. north of Rome; it dominated a ford of the Tiber. The first Etruscan city conquered by Rome (396).

**Villanovan:** (Named from the site of Villanova, near Bologna) proto-historic culture of Etruria, tenth to eighth centuries B.C.

**Vulci:** city of mid-coastal Etruria on the Fiora river. Its principal port was at Regae.

# Illustration Credits

1.1. S. Haynes, *Etruscan Civilization: A Cultural History* (Los Angeles 2000) 280.
1.3. M. Cataldi, *I sarcophagi etruschi delle famiglie Partunu, Camna, Pulena* (Rome 1988).
1.4. *CIE Tarq.* 5430.
1.5. F. Roncalli, *Scrivere etrusco* (Milan 1985) 30 [III].
1.6. S. Haynes, *Etruscan Civilization*, 271, fig. 219.
1.8. M. Cristofani, *Tabula Capuana* (Florence 1995).
2.2. B. van der Meer, *The Bronze Liver of Piacenza* (Amsterdam 1987).
2.4. Catalogue, *The Etruscans* (Venice 2000) no. 158.
2.6. Catalogue, *Antichità dell'Umbria a New York* (Perugia 1991) fig. 1.6.
2.7. *Antichità dell'Umbria a New York*, 275, fig. 6.5.
2.8. F. Buranelli, *La Tomba François di Vulci* (Rome 1987).
2.9. A. Maggiani, *La divination dans le monde italique* 3 (Tours 1986) 28.
2.10. Maggiani, *La divination dans le monde italique*, 3.
3.2. M. Cristofani, *Tabula Capuana* (Florence 1995).
3.3. *CIE* 5237.
3.4. J.-R. Jannot, *Les reliefs archaïques de Chiusi* (Rome 1984) D,I,14.
3.5. M. Cristofani, *Le lastre dipinte da Cerveteri* (Florence 1965) no. 3.
4.1. H. Blanck and C. Weber Lehmann, *Malerei der Etrusker* (Mainz 1987) 209.
4.2. Catalogue, *Les Étrusques et l'Europe* (Paris 1992) 93.
4.3. M. F. Briguet, *Le sarcophage des epoux de Cerveteri du Musée du Louvre* (Florence 1989).
4.4. S. Haynes, *Etruscan Civilization*, 336, and figs. b and c.
4.5. G. Becatti and F. Magi, *Le pitture della Tomba degli Auguri* (Rome 1956).
4.6. L. Banti, *StEtr* 24 (1955–56) 143ff.
4.7. M. Cataldi Dini, "La Tomba dei Demoni Azzuri," in *Tarquinia: ricerche, scavi, prospettive* (Milan 1986).
4.8. J.-R. Jannot, "Charu, Tuchulcha et les autres," *RM* 100 (1993) 59ff.
4.10. J.-R. Jannot, "The Etruscans and the Afterworld," *EtrSt* 7 (2000) 93.
4.11. J.-R. Jannot, "The Etruscans and the Afterworld," 93.
4.13. J.-R. Jannot, in *LPRH*, 153.
5.1. G. Colonna, ed., *Il santuario di Portonaccio a Veio* (Rome 2002).
5.3. M. Bonghi Jovino, *LPRH*, 69ff.
5.5. Catalogue, *Santuari d'Etruria* (Milan 1985) fig. 4.7.
5.6. G. Mansuelli, "La città etrusca di Misano," in *Arte Antica e Moderna* 17 (1962) 14ff.
5.9. G. Colonna, in *Santuari d'Etruria*, 127ff.
5.10. K. M. Phillips, "Excavations in Murlo," *AJA*, 1967–87; idem, *In the Hills of Tuscany* (Philadelphia 1993).
6.1. D. Steurnagel, *Menschenopfer und Mord am Altar* (Wiesbaden 1998) fig. 175.
6.2. S. Bruni, *Archeologia Classica* 46 (1994) 55ff.
6.3. S. Stopponi, *Santuari d'Etruria* (Milan 1985) 150.
6.4. R. Staccioli, *Modelli di edifici etrusco-italici* (Florence 1968) fig. 38; plan: after H. Knell, "Der etruskische Tempel nach Vitruvius," *RM* 90 (1983) 91–101.

## Illustration Credits

6.7. Haynes, *Etruscan Civilization*, 354.
6.8. F. R. Fortunati in *La grande Roma dei Tarquini* (catalogue, Rome 1990) 201ff.
6.9. Staccioli, *Modelli di edifici etrusco-italici*, no. 30.
6.10. F. Brown, "Cosa II, The Temples of the Arx," *MAAR* 26 (1960).
6.11. S. Quilici Gigli in *La grande Roma dei Tarquini*, 251ff.
6.17. *La grande Roma dei Tarquini* (Rome 1990) 133ff.
6.18. A. Somella Mura, in *PP* 172–173 (1977) 62 sq.
6.22. M. Pallottino, "La scuola di Vulca," in *Saggi di Antichità* 3 (Rome 1979) pl. 49.4.
6.23. Pallottino, "La scuola di Vulca," 1005s, fig. 28–39.
6.24. M. Pallottino, "Il grande acroterio femminile," in *Saggi di Antichità* 3, 1037ff.
6.25. Pallottino, "La scuola di Vulca," 1005, figs. 28–39.
6.30. B. von Freitag-Löringhoff, *Das Giebel von Telamon* (Mainz 1986). Soprintendenza Archeologica per la Toscana Firenze.
7.3. J.-R. Jannot, *Les reliefs archaïques de Chiusi* (Rome 1984) 59ff.
7.4. Jannot, *Les reliefs archaïques de Chiusi*, 90ff.
7.6. H. Nagy, "Divinities in the Context of Sacrifice and Cult on Caeretan Votive Terracottas," in R. De Puma and J. P. Small, eds., *Murlo and the Etruscans* (Madison 1994) 212, fig. 19.1.
7.10. S. Haynes, *Etruscan Bronzes* (London 1985) 282, no. 101; E. H. Richardson, *Etruscan Votive Bronzes* (Mainz 1983) 240.
7.11. F. Buranelli, *Bronzi a figura umana* (Vatican City 1999) 120ff., no. 3.
8.1. A.-M. Adam, *Bronzes etrusques et italiques de la Bibliothèque Nationale* (Paris 1984) 166, no. 244; inscription: A. J. Pfiffig, *StEtr* 29 (1961) 150.
8.4. M. Cristofani, "Masculin/féminin dans la théonymie étrusque," in *LPRH*, 209ff.
8.5. Cristofani, "Masculin/féminin dans la théonymie étrusque," 211, fig. 6.
8.7. D. Steurnagel, *Menschenopfer und Mord am Altar* (Wiesbaden 1998) 22ff.
8.8. T. Dohrn, *Die etruskische Kunst im Zeitalter der griechischen Klassik* (Mainz 1982) 52.
9.2. B. von Freitag, "Die Bronzestatuette 1449: etruskische Vanth oder unteritalische Erinys?" in *Italian Iron Age Artefacts* (London 1986) 453ff.

# Index

Achilles, 55 (4.1), 66, 154 (8.7)
Acquarossa, 99, 101, 165
acropolis sanctuaries, 75, 76, 79 (5.6), 79–80
acroterial figures, 85, 94 (5.10), 102, 104, 108, 114 (6.19), 116 (6.21), 117, 118 (6.23), 127, 134, 144
Adonis. *See* Atunis/Adonis
Afterlife, Greek, 54, 62, 65, 70, 71, 180
Afterworld, 4, 9, 9 (1.6), 53, 54, 58, 60, 62, 63, 65, 66, 68, 71, 85, 89, 97, 98, 148, 152 (8.6), 183; animals of, 50, 59–62; doors to, 56, 63 (4.9), 64 (4.10); games and, 48–50, 92–93; Greek influences on, 67–68, 71, 180; journeys to, 59–63, 61 (4.6), 62 (4.7), 64 (4.11); reunion with predeceased relatives in, 64 (4.10), 65. *See also* Aita/Hades; Calu; Charu(n); Culsans/Culsu; Vanth
Aides. *See* Aita/Hades
*Aiser/Eiser*, 173, 178
Aita/Hades, 66, 67, 69, 70, 71, 81, 153, 154 (8.7), 172; on cinerary urns from Perugia, 70–71; deities associated with, 69, 79, 152 (8.6), 152–54, 156, 164, 172, 177, 181; dogs and, 50, 153; at sacrifice of Trojan prisoners for Patroclus, 154 (8.7); in tomb paintings, 64, 66, 70, 153, 191n30 (8.7); on Torre San Severo sarcophagus, 154 (8.7); wolf skin worn by, 66, 70, 153
Alatri temple, 105 (6.9b)
Alpan (attendant of Aphrodite), 150, 150 (8.5), 163, 174
altars, 38, 43, 52, 96, 97 (6.3); with *bothros* (sacrificial pit), 85, 89, 97, 98, 148; on Campana plaques, 38 (3.5), 96; for chthonic sacrifices, 97, 181; deities and, 91, 148, 151; at Fiesole, 96, 97 (6.2); for funerary sacrifices, 39, 51 (3.15), 97, 98; Guglielmi altar, 51 (3.15); for libations, 39, 41 (3.8), 51, 52, 79; at Marzabotto, 79 (5.6), 79–80, 96; at Populonia, 39, 159, 162; at Portonaccio Sanctuary at Veii, 85, 86; at Pyrgi, 80, 89, 90; shapes of, 96, 97 (6.3), 151; urns depicting, 96, 97 (6.1)
Ammianus Marcellinus, 8, 24
Amphiarios, myths of, 174 (9.1), 181
amphorae, 41–43, 42 (3.9), 48, 60, 96, 131
Aninas, Tomb of the (Tarquinia), 63 (4.8)
antefixes, 110, 122
antepagmenta, 105 (6.9a, 6.9b), 110, 111 (6.16), 117. *See also* pediments
Aphrodite. *See* Turan/Aphrodite
Aplu/Apollo, 77, 94 (8.1), 146, 146 (8.2), 147, 180; attributes of, 10, 31–32, 144–45, 146, 160; deities associated with, 4, 5 (1.1), 77, 80, 89–91, 94, 140, 144, 146, 147, 155, 159, 160–61, 161, 165, 171, 180; Greek models for, 140, 143, 144 (8.1), 145–46, 146 (8.2); name on lots, 30, 159; at Pyrgi, 89, 90–91, 146; at Veii, 118 (6.23), 144
Apollo. *See* Aplu/Apollo
Appian, 23
aquatic beasts, 59–60, 153
Ara della Regina Temple, 3, 76 (5.2), 76–78, 77 (5.3), 78 (5.4), 94
architectural features: antefixes, 110, 122; antepagmenta, 105 (6.9a, 6.9b), 110, 111 (6.16), 117; bases, 38 (3.4), 130 (7.4); columns, 101, 102 (6.6); Greek influence in, 91, 99 (6.4a, 6.4b), 100–101, 103–4, 104 (6.8), 105–6, 108; *naiskos*, 52, 91, 98, 121 (6.29), 139; *oikos*, 99, 100; orthogonal scheme, 72, 75; pediments, 78 (5.4), 83–85, 84 (5.7), 102, 105 (6.9a, 6.9b), 110, 121 (6.29), 123; podium, 72, 73, 76, 79, 100, 102, 119 (6.26); Roman influence, 105–6, 106 (6.10); south/southern orientation, 20, 28, 43, 89, 100, 101–2, 116; terraces, 41–42, 52, 76, 80, 86, 96; Vitruvius on, 74, 98, 101–4, 102 (6.6), 107
architecture, Greek, 72, 91, 99 (6.4a, 6.4b), 100, 103–4, 104 (6.8), 105–6, 108
Arezzo, 20 (2.4), 30–31, 31 (2.9), 44–45, 45 (3.10), 80, 82, 88, 123, 135 (7.8), 135–36, 157
Aritimi. *See* Artumes/Artemis
Arnobius, 24, 53
Artames. *See* Artumes/Artemis
Artemis. *See* Artumes/Artemis
Artumes/Artemis, 77, 85, 94, 147, 180
Astarte, 81, 89–91, 109, 157, 194n47. *See also* Uni/Hera/Juno/Mae
*asylon/asyla*, 110, 143, 145, 164
Athena. *See* Menrva/Tecvm/Minerva
Athrpa/Atropos, 14
Atunis/Adonis, 31, 32 (2.10), 91, 150 (8.5)
Augurs, Tomb of the (Tarquinia), 56, 60 (4.5), 129
Augustus, 5, 6–7, 14, 15, 182
Aule Lecu, 18, 19 (2.3), 20, 21
aulos players, 38, 39, 41, 43, 45, 66, 127, 131, 132 (7.6); Roman, 131–32, 132 (7.6)
Aurora. *See* Thesan/Eos/Aurora
auspication, 27, 28, 28 (2.8), 29–30, 43, 178; in *libri rituales*, 29–30
Avl Tarchunus, 125, 126 (7.1). *See also* Tarchunus

Bacchus. *See* Fufluns/Dionysus/Pacha/Bacchus
Banditaccia necropolis (Caere), 55–56
banquets, 46–47, 47 (3.13), 48–49, 55, 57–58, 58 (4.3), 64, 66, 191n35
Baron, Tomb of the (Tarquinia), 41 (3.8)
Bellerophon killing the Chimaera, 16, 82, 135 (7.8)
Belvedere sanctuary (Orvieto), 77, 78 (5.5), 79, 93, 119 (6.26), 120 (6.27, 6.28)

221

# Index

birds, 27, 28, 28 (2.8), 29, 43, 100 (6.14), 178
black-figure amphorae, 41, 48, 60, 96
Blera, 51, 81, 86, 102
Blue Demons, Tomb of the (Tarquinia), 62 (4.7), 68
Bolsena, 6 (1.2), 45, 72, 100, 157, 160, 168
Bomarzo, 41, 132 (7.7), 132–33
*bothros* (sacrificial pit), 85, 89, 97, 98, 148
Brolio sanctuary (Chiusi), 88
bronzes, 26 (2.6), 88, 144 (8.1); Arezzo plowman, 44, 45 (3.10); from Bomarzo, 41, 132 (7.7), 132–33; chariots, 26 (2.6); Chimaera of Arezzo, 82, 135 (7.8), 157; reliefs, 41, 144; from Tuscania, 125, 126 (7.1); urns, 99–100, 100 (6.5); votives, 125, 126 (7.1), 129–30, 138, 139 (7.10)
Bruschi sarcophagus, 65 (4.11)
Bulls, Tomb of the (Tarquinia), 60–61, 61 (4.6), 169

Cacu, 5–6, 6 (1.2), 7, 31
Caecina, 23, 24, 172
Caere/Cerveteri, 9, 10 (1.6), 35, 39 (3.6), 48, 57–58, 58 (4.3), 59 (4.4), 66, 68, 81, 154 (8.7); Aplu/Apollo images from, 144, 145; La Vignaccia, 140, 151; Montetosto complex, 93–94; necropoleis at, 41, 55–56; sanctuaries at, 86–87, 87, 108 (6.12), 109; Tomb of the Sarcophagi, 9, 10 (1.6), 35, 39 (3.6), 48, 59 (4.4), 66, 68, 154 (8.7); tombs at, 9, 10 (1.6), 35, 39 (3.6), 48, 55–56, 59 (4.4), 66, 68, 100, 154 (8.7); Uni temple at, 157; votive terracottas from, 151. *See also* Pyrgi
calendars, 8–9, 9 (1.5), 11 (1.8), 34–36, 36 (3.2), 38–39, 133
Calu, 50, 70, 71, 79, 153–54, 156, 177, 180–81
Campana plaques, 38 (3.5), 96
Campana Tomb (Veii), 99
Campania, 44, 86, 87, 107, 108
Cannicella necropolis sanctuary (Orvieto), 80–81, 149 (8.4), 151, 176
Capitoline Temple of Jupiter Optimus Maximus (Rome), 14, 74, 98, 105–6, 114
Capua, 11 (1.8), 35–36, 36 (3.2), 37–39, 44, 48, 81, 153, 157, 162
Capua tablet (Capua tile), 1 (1.8), 35–39, 36 (3.2), 81, 136, 153
Castel d'Asso, 41–42, 51, 52
Castel San Marino, 26 (2.6)
Castor and Pollux/Castur and Pultuce. *See* Dioskouri/Dioscuri
Cath. *See* Cautha/Cath/Cathesan
Catha, 7 (1.4), 129, 177, 193n28
Cathesan. *See* Cautha/Cath/Cathesan
Cautha/Cath/Cathesan, 21, 34, 89, 90–91, 146, 155, 158–59, 171
Ceicna Fetiu, urn of, 97 (6.1)
Cel/Cels/Ge/Gaia, 4, 5 (1.1), 21, 162
Cels. *See* Cel/Cels/Ge/Gaia
Censorinus, 15
Cerveteri. *See* Caere/Cerveteri
Chalchas Mirror (Vulci), 22 (2.5)
Chaldean heptoscopy, 23–24

chariots, 26 (2.6), 50, 78 (5.4), 83, 160
Charu(n), 61–66, 71, 152, 154, 176; as Charon of Greek mythology, 65; at funeral banquet, 66; as gatekeeper, 64 (4.10), 64–65; identity of, 64, 176, 191nn34, 35; in journey to Afterworld, 65 (4.11); mallet of, 61, 62–63, 63 (4.8), 64–65, 66; Oltos sherd and, 71; at sacrifice of Trojan prisoners by the Greeks (François Tomb, Vulci), 55 (4.1); at Tomb of the Cardinal (Tarquinia), 176; Turms/Hermes and, 152, 154
Chianciano, 35 (3.1), 83–85, 84 (5.7), 129, 130 (7.4), 134, 168
children, 3, 123, 140–41, 141 (7.11), 157, 158; Artumes/Artames as protectress, 147; depictions of, 3, 140–41, 141 (7.11), 158; Hercle as child, 165; of Laran/Mars, 150, 164; Maris, 147, 150, 164–65, 173, 177; maternity goddesses, 140; Mean at childbirth, 174; Menrva and, 140, 148, 164–65; Tinia as child, 179; of Turan/Aphrodite, 150; Uni as protector of, 157; votives and, 123, 140–41, 141 (7.11)
Chimaera of Arezzo, 82, 135 (7.8), 157
Chiusi, 3, 4, 11, 13, 24, 25, 34, 38 (3.4), 39 (3.6), 42, 46 (3.11, 3.12), 48, 57–58, 52, 58 (4.4), 85–88, 69 (4.13), 127 (7.3), 144, 165, 181; aristocratic tombs at, 55; Arno sanctuary, 87; border sanctuaries, 86, 88; Brolio sanctuary, 88; forced migration from, 181; funerary monuments at, 38 (3.4), 39 (3.6), 42, 46 (3.11, 3.12), 48, 57–58, 81; mirror from, 31, 32 (2.10); ossuaries, 57 (4.2); reliefs at, 38 (3.4), 48, 50, 55, 81, 129–30; Roman political alliance with, 85; Vegoia/Vegoe at, 3, 4, 11, 13, 24, 25, 34
Christianity, 3, 8, 83, 96, 183
chthonian world. *See* Afterworld; Piacenza liver
chthonic deities, 36, 41, 50, 53, 61–68, 69–71, 98, 148, 149–51, 152, 153–54, 156, 158, 162, 163–64, 171, 172, 173, 174–76, 177–78, 180; Calu, 50, 70, 71, 79, 153–54, 156, 177, 180–81; Nethuns, 21, 34, 60, 133, 153, 158, 159 (8.9), 180; Tuchulcha, 67. *See also* Aita/Hades; Charu(n); Tinia/Zeus/Jupiter; Vanth
Cicero, 3, 7, 8, 19–20, 23, 24, 127, 128
Cilen, 4, 5 (1.1), 21, 162, 164
cippus/cippi, 13, 37, 51, 72
cities, 13, 14 (1.10), 43–45, 72, 75–76; foundation rites, 43–45; planning of, 43–45, 45 (3.10); Greek influence on Etruscan planning, 44, 45. *See also* sanctuaries; temples; *individual cities*
Claudius, 8
college of deities, 15, 25, 172, 173
Comeana, 165
Cortona, 52, 53 (3.16), 81, 83, 134, 152, 157, 159, 163 (8.11)
Cosa, 105–6, 106 (6.10)
"couples" sarcophagi, 57–58, 58 (4.3)
cremation, 46, 55
Culsans/Culsu, 7 (1.4), 21, 64, 129, 162, 163 (8.11), 178; associated with Vanth, 63, 163

# Index

Culsu. *See* Culsans/Culsu
curative functions, 85, 86, 87, 134, 141 (7.12), 141–42, 145, 148, 176

dancing, 42 (3.9), 42–43, 46 (3.12), 48, 49 (3.14), 55, 57 (4.2), 100 (6.14); reanimation, 48, 49 (3.14), 55
Daunians, 105–6, 106 (6.10)
Delphi, 10, 32–33, 117, 145, 178
*De rebus divinis* (Tarquitius Priscus), 7–8, 29
*di animales*, 41, 52–53, 69–70, 71, 172
*di consentes*, 15, 25, 172, 173
die-shaped tombs (*tombe a dado*), 52, 98
*di involuti*, 172
Dionysus, 81, 83, 123, 129, 160, 176, 181. *See also* Fufluns/Dionysus/Pacha/Bacchus
Dionysius of Halicarnassus, 27, 42–43, 94–95
*Dioskouri*/Dioscuri (sons of Zeus), 47, 154–55, 156, 168, 180
distyle temple (Vulci), 121 (6.29)
divination, 13, 15, 20–23, 27, 28 (2.8), 30–31, 31 (2.9), 33, 146, 148, 159, 178; auspication, 27, 28, 28 (2.8), 29, 43, 178; fate and, 13, 15, 33; friendly v. hostile parts of the liver, 20; gods' silence (*muta exta*), 23; Greek, 23, 24, 31–33; haruspices holding liver in left hand, 20, 21, 22 (2.5); liver morphology in, 23; lots, consultation of, 30–31, 31 (2.9), 146, 148, 159; before military encounters, 27, 28 (2.8); by observation not interrogation, 178; orientation of liver for, 20; Roman, 4, 5 (1.1), 23, 24, 27
doors, 13, 21, 51 (3.5), 56, 60 (4.5), 63–64, 64 (4.10), 101, 102 (6.6), 129, 162, 163 (8.11), 178; to Afterworld, 56, 63–64, 64 (4.10); Culsans/Culsu/Vanth as god of, 13, 21, 63–64, 129, 162, 163 (8.11), 178; Culsl as god of, 7 (1.4); false door motif in painted tombs, 56, 60 (4.5), 129; in Guglielmi altar, 51 (3.15); in temple architecture of Vitruvius, 101, 102 (6.6)

Eos. *See* Thesan/Eos/Aurora
Epiur, 165, 198n14
Ethausva, 148

Falerii, 72, 75–76, 82, 92, 121; Temple of Uni/Juno Curite at, 83
false door motif, 56, 60 (4.5), 129
Falterona, 87, 137–38
Fanum Voltumnae, 77, 93, 136, 155, 157
Farthan, 30, 31 (2.9)
fate, 8, 12 (1.9), 13, 15, 17, 21, 27, 33, 34, 41, 70
Ferrara, 144 (8.1), 146
Fidenae, 92
Fiesole, 82, 96, 97 (6.2), 131 (7.5)
flamen/flamines, 126, 127 (7.2)
Fortuna, 30, 105, 112
Fortuna and the Mater Matuta, temple of (Rome), 105, 114
Forum Romanum, 96, 112

François Tomb (Vulci), 16, 27, 28 (2.8), 54, 55 (4.1), 63, 168; scene of sacrifice of Trojan prisoners, 16, 54, 55 (4.1), 63, 154 (8.7)
Fucoli sanctuary, 83–85, 84 (5.7), 168
Fufluns/Dionysus/Pacha/Bacchus, 21, 129, 160–61, 177, 183–84; Bacchus identified with, 160; Bolsena sanctuary of, 45; Catha associated with, 7 (1.4); at Fucoli sanctuary, 85; Greek models for, 140; musicians and, 132; offerings to, 136; Pacha, 129, 160, 177; on Piacenza liver, 21, 160; Populonia (Fufluna), 39, 159, 161, 162; priestesses and, 129; wine growers' chant to, 183–84
Funeral Bed, Tomb of the (Tarquinia), 47 (3.13), 49
funerary rites, 34–53, 55, 57 (4.2), 130 (7.4); Afterworld and, 52–53; banquets, 46–47, 47 (3.13), 48–49, 55, 57–58, 58 (4.3), 64, 66, 191n35; bloodshed as, 50; cremation, 46, 55; dances of, 48, 49 (3.14), 55, 57 (4.2); games and, 48–50; inhumation, 55, 83; *kline* (funeral bed), 47, 48, 66; lamentations and praise of the dead, 46 (3.12), 55; music at, 38, 40 (3.7), 41, 42–43, 47, 66; orant gestures at, 133; ossuaries, 56–57, 57 (4.2), 175; processions at, 38 (3.4), 42 (3.9), 42–43, 130 (7.4); *prothesis* (laying out of corpse), 45, 46 (3.11); sacred laurel groves and, 144; Turan/Aphrodite and, 149 (8.4), 176

Gaia. *See* Cel/Cels/Ge/Gaia
games, 42, 48–50, 59–60, 92–95, 98; funeral, Greek, 48–49; Roman, 42
gates and gateways, 13, 21, 56, 63–65, 72, 74, 75, 80, 129, 162–63; to Afterworld, 56, 63–64, 64 (4.10), 163; Charu(n) and, 64 (4.10), 64–65; to cities, 74; Culsu as keeper of, 13, 21, 63–64, 129, 162–63, 163 (8.11), 178; false door motif in painted tombs, 56, 60 (4.5), 129; of sanctuaries, 72, 75, 80
Ge. *See* Cel/Cels/Ge/Gaia
genies, 8, 21, 63–64, 129, 150, 162–63, 163 (8.11), 174 (9.1), 174–75, 178, 182
Geryon, 67, 68, 165
Golini tombs (Orvieto), 66, 70, 127, 153, 191n35
Graviscae, 91–92, 145, 149, 151, 157
*gromatici* (Roman surveyors), 13, 14, 161
Grotta Porcina, 52, 81, 86, 98
Guglielmi altar, 51 (3.15)

Hades. *See* Aita/Hades
haruspices, 4, 125–28, 182; costume of, 125, 126 (7.1, 7.2); Laris Pulenas, 7 (1.3, 1.4), 23; on mirrors, 4, 5 (1.1); Pava Tarchies, 4, 5 (1.1); sacrificial victims interrogated by, 41; Tages, 3–4, 5 (1.1), 7, 11, 24, 77, 178, 183; Tarchunus, 4, 5 (1.1); Temple of Jupiter Optimus Maximus and, 98, 114; tombs of, 35 (3.1), 127; Vel Sveitus, 125–26, 126 (7.1)
haruspicy, 4, 5 (1.1), 19 (2.3), 20 (2.4), 21–23, 29–30; Chaldean heptoscopy compared with, 23–24; divination before war, 28, 28 (2.8); divination by

# Index

haruspicy (*continued*)
  observation not interrogation, 178; division of space, 12 (1.9), 12–13; gallbladder, 18, 20, 21, 22; *libri tagetici*, 4; liver held in left hand, 19 (2.3), 20 (2.4), 21, 22 (2.5); Pesaro bilingual inscription, 125; Roman, 183; Roman sources for, 20 (2.4), 21, 23, 29–30; as science, 23; Tages, 3–4, 5 (1.1), 7, 11, 24, 77, 178, 183. *See also* oracular consultations; Piacenza liver
Hasti Afunei sarcophagus, 163
healing rites, 85, 86, 87, 134, 141 (7.12), 141–42, 145, 148, 176
Hephaistos. *See* Sethlans/Velchans/Vulcan
Hera. *See* Uni/Hera/Juno/Mae
Heracles. *See* Hercle/Hercules/Heracles
Hercle/Hercules/Heracles, 80, 87, 114 (6.19), 118 (6.25), 134, 147, 150, 157, 165–66, 166 (8.2); children of, 147, 150, 165, 177; deities associated with, 147, 150, 157, 165–66, 166 (8.12); depictions of, 65, 83–85, 134, 165, 168; derivation of name, 179; Greek models for, 140; Montefortini Tomb (Comeana), 165; on Piacenza liver, 164, 165; sanctuaries of, 80, 87, 118 (6.25), 134; at Sant'Omobono (Rome), 114 (6.19), 134; on Tarquinia plaque, 165
Hercules. *See* Hercle/Hercules/Heracles
Hermes. *See* Turms/Hermes/Mercury
Herodotus, 31–32, 145, 173
heroization rituals, 39–42, 52–53
hierdules (in sacred prostitution), 89, 90, 151, 194n48
*hinthial*, 54, 58, 60
hippocamps, 60, 61 (4.6), 62, 63
horses/horse races, 48–50, 59–60, 78 (5.4), 95, 110

imported deities. *See* Aplu/Apollo; Artumes/Artemis; Cautha/Cath/Cathesan; Sethlans/Velchans/Vulcan
individuation of deities, 180
inhumation, 55, 83
Ino. *See* Leucothea/Ino
Inscriptions, Tomb of the (Tarquinia), 50

Juno. *See* Uni/Hera/Juno/Mae
Juno Curite, temple of (Falerii), 83
Juno Moneta, temple of (Rome), 34
Jupiter. *See* Tinia/Zeus/Jupiter
Jupiter Optimus Maximus, Temple of (Rome), 14, 74, 98, 105–6, 114

*kline* (funeral bed), 10 (1.6), 35 (3.1), 47, 48, 66; Tomb of the Funeral Bed (Tarquinia), 47 (3.13), 49

Lake Trasimene, 140, 141, 159
land, sacred division of, 13, 14 (1.10), 161; Vegoia/Vegoe and, 3, 4, 11, 13, 24, 25, 34
Laran/Mars, 136, 137 (7.9), 140, 164–65, 179; children of, 150, 164, 165, 177; derivation of name, 179; Greek models for, 140; lightning attributed to, 25; on Magliano Lead Tablet, 198n14; Mars of Todi statue, 136, 137 (7.9), 165; Turan and, 150, 164, 177; woodpecker sacred to, 28 (2.8)
Lares, 69–70, 172–73
Laris Pulenas, 7 (1.3, 1.4), 8, 23, 128–29
Larissa, terracotta plaques of, 103, 104 (6.8)
Larthia Seianti, 58
Lasa, 8, 150, 163, 174 (9.1), 174–75, 182
Latona. *See* Leto/Latona
laurel groves/trees, 48, 49 (3.14), 66, 144
Letham, 21, 36 (3.2), 38, 43, 161 (8.10), 162, 176, 178
Leto/Latona, 85, 118n6.24
Leucothea/Ino, 90, 157, 160
libations, 39, 41 (3.8), 51, 52, 79, 131, 138, 139 (7.10)
*liber linteus* (linen book), 9, 9 (1.5), 10 (1.6), 34, 35 (3.1), 35–37, 39, 127 (7.3), 157, 158, 173, 178; afterlife and, 9, 9 (1.6); dating of, 34; deities associated with, 157, 158, 173, 178; images of, 9, 9 (1.5), 10 (1.6), 35 (3.1); prayers in, 178; sacrifices described in, 9, 9 (1.6), 39; as sign of social rank, 10 (1.6), 35 (3.1), 35–36, 127 (7.3); writing in religious life, 36–37; the Zagreb Book as, 8, 9 (1.5), 34–35, 128, 181
*libri acherontici*, 4, 53, 65, 68, 71, 183
*libri fatales*, 15, 34
*libri fulgurales*, 24–25
*libri rituales*, 4, 15, 24–25, 29–30, 34, 37–38, 53, 65, 68, 71, 183; auspication in, 29–30; foundation rites for cities in, 43–45; on sacrifices (*nuntheri/nunthen*), 37–38. *See also* liber linteus
*libri tagetici*, 4
lightning, divination by, 4, 7–8, 10, 15, 24–27, 26 (2.6, 2.7), 125, 147, 152, 178, 188n8
linen books. *See* liber linteus
*lituus*, 38 (3.4), 129, 130, 131 (7.5)
liver divination. *See* haruspicy; Piacenza liver
Livy, 75, 86, 92
Lorenzini Kouros, 146 (8.2)
lots, consultation of, 30–31, 31 (2.9), 146, 148, 159
Lusl/Lusa, 158
Lydos, John, 8

Macstrna, 168, 173
Macchia Grande sanctuary (Veii), 80
Mae. *See* Uni/Hera/Juno/Mae
Magliano Lead Tablet, 36–37, 37 (3.3), 153, 156–57, 173, 198n14
Magna Graecia, 41, 52, 61, 62 (4.7), 87, 108, 180
Malavisch, 150
mantic deities, 4, 12 (1.9), 13, 21, 25, 28, 30–33; Cel/Cels/Ge/Gaia, 4, 5 (1.1), 21, 162; Menrva/Tecum, 118, 149, 155; Śuri, 80, 89, 90–91, 146, 155, 159, 161, 171; Turan, 28, 81, 85, 91, 140, 147–51, 149 (8.4), 150 (8.5), 157, 163, 165, 174, 176, 177. *See also* Aplu/Apollo

224

# Index

Maris, 147, 150, 164–65, 173, 177
Mars. *See* Laran/Mars
Mars of Todi statue, 136, 137 (7.9), 165
Martianus Capella, 19–20, 21, 29, 79, 155, 188n3
Marzabotto, 14 (1.10), 44, 75–76, 79 (5.6), 79–80, 83, 96
Mater Matuta, 90, 112 (6.17), 157, 160
Mater Matuta, temple of (Satricum), 106–8, 107 (6.11), 109
Mean, 174
Melone del Sodo II (Cortona), 52, 53 (3.16)
Menrva/Tecvm/Minerva, 85, 114 (6.19), 144, 147–49, 150, 157, 165, 176, 179; altars of, 148; Athena as, 111 (6.16), 114 (6.19), 140, 147–48, 148 (8.3), 179; children and, 140, 148, 164–65; deities associated with, 14, 85, 114 (6.19), 144, 147–48, 150, 157, 165; depictions of, 147–49, 148 (8.3); as healer, 148; lightning and, 25, 147; lots and, 30, 148; mantic function of, 155; mirrors, 148–49, 167; Piacenza liver and, 21, 147, 148, 149, 158; sanctuaries of, 87, 134, 147; as warrior goddess, 148–49, 176, 179
Mercury. *See* Turms/Hermes/Mercury
Minerva, 14, 147. *See also* Menrva/Tecvm/Minerva
mirrors: Cacu prophesying on, 6 (1.2), 31; Chalchas Mirror (Vulci), 22 (2.5); from Chiusi, 31, 32 (2.10); deities depicted on, 4–5, 5 (1.1), 31–32, 32 (2.10), 41, 148–49, 150 (8.5), 152–57, 159 (8.9), 160, 162, 166 (8.12), 167; haruspices depicted on, 20, 22 (2.5), 125; *Lasa* depicted on, 174, 174 (9.1); oracle consultations on, 6 (1.2), 31, 32 (2.10); from Praeneste, 38, 41; sacrificial rites depicted on, 38, 39 (3.6), 40 (3.7), 131; Tiresias depicted on (Vulci), 54
Monte Acuto Ragazza, 88, 138, 139 (7.10)
Montefortini Tomb (Comeana), 165
Montetosto complex (Caere), 93–94
moon, deity of. *See* Tivs
Munthuc (attendant of Turan/Aphrodite), 150, 174
Murlo complex, 45, 48, 93 (5.9), 94 (5.10), 94–95, 117, 127
music, funerary, 38, 40 (3.7), 41, 42–43, 47, 66
mythology, Greek, 101, 167–70

*naiskos*, 52, 91, 98, 121 (6.29), 139
necropoleis: at Blera, 51; at Caere, 41, 55–56; La Cannicella (Orvieto), 80–81, 149 (8.4), 151, 176; Cavalupo (Vulci), 75; funerary altars at, 98; Grotta Porcina (Tarquinia), 52; at Norchia, 102, 103 (6.7); sacred laurel groves in, 144; at Tarquinia, 41, 52. *See also* sanctuaries
Nethuns/Neptune, 21, 34, 60, 133, 153, 158, 159 (8.9), 180
Nigidius Figulus, 8, 20, 26–27
*nomen etruscum* (Twelve Peoples), 3–4, 92–93, 155
Norchia, 52, 81, 102, 103 (6.7)

Nortia, 171
Numa, 5, 11

Ogre II, Tomb of the (Tarquinia), 153
*oikos*, 99, 100
Oltos, 71
omens/*ostenta*, 7–8, 14, 25–26, 27, 28, 28 (2.8), 29–30, 43, 178; by auspication, 27, 28, 28 (2.8), 29, 43, 178; Bellerophon killing the Chimaera as, 16, 135 (7.8); *De rebus divinis* (Tarquitius Priscus), 7–8, 29; of historical events, 16–17; lightning as, 25–26; by haruspicy, 22; of saeculum, 16. *See also* haruspicy
oracles, Greek, 31–33, 32 (2.10)
oracular consultations, 5–6, 6 (1.2), 10, 31–33, 32 (2.10), 117, 145, 178; Cacu and, 5–6, 6 (1.2), 31; at Delphi, 10, 32–33, 117, 145, 178; Etruscans and, 33; Hellenization of, 31–32, 32 (2.10); musical accompaniment for, 31; of Pythian Apollo, 31–32; transcription of, 6 (1.2)
orant gesture, 133
Orbetello, 121, 160
Orco, Tomba dell' (Tarquinia). *See* Orcus, Tomb of
Orcus, Tomb of (Tarquinia), 54, 64, 66, 67, 70, 191n30
orientation of temples, 20, 28, 43, 89, 100, 101–2, 116
Orpheus. *See* Urphe/Orpheus
orthogonal scheme, 72, 75
Orvieto: Belvedere sanctuary, 77, 78 (5.5), 79, 93, 119 (6.26), 120 (6.27, 6.28); Cannicella necropolis at, 80–81, 149 (8.4), 151, 176; Golini tombs, 66, 70, 127, 153, 191n35; sanctuaries at, 77, 78 (5.5), 79, 93, 119 (6.26), 120 (6.27, 6.28), 164; San Leonardo temple at, 156 (8.8), 180; Tinia representations at, 154, 157; Torre San Severo sarcophagus, 66, 154 (8.7), 168; Turan/Aphrodite at, 149 (8.4), 151
ossuaries, 56–57, 57 (4.2), 175
*ostenta. See* omens/*ostenta*

Pacha. *See* Fufluns/Dionysus/Pacha/Bacchus
Palatine Apollo, Temple of (Rome), 5
Parzalii (Lycia), 103, 104 (6.8)
Patroclus, 40, 46, 54, 55 (4.1), 63, 154 (8.7)
Pava Tarchies, 4, 5 (1.1), 125, 126 (7.1)
pediments, 78 (5.4), 83–85, 84 (5.7), 102, 105 (6.9a, 6.9b), 110, 121 (6.29), 123
Penates, 69, 172
Perugia, 37, 38 (3.4), 70–71, 157
Pesaro bilingual inscription, 125
Phersipnai/Persephone, 66, 67, 70, 71, 81, 153, 154 (8.7)
Phineas, myth of, 169
Piacenza liver, 18–21, 19 (2.1, 2.2); Alpan, 150, 150 (8.5), 163; Aplu/Apollo, 146; Artumes/Artames, 147; Aule Lecu, 18, 19 (2.3), 20, 21; Cautha, 155; Cilensl/Cilen/Tin Cilen, 164; Culsans/Culsu/Vanth, 162; dating of, 18; divisions of, 18–19, 19

# Index

Piacenza liver (*continued*)
(2.2), 21, 28–29; Epiur on, 165, 198n14; Fufluns on, 160; gallbladder, 18, 20, 21; Hercle on, 164, 165; Lasa on, 174; Lusl/Lusa on, 158; Maris and, 164; Menrva/Tecvm absent from, 21, 147, 148, 149, 158; Nethuns on, 158; orthography of, 18; Satre on, 165; Selvans on, 13, 161; Tinia on, 79, 156; Tluscv on, 21, 162; Turan on, 151; Uni/Hera/Juno/Mae on, 19, 21, 147, 157; Usil on, 18, 159–60; Velchans on, 153
Piazza d'Armi (Veii), 75, 100
Pieve a Socana, 96
plaques, terracotta, 38 (3.5), 75, 95, 96, 103–5, 104 (6.8), 105 (6.9a, 6.9b), 113, 113 (6.18), 119, 165; Campana, 38 (3.5), 96; Capua tablet, 11 (1.8), 36 (3.2); at Corinth, 103, 104 (6.8); at Murlo complex, 95; pediment of Temple B at Pyrgi, 110; revetment plaques, 103–5, 104 (6.8), 105 (6.9a, 6.9b); temple at Sant'Omobono (Rome), 113 (6.18); at Velletri, 104 (6.8), 113
Pliny the Elder, 8, 12 (1.9), 19–20, 23, 27, 29, 103
plural deities, 174–76. *See also* Charu(n); Lasa; Vanth
Plutarch, 16, 44
Pluto. *See* Aita/Hades
podium of temple, 72, 73, 76, 79, 100, 102, 119 (6.26)
Populonia (Fufluna), 39, 159, 161, 162
Po region, 44, 144 (8.1), 145, 147, 151
Porsenna, 27, 70
Portonaccio Sanctuary (Veii), 72, 73 (5.1), 82, 85–86, 96, 116 (6.21), 134, 147
Praeneste, 30, 38, 41
prayers, Greek liturgical, 133–34
priests, 128–33; costume of, 44, 45 (3.10), 125, 126 (7.1, 7.2); etymology of *sacerdos*, 128; haruspices compared with, 125, 127; images of, 129–33, 130 (7.4), 131 (7.5), 132 (7.6, 7.7); instruments of, 126 (7.2), 127, 131; on Chianciano base, 129, 130 (7.4); lituus of, 38 (3.4), 129, 130, 131 (7.5); tombs of, 35 (3.1), 127; women as priestesses, 129, 131
processions, 38 (3.4), 42 (3.9), 42–43, 130 (7.4)
*prothesis*, 45, 46 (3.11)
*psychopompoi*, 60, 62, 63, 66, 71, 152 (8.6)
Punics, 14–15, 15, 89, 90, 90 (5.8), 92, 194n47
Punta della Vipera, 87, 97 (6.3)
Pyrgi, 9, 11 (1.7), 72, 88–92, 90 (5.8), 108 (6.12), 109 (6.13), 146, 159, 160, 171; *antepagmenta* of, 111 (6.16), 168; deities represented at, 89, 90–91, 146, 159, 160, 171; gold tablets, 9, 11 (1.7), 14–15, 89, 90 (5.8), 194n47; Greek presence at, 88, 108; prostitution at, 151; sanctuaries at, 9, 11 (1.7), 72, 88–92, 90 (5.8), 108 (6.12), 109 (6.13); Temple A, 89, 90, 110, 111 (6.16); Temple B, 80, 89–90, 98, 109 (6.13), 110 (6.14), 194nn47, 48; temples at, 80, 89–90, 98, 109 (6.13), 110 (6.14), 111 (6.16), 194nn47–48

reliefs: bronze, 41, 144; Roman polychrome, 112; stone ash urns, 8, 18–21, 19 (2.3), 39 (3.6), 55, 57 (4.2), 69 (4.13), 70–71, 99; stone *cippi*, 13, 37, 51, 72; terracotta, 75, 95, 99, 103–5, 104 (6.8), 105 (6.9a, 6.9b), 108, 110, 111 (6.16), 117, 168. *See also* sarcophagi
Reliefs, Tomb of the (Caere), 35
rituals, Roman, 14–15, 37, 39–40, 44, 181
Rome, 5, 6, 12, 16, 23, 24, 27, 28, 39, 40, 42, 43, 69, 74, 80, 82, 85, 88, 102, 105, 107, 108, 110–13, 115–16, 117, 130, 136, 142, 145, 147, 155, 157, 165, 168, 172, 173, 181, 182; Capitoline Temple of Jupiter Optimus Maximus, 14, 74, 98, 105–6, 114; Fortuna and the Mater Matuta temple, 105, 114; Forum, 96, 112; Juno Moneta temple, 34; Palatine Apollo temple, 5; Sant'Omobono temple, 107, 112 (6.17), 113 (6.18), 114 (6.19), 134

sacred divisions, 11, 12–14, 12 (1.9), 14 (1.10), 15, 16, 161; *cippi* (boundary stones), 13, 51, 72; division of celestial and terrestrial space, 11, 12–14, 12 (1.9); of human life, 15, 16; of land, 13, 14 (1.10), 161; time as, 13–16; Vegoia/Vegoe and, 3, 4, 11, 13, 24, 25, 34
sacred literature, 5–11, 34–36; calendars, 8, 9, 9 (1.5), 11 (1.8), 34, 35, 36 (3.2), 38–39, 133; Roman interest in Etruscan, 6–8; on *saeculum/saecula*, 5, 13, 14, 15, 16, 182; the Zagreb Book (*liber linteus*), 8, 9 (1.5), 34–35, 128, 181. *See also* liber linteus; libri
sacred prostitution, 89, 90, 151, 194n48
sacrifices, 34–53; to *Aiser/Eiser*, 173; animals in, 38–39, 39 (3.6), 39–40, 40 (3.7); calendars for, 36; on Campana plaque from Caere, 38 (3.5), 96; dead present at, 51; depictions of, 38 (3.4, 3.5), 39 (3.6); for freeing of souls, 41; Greek rituals for, 38–39; haruspices' interrogation of victims, 41; human sacrifice, 39–40, 70; libations as, 39, 41 (3.8), 51, 52, 79, 131, 138, 139 (7.10); lightning strikes and, 26, 188n7; music at, 38, 40 (3.7), 41, 42–43; prayer at, 15, 133–34, 178; priests in, 38 (3.4); sacrificial knife in, 38; Silenus/Sileni at, 38, 39 (3.7), 42–43; victims for, 38–39, 39 (3.6), 39–40, 40 (3.7); worshippers and, 132 (7.7), 132–33
*saeculum/saecula*, 5, 13, 14, 15, 16, 182
Samnites, 105–6, 106 (6.10)
San Bartolomeo temple (Arezzo), 80
sanctuaries, 72–95; Belvedere sanctuary (Orvieto), 77, 78 (5.5), 79, 93, 119 (6.26), 120 (6.27, 6.28); border sanctuaries, 86–87, 88, 137; Cannicella necropolis (Orvieto), 80–81, 149 (8.4), 151, 176; of the Chimaera (Arezzo), 82, 135 (7.8); excavations of, 82, 83, 87; of family cults, 81–82; federal sanctuaries, 75, 77, 92–93, 93 (5.9), 115, 155; gates of, 72, 75, 80; open-air sanctuary at Thesmophoria, 91; orientation of, 89; port sanc-

# Index

tuaries, 74–75, 89–91; Punta della Vipera sanctuary, 87; at Pyrgi, 9, 11 (1.7), 72, 88–92, 90 (5.8), 108 (6.12), 109 (6.13); rural sites for, 74, 88; *temenos/temene* and, 72, 85, 86, 88, 91, 100, 112, 139; of Tinia, 157; urban sanctuaries, 73–74, 77, 78 (5.5), 79; water and, 83, 85. *See also* altars

San Giuliano, 41, 51, 55, 86
San Leonardo temple (Orvieto), 156 (8.8), 180
Santa Marinella, 98, 148
Sant'Omobono temple (Rome), 107, 112 (6.17), 113 (6.18), 114 (6.19), 134
sarcophagi: Bellerophon killing the Chimaera on, 16, 135 (7.8); Bruschi sarcophagus, 65 (4.11); couples groups on, 57–58, 58 (4.3); of Hasti Afunei, 163; of Laris Pulenas, 7 (1.3, 1.4), 8, 23, 128–29; Sarcophagus of the Priest (Tarquinia), 168; of Seianti Hanunia Tlesnasa, 59 (4.4); at Tarquinia, 58, 65 (4.11); Tomb of the Sarcophagi (Caere), 9, 10 (1.6), 35, 39 (3.6), 48, 59 (4.4), 66, 68, 154 (8.7); from Torre San Severo, 66, 154 (8.7), 168; from Vulci, 48, 58
Sarcophagi, Tomb of the (Cerveteri), 9, 10 (1.6), 35, 39 (3.6), 48, 59 (4.4), 66, 68, 154 (8.7)
Sarteano tomb, 66, 191n35
Sassi Caduti Temple (Falerii), 72, 83
Satricum, 106–8, 107 (6.11), 109; Temple of the Mater Matuta, 106–8, 107 (6.11), 109
Scrofa Nera, Tomba della (Tarquinia), 47, 168
Seianti Hanunia Tlesnasa sarcophagus, 59 (4.4)
Selva. *See* Selvans/Selva/Sylvanus
Selvans/Selva/Sylvanus, 13, 21, 72, 140, 161–62, 171
Seneca the Elder, 8, 10, 24, 25
Servius Tullius, 74, 105, 107, 112, 168, 173
Sethlans/Velchans/Vulcan, 25, 147, 152–53
Seven against Thebes, 110, 111 (6.16), 122 (6.11)
Silenus/Sileni, 38, 39 (3.7), 42–43, 132 (7.7)
Sillene spring (Chianciano Terme), 83, 193n28
solar deities, 18, 19 (2.2), 21, 89, 90–91, 100 (6.14), 129, 146, 155, 158–59, 171, 179; Apollo as, 146, 159; associated with Dionysus, 129; Cautha/Cath/Usil/Cathesan as, 21, 89, 90–91, 146, 155, 158–59, 171; dancer with a bird's head (Pyrgi), 100 (6.14); on Piacenza liver, 21; Pyrgi Temple B, 194n47; sexual identity of, 179; Tinia, 179; Usil/Usils, 18, 19 (2.2), 159
souls, 41, 52–53, 54–55, 66, 69
sources for *etrusca disciplina*, historical, 29–30
south/southern orientation (*pars antica*), 20, 28, 43, 89, 100, 101–2, 116
space, sacred division of, 12–13, 12 (1.9)
Spina, 145, 152, 152 (8.6), 154
Stigmata, temple of the (Velletri), 104 (6.8)
Sulla, 16, 18
sun, deities of. *See* solar deities
Śuri, 80, 89, 90–91, 146, 155, 159, 161, 171
Sylvanus. *See* Selvans/Selva/Sylvanus

*tabula capuana*. *See* Capua tablet
Tages, 3–4, 5 (1.1), 7, 11, 24, 77, 178, 183
Talamone, temple at, 122 (6.30), 169
Tarchon. *See* Avl Tarchunus; Tarchunus
Tarchunus, 4, 5 (1.1). *See also* Avl Tarchunus
Tarquinia, 3, 16, 40, 41, 41 (3.8), 47, 48, 55, 56, 60–64, 76 (5.2), 76–78, 77 (5.3), 78 (5.4), 80, 81, 86, 91, 94–95, 98, 105, 129, 168, 169, 176; Achilles at, 169; altars at, 98; Ara della Regina Temple, 3, 76 (5.2), 76–78, 77 (5.3), 78 (5.4), 94; commerce in, 81, 91; cult of Cautha and Pacha, 159; deities at, 157, 159, 161, 165, 171; games at, 94–95; Gravisca (port of Tarquinia), 91–92, 145, 149, 151, 157; haruspices and, 4, 127; Laris Pulenas, 7 (1.3, 1.4), 23, 128–29; prisoner massacre at, 40; sanctuaries at, 76, 80, 86; sarcophagi from, 58, 65 (4.11), 168; slaughter of Roman prisoners at, 16; Tages, 3–4, 5 (1.1), 7, 11, 24, 77, 178, 183; tombs at, 41, 41 (3.8), 47, 55, 56, 60–64, 68, 105, 129, 168, 169, 176
Tarquinia, tombs: Tomba della Scrofa Nera, 47, 168; Tomb of the Aninas, 63 (4.8); Tomb of the Augurs, 56, 60 (4.5), 129; Tomb of the Baron, 41 (3.8); Tomb of the Blue Demons, 62 (4.7), 68; Tomb of the Bulls, 60–61, 61 (4.6), 169; Tomb of the Funeral Bed, 47 (3.13), 49; Tomb of the Inscriptions, 50; Tomb of the Ogre II, 153; Tomb of Orcus, 54, 64, 66, 67, 70, 191n30; Tomb of the Triclinium, 47, 49 (3.14), 129
Tarquinius Priscus, 27, 29
Tarquitius Priscus, 7–8, 13, 29
Tecvm, 21, 25, 30, 140, 141 (7.11), 158. *See also* Menrva/Tecvm/Minerva
Temple A (Pyrgi), 89, 90, 110, 111 (6.16)
Temple B (Pyrgi), 80, 89–90, 98, 109 (6.13), 110 (6.14), 194nn47, 48
temples, 74, 75–80, 98–124; architecture of, 98–100, 99 (6.4a, 6.4b), 100 (6.5), 114–15; cellae in, 75, 76, 79, 80, 86, 89, 98, 100, 110, 116, 119, 147; Etrusco-Italic, 98, 102; models of, 98–99, 99 (6.4a, 6.4b); of multiple divinities (*synnaoi*), 21; *naiskos/naiskoi*, 52, 91, 98, 121 (6.29), 139; national characteristics of, 75; orientation of, 12 (1.9); period renovations of, 105; Roman, 14, 72–74, 98, 103, 105–6, 114; tripartite division of, 74; urban sites for, 73, 74. *See also* sanctuaries; *specific temples by site and/or deity*
terraces, 41–42, 52, 76, 80, 86, 96
Thalna, 147, 163
Thanr, 147, 163
Thefarie Velianas, 11 (1.7), 89, 109
Thesan/Eos/Aurora, 90, 157, 158, 159 (8.9), 160
*thiasos/thiasoi*, 84, 180
Thufltha, 80, 140, 171
Thuluter, 155
*thymiaterion* (incense burner), 38, 43
time, sacred division of, 13–16
Tinia/Zeus/Jupiter, 19, 21, 25, 26 (2.6, 2.7), 79,

# Index

Tinia/Zeus/Jupiter (*continued*)
126, 147, 155–57, 169, 179–80; altars of, 79, 98; at Belvedere sanctuary (Orvieto), 77, 78 (5.5), 79; Capitoline Temple of Jupiter Optimus Maximus and, 14, 74, 98, 105–6, 114; Chimaera of Arezzo and, 135 (7.8); as chthonic figure, 156, 157, 179; *di consentes*, 15, 172; *di involuti* and, 172; deities associated with, 79, 147, 152 (8.6), 153–58, 164, 165, 173, 177, 180; depictions of, 126, 156 (8.8), 156–57; Dioscuri as sons of (*Tinas Clinarii*), 47, 154–55, 156, 168, 180; on division of celestial and terrestrial space, 12 (1.9), 13; eagles as messengers of, 28, 29; Greek characteristics of, 169, 179–80; *liber linteus* (linen books) and, 157, 178; lightning attributed to, 25, 26 (2.6, 2.7), 156, 179; Penates and, 69, 172; on Piacenza liver, 19, 21, 79, 147, 156; Severe Style and, 140; temples of, 75, 80, 192n9; Tinia Calusna, 79, 154, 156, 164, 177. *See also* Velthumna/Velthumena/Voltumna

Tiresias, 54, 66, 67

*Tivs* (moon), 18, 19 (2.2), 21, 83

Tluscv, 21, 162

Todi, Mars of, 136, 137 (7.9), 165

Tomb 5636 (Tarquinia), 64 (4.10)

tombs: aquatic beasts on, 59–60; die-shaped tombs (*tombe a dado*), 52, 98; doors in, 56, 59, 60 (4.5); false door motif in painted tombs, 56; of families, 66, 67; funeral banquets depicted on, 64, 66, 191n35; Greek Underworld depictions on, 67; as huts, 55–56; laurel depictions in paintings, 144; mirrors, 4, 5 (1.1); of priests, 35 (3.1), 127; as resembling houses, 56, 58–59; rock in construction of, 105; terraces, 41–42; tromp-l'oeil painting in, 56. *See also individual tomb headings*

Torre San Severo sarcophagus, 66, 154 (8.7), 168

translations of *etrusca disciplina*, 7–8

Tretu, 152

Triclinium, Tomb of the (Tarquinia), 47, 49 (3.14), 129

Turan/Aphrodite, 28, 81, 85, 91, 140, 147–51, 149 (8.4), 150 (8.5), 157, 163, 165, 174, 176, 177

Turms/Hermes/Mercury, 7 (1.4), 83, 117 (6.22), 129, 151–52, 152 (8.6), 154, 173, 177

Twelve Peoples (of *nomen etruscum*), 3–4, 92–93, 155

Tyrrhenians, 145, 162, 182

Uni/Hera/Juno/Mae, 19, 21, 25, 91, 147, 157, 165–66, 166 (8.12), 167, 179; Astarte and, 81, 89–91, 109, 157, 194n47; on Capua tablet, 36 (3.2); depictions of, 157, 166 (8.12); etymology of name, 157; Gravisca sanctuary, 91; in Greek mythology, 167; Hercle and, 165–66, 166 (8.12); lightning attributed to, 25; on Piacenza liver, 19, 21, 147, 157; on Pyrgi gold tablets, 81, 89–91, 109, 157, 194n47; temple at Caere, 157; Uni/Juno Curite temple (Falerii), 8

urns: altars depicted on, 96, 97 (6.1); bronze, 99–100, 100 (6.5); canopic urns, 56–57; of *Ceicna Fetiu*, 97 (6.1); cinerary urns, 18–21, 19 (2.3), 39 (3.6), 55, 57 (4.2), 69 (4.13), 70–71, 99; hut urns, 55, 56, 99–100, 100 (6.5); terracotta, 99; Villanovan urns, 99; of Volterra, 18, 19 (2.3), 42, 61–62, 96, 97 (6.1)

Urphe/Orpheus, 31, 32 (2.10), 71

Usil/Usils, 18, 19 (2.2), 21, 34, 89–91, 146, 155, 159 (8.9), 159–60, 171, 177

Vanth, 8, 21, 55 (4.1), 57, 61, 63 (4.8), 63–64, 65 (4.11), 70–71, 122 (6.30), 129, 162, 163 (8.11), 175 (9.2); Culsans associated with, 21, 63–64, 129, 162, 163 (8.11), 178; cult of, 70–71; depictions of, 8, 55 (4.1), 57, 63 (4.8), 175 (9.2); on journey to Afterworld, 61, 63, 65 (4.11); sacrifice of Trojan prisoners by the Greeks and, 55 (4.1), 63; at temple at Talamone, 122 (6.30)

Varro, 8, 94, 155, 172

vases, 8, 56–57, 60, 144, 149–50

Vea, 81, 91, 149 (8.4), 151

Vegoia/Vegoe, 3, 4, 11, 13, 24, 25, 34

Veii, 72, 73 (5.1), 75, 80, 82, 85–86, 92, 96, 99, 100, 112, 116 (6.21), 117 (6.22), 118 (6.23, 6.24, 6.25), 134, 147; acropolis of, 75; acroteria at, 116 (6.21), 117 (6.22), 118 (6.23, 6.24, 6.25), 144; Campana Tomb of, 99; capture of Fidenae and, 92; deities represented at, 148, 157, 165; Macchia Grande sanctuary at, 80; Piazza d'Armi at, 75, 100; Portonaccio Sanctuary at, 72, 73 (5.1), 82, 85–86, 96, 116 (6.21), 117 (6.22), 118 (6.23, 6.24, 6.25), 134, 147; terracotta objects at, 75, 85, 100, 116, 134

Veiovis. *See* Vetisl/Veive/Veiovis

Veive. *See* Vetisl/Veive/Veiovis

Velchans. *See* Sethlans/Velchans/Vulcan

Velletri, 100 (6.5), 104 (6.8), 112, 113; Temple of the Stigmata at, 104 (6.8)

Vel Saties, 27, 28 (2.8)

Vel Sveitus, 125–26, 126 (7.1)

Velthumna/Velthumena/Voltumna, 4, 5 (1.1), 50, 77, 81, 92–93, 136, 155–57, 176, 177. *See also* Tinia/Zeus/Jupiter

Vetisl/Veive/Veiovis, 21, 34, 39–40, 164

Vibenna brothers, Aulus and Caelius, 5–6, 6 (1.2)

Vignaccia votive deposit (Caere), 140, 151

*vinum*, 39

Virgil, 14, 68, 69, 70, 71

Vitruvius, 74, 98, 101–4, 102 (6.6), 107

Volsinian region, 6 (1.2), 45, 72, 79, 100, 157, 160, 168. *See also* Orvieto

Volsinii, 27, 81, 93, 171

Volta, 27, 70

Volterra, 18, 19 (2.3), 42, 61–62, 87, 96, 97 (6.1), 166 (8.12), 181

Voltumna. *See* Velthumna/Velthumena/Voltumna; Tinia/Zeus/Jupiter

votives: anatomical, 91; from Ara della Regina Temple, 77; aulos players, 132 (7.6); from Brolio

# Index

sanctuary, 88; bronze, 125, 126 (7.1), 129–30, 138, 139 (7.10); children and, 123, 140–41, 141 (7.11); to deities, 79, 157, 160, 163 (8.11); female figurines, 140; from Grasceta dei Cavallari border sanctuary, 87; Hellenistic influence on, 87; inscriptions on, 178; personalized busts, 142; requests for cures, 123, 141 (7.12), 141–42; from Sanctuary of the Chimaera (Arezzo), 82, 135 (7.8); from Sant'Omobono (Rome), 114 (6.19); social class and, 134, 136–37, 137 (7.9); statues as, 88, 136, 137 (7.9), 138, 165; stele of the Tyrrhenians as, 145; terracotta, 66, 132 (7.6), 151; Vea depicted on, 151

Vulcan. *See* Sethlans/Velchans/Vulcan

Vulci, 16, 27, 28 (2.8), 54, 55 (4.1), 56, 63, 80, 86, 105, 121 (6.29), 168; amphorae from, 42 (3.9), 48; Chalchas Mirror of, 22 (2.5); distyle temple at, 121 (6.29); false door motif in painted tombs at, 56; François Tomb at, 16, 27, 28 (2.8), 54, 55 (4.1), 63, 168; Guglielmi Altar, 51 (3.15); rock tombs, 105; sanctuaries of, 80, 86; sarcophagi at, 48, 58; seahorse group at, 59–60; Śuri at, 171

war, 16, 27–28, 28 (2.8), 40, 54, 55 (4.1), 63, 75, 154 (8.7), 176, 179

Zagreb Book (*liber linteus*), 8, 9 (1.5), 34–35, 128, 181

Zeus, 15, 84, 97, 98, 111 (6.16), 154–56, 156 (8.8), 179, 180. *See also* Tinia/Zeus/Jupiter

Zipna (attendant of Turan/Aphrodite), 150, 174

# Wisconsin Studies in Classics

GENERAL EDITORS
Richard Daniel De Puma and Patricia A. Rosenmeyer

E. A. THOMPSON
*Romans and Barbarians: The Decline of the Western Empire*

JENNIFER TOLBERT ROBERTS
*Accountability in Athenian Government*

H. I. MARROU
*A History of Education in Antiquity*
*Histoire de l'Education dans l'Antiquité,* translated by GEORGE LAMB

ERIKA SIMON
*Festivals of Attica: An Archaeological Commentary*

G. MICHAEL WOLOCH
*Roman Cities: Les villes romaines* by Pierre Grimal, translated and edited by
G. Michael Woloch, together with A Descriptive Catalogue of Roman Cities by
G. Michael Woloch

WARREN G. MOON, editor
*Ancient Greek Art and Iconography*

KATHERINE DOHAN MORROW
*Greek Footwear and the Dating of Sculpture*

JOHN KEVIN NEWMAN
*The Classical Epic Tradition*

JEANNY VORYS CANBY, EDITH PORADA, BRUNILDE SISMONDO RIDGWAY, and TAMARA STECH, editors
*Ancient Anatolia: Aspects of Change and Cultural Development*

ANN NORRIS MICHELINI
*Euripides and the Tragic Tradition*

WENDY J. RASCHKE, editor
*The Archaeology of the Olympics: The Olympics and Other Festivals in Antiquity*

PAUL PLASS
*Wit and the Writing of History: The Rhetoric of Historiography in Imperial Rome*

BARBARA HUGHES FOWLER
*The Hellenistic Aesthetic*

F. M. CLOVER and R. S. HUMPHREYS, editors
*Tradition and Innovation in Late Antiquity*

BRUNILDE SISMONDO RIDGWAY
*Hellenistic Sculpture I: The Styles of ca. 331–200 B.C.*

BARBARA HUGHES FOWLER, editor and translator
*Hellenistic Poetry: An Anthology*

KATHRYN J. GUTZWILLER
*Theocritus' Pastoral Analogies: The Formation of a Genre*

VIMALA BEGLEY and RICHARD DANIEL DE PUMA, editors
*Rome and India: The Ancient Sea Trade*

RUDOLF BLUM and HANS H. WELLISCH, translators
*Kallimachos: The Alexandrian Library and the Origins of Bibliography*

DAVID CASTRIOTA
*Myth, Ethos, and Actuality: Official Art in Fifth Century B.C. Athens*

BARBARA HUGHES FOWLER, editor and translator
*Archaic Greek Poetry: An Anthology*

JOHN H. OAKLEY and REBECCA H. SINOS
*The Wedding in Ancient Athens*

RICHARD DANIEL DE PUMA and JOCELYN PENNY SMALL, editors
*Murlo and the Etruscans: Art and Society in Ancient Etruria*

JUDITH LYNN SEBESTA and LARISSA BONFANTE, editors
*The World of Roman Costume*

JENNIFER LARSON
*Greek Heroine Cults*

WARREN G. MOON, editor
*Polykleitos, the Doryphoros, and Tradition*

PAUL PLASS
*The Game of Death in Ancient Rome: Arena Sport and Political Suicide*

MARGARET S. DROWER
*Flinders Petrie: A Life in Archaeology*

SUSAN B. MATHESON
*Polygnotos and Vase Painting in Classical Athens*

JENIFER NEILS, editor
*Worshipping Athena: Panathenaia and Parthenon*

PAMELA WEBB
*Hellenistic Architectural Sculpture: Figural Motifs in Western Anatolia and the Aegean Islands*

BRUNILDE SISMONDO RIDGWAY
*Fourth-Century Styles in Greek Sculpture*

LUCY GOODISON and CHRISTINE MORRIS, editors
*Ancient Goddesses: The Myths and the Evidence*

JO-MARIE CLAASSEN
*Displaced Persons: The Literature of Exile from Cicero to Boethius*

BRUNILDE SISMONDO RIDGWAY
*Hellenistic Sculpture II: The Styles of ca. 200–100 B.C.*

PAT GETZ-GENTLE
*Personal Styles in Early Cycladic Sculpture*

CATULLUS
DAVID MULROY, translator and commentator
*The Complete Poetry of Catullus*

BRUNILDE SISMONDO RIDGWAY
*Hellenistic Sculpture III: The Styles of ca. 100–31 B.C.*

ANGELIKI KOSMOPOULOU
*The Iconography of Sculptured Statue Bases in the Archaic and Classical Periods*

SARA H. LINDHEIM
*Mail and Female: Epistolary Narrative and Desire in Ovid's Heroides*

GRAHAM ZANKER
*Modes of Viewing Hellenistic Poetry and Art*

ALEXANDRA ANN CARPINO
*Discs of Splendor: The Relief Mirrors of the Etruscans*

TIMOTHY S. JOHNSON
*A Symposium of Praise: Horace Returns to Lyric in Odes IV*

JEAN-RENÉ JANNOT
*Religion in Ancient Etruria*
*Devins, Dieux et Démons: Regards sur la religion de l'Etrurie antique,* translated by JANE K. WHITEHEAD

CATHERINE SCHLEGEL
*Satire and the Threat of Speech: Horace's* Satires, Book 1

CHRISTOPHER A. FARAONE and LAURA K. MCCLURE, editors
*Prostitutes and Courtesans in the Ancient World*

www.ingramcontent.com/pod-product-compliance
Lightning Source LLC
Chambersburg PA
CBHW082316230426
43666CB00036B/2725